POSITIVE

PARENTING

YOUR TEENS

ALSO BY KAREN RENSHAW JOSLIN

Positive Parenting from A to Z

POSITIVE

PARENTING

YOUR

TEENS

Karen Renshaw Joslin
and
Mary Bunting Decher

FAWCETT COLUMBINE
NEW YORK

A Fawcett Columbine Book
Published by Ballantine Books

Copyright © 1997 by Karen Renshaw Joslin and Mary Bunting Decher

All rights reserved under International and Pan-American Copyright Conventions.
Published in the United States by Ballantine Books, a division of Random
House, Inc., New York, and simultaneously in Canada by Random
House of Canada Limited, Toronto.

http://www.randomhouse.com

LIBRARY OF CONGRESS CATALOGING-IN-PUBLICATION DATA
Joslin, Karen Renshaw.
  Positive parenting your teens / Karen Renshaw Joslin and Mary
Bunting Decher.
    p.   cm.
  Includes index.
  ISBN 0-449-90996-4
  1. Parent and teenager.   2. Parenting.   I. Decher, Mary Bunting.
II. Title.
HQ799.15.J67   1997
649'.125—dc21   96-49385
                                                                   CIP
Manufactured in the United States of America

First Edition: May 1997

10 9 8 7 6 5 4 3 2 1

We dedicate this book to all parents and their teens who, because of their struggles, have become more thoughtful, accountable, and satisfied than if it had been otherwise.

SPECIAL RECOGNITION

This book started with our families; their patience, understanding and personal experiences. Our heartfelt appreciation to Reiner and Richard, Laura, Meika, Brett, Malia, and our resident teen resource, Elizabeth. All provided often needed inspiration and have allowed us to experience interdependence firsthand!

CONTENTS

ACKNOWLEDGMENTS

Our ideas are a collaboration of stimulating conversation with teens, parents, and experts. Parent questions, teen concerns, and their moments of joy have been instrumental in helping us write this book.

We want to thank all who have helped make this book possible both through their direct support, their ideas, and their belief that it could be done!

Arnold and Joan Kerzner
Ken Wong
Judy Lipton
Mary Ann Bailey
Denise Ward
Dick Gode
Elaine Percival
Maureen and Page
  Jenner
Tom Bradley
Joanne Holt
Lorna Cook
Tom and Jeannie Blank
Robin Gilleland
Belinda Lafferty

Mary "Pete" Becker
Marsha Meyers
Mary Ann Dewing
Mehri Moore
Stan and Charlene
  Relyea
Robert B. Penny
Greg Burdette
Debbie Halela
Bob Fitzgerald
Dana Hayes
Lark Young
Fred Wier
Peter Carl
Barbara Milam

Kathryn Koelemay
William Joslin
Ruth Crosby
Monica Rictor
Ann Skutt and the
  Puget Sound
  Adlerian Society
Youth Eastside Services
Party Patrol
Eastside Sexual
  Assault Center
  for Children
Missy McIver
Jerry and Martha
  Neyland

Babette, Cathy, Marion, Carol, Janet, Diane, Joan, Chooch, Kathy and Pete, Jennifer, Jeff, Sue and Tom, Jill, Annie, K.C., Shelby, Zac, Katy, Lisa, Jamie, Kirsten, Karen, Mary, Monica, Kelsea, Emily, Jill, Suzanne, Toby, Amy, Jeanne, Becky, Rachael, Peggy, and Ellen.

A NOTE FROM THE AUTHORS

We wanted to call this book "Positive Parenting with Your Teen," but our editor said that "with" wouldn't be grammatical, suggesting, as it does, that your teen will be parenting herself. Of course we want to be correct, but we also want you to know that parenting a teenager is not something you do to them, but something you and your teen work at together, through communication, understanding, and love. "With," therefore, is very much at the heart of our approach.

In "positive parenting," the participation of your teen is vital. We invite you to ask him to read this book along with you and hope that doing so will stimulate some good discussions. Communication between parents and teenagers can be testy during these years, and the misunderstandings that result can be painful. Lost privileges and hard feelings abound. We hope you use this book as a springboard for discussion. This will show your teen that you respect her feelings and desires. We hope that talking and working things out together will help you both in your voyage through your teen's adolescence.

Note: There are differences in how teen boys and girls experience adolescence, but in most instances gender is not crucial. We have used "he" or "she" singly throughout this book to simplify the text, unless otherwise stated.

INTRODUCTION

Though our editor thought a book written for parents with teens would be a great sequel to *Positive Parenting from A to Z,* the professional community seemed to warn, *"It would be terrific, but the subject is too complex; it can't possibly be done."* That was enough to persuade us to try. We both have a personal commitment to teach the most current understanding of the many issues that create barriers between parents and teens. We recognize the challenges that confront teenagers and their parents. We hope this book will provide a sense of comfort and reassurance that you are not facing the challenges alone. And we hope it leaves you with the feelings of faith and trust that we have for the majority of the adolescent population today.

Ideas are changing rapidly, and we stress that parents need to keep up with the times. One example: When we started writing this book two years ago, the current research regarding the dangers of smoking and the use of alcohol and other drugs was not available. Today, we know that teens who use are facing more serious addiction than we had imagined.

We caution parents not to feel that their job is finished when their kids are junior-high age. As you probably already know if you have picked up this book, the adolescent years are challenging! Most of us have insecurities based on our misperceptions, and teens are no different. As mature adults, we need to make more time to be with our teens, to listen to their concerns, and to convey our interest, faith, and trust in them. Listening is an act of love.

We need to understand that adolescence is a time when our children are practicing being adults. What they learn from their experiences today may mean the difference between feeling prepared or not for the future. Anyone who has raised teens or has worked with them in counseling, in Scouts, at school, or on the baseball field knows they can be witty, fun-loving, determined, interesting, and creative people. They are energetic, hopeful, and excited. They refuse limitations and reject warnings. They challenge the ways of their parents, teachers, and community. Their dreams do not admit the impossible. When harsh reality intrudes, we can only hope they will be mature enough to cope. Parents play a vital role in being a sounding board during these years. Every teen is vulnerable and needs to be nurtured and supported in a loving, stable home. In order for teens to mature, parents need to let go as well as to be there to guide them through mistakes, to listen, to comfort, and to give occasional advice. With an encouraging support system, a young teen facing great disappointment, or making common mistakes, will learn important life lessons that will prepare him for future successes.

This book offers new approaches to replace old ones that aren't working and new ways to create an atmosphere of co-operation and responsibility. Your teen will make mistakes, and so will you, innumerable times. No one is perfect—a fact that your teen will remind you of with infuriating frequency. We want you to risk listening and learning from your teen as he moves into adulthood faster than seems humanly possible. This change is as great as the metamorphosis of a caterpillar to a butterfly.

Teenagers are impatient and skeptical. They will do as we do, not as we say. They may wander, but ultimately they will follow the examples we set. We are reminded of the saying "The apple doesn't fall far from the tree, when the tree is well rooted." Both of us have lived firsthand with the many issues discussed in this book. We know the feeling of fear as the sixteen-year-old drives the family car off into the night, the shock to hear she was at a busted, unchaperoned party, the relief at learning that she chose not to ride with the kid who was drunk and totaled his car. We've been amazed to see our own teens emerge into their twenties as capable citizens with good judgment and strong values.

Your child's adolescence means growth on your part, too. Parenting styles must change. *Discussions* replace steadfast rules and arguments; *faith and trust* replace worry; *consistent follow-through* replaces rescuing or punishing.

As your teen's future takes form, you face the limitations of advancing age. Worries about forgetfulness, receding hairlines, and widening waistlines take hold while your teen's budding body embarks on new romances and exciting plans. Will it make you feel envious? *"Sometimes"* is the only honest answer. Are you afraid that your teen may be disappointed and hurt, that her dreams might crash? *"Of course."* Can you become overly invested in your child's successes? *"Certainly."* These are the kinds of issues that can get tangled as you and your teen develop new ways to look at and react to the world.

It was once commonly thought that the adolescent's job was to become independent from her parents and the parents' job was to raise their adolescent to be independent. Supposedly, the dependency part of the child-parent relationship would disappear, as if by magic, and in its place would be an adult—ideally, at age eighteen! This concept of separation was resisted by both teens and parents because it seemed so final and abrupt.

We have adopted a more helpful and realistic approach to understanding adolescence, which is the process of learning to become mutually interdependent with others. To understand interdependence, it helps to work backward. A successful, mature adult needs to be able to function independently as well as to collaborate positively in work, in marriage, and in the community. This requires a basic sense of respect and trust, the ability to share feelings, thoughts, and ideas appropriately, honestly, and without fear of ridicule or rejection, and to be comfortable asking for help and offering to help others. We begin to develop these qualities before reaching adulthood. Adolescence is the key time when caring adults can make a difference with guidance, encouragement, and support.

We have interviewed many parents and teens in the past two years. We know that many parents feel on the verge of panic, while many teens feel that no one listens to or respects them. We also know that most adolescents' future successes are based on these major, "practice" years. We hope that by sharing both our experience and our research we can help you and your teen to understand, feel in control, and feel confident during the adolescent stage.

First, it is important that you untangle your own adolescent experiences from your feelings about your teen's behavior. Ask yourself, *"Why is this a problem for me? Is this especially hard because I experienced this as a teen?"* Your past experiences are not your teen's. Do not confuse what she is facing with what you faced at that age. For example, one mother grew up poor, in the bad part of a large city. She says, *"I've seen it all."* Because of her experiences, she feels she has to put the clamps on her fourteen-year-old daughter, who is growing up in a very different kind of neighborhood. Her daughter says, *"My mom won't even let me go to a movie with friends. She doesn't trust me."*

The family is the single most important source of love and support; however, most communities provide teens a variety of opportunities to show their capabilities. A middle-aged man interviewed during the disastrous 1996 floods in Oregon said, *"I don't know what we would have done without the teenagers. They were there by the hundreds, helping with the sandbagging, not even taking breaks."* Those teens have reason to feel proud: they felt capable and needed, possibly for the first time, and gleaned citywide approval. As an identity and morale booster, they will never forget that day. Adults need to compliment teens more when they do good things. Volunteering in a soup kitchen, tutoring a recent immigrant, or returning a found wallet are other ways for teens to gain good feelings about themselves.

When teens are appreciated and valued, they will resist many negative pulls.

These are very complicated times. Parents must be extremely patient and allow time for change. Teens' emotions are so random that a problem may disappear in a day. Other issues take more time. This book will remind you again and again, *"Keep the faith."* You must believe that your teen is capable. Believe it, and, with your encouraging guidance, you will see it. Our communities are full of terrific teenagers.

1

WHAT HAPPENS DURING
THE TEEN YEARS

Maturing from a child to an adult is a big move and it happens *fast*. Teens are searching for their identity, trying out new roles and ideas that often challenge the status quo in their families. They argue their points vehemently one day, and a day later they deny having said those things. All teens need to create a new identity for themselves and leave parts of the child behind. This is the major process of adolescence—and the fact that it's not an easy task is made apparent by their mood swings and inner turmoil.

Puberty neither begins nor ends on schedule. The genetic calendar has a life of its own. One boy reflects, *"I was nicknamed Shorty. I grew eight inches in two years. The name stuck but I stood taller than most kids in my senior class."* Testosterone makes shoulders wider and muscles larger and stronger. Estrogen causes hips to widen and breasts to develop. Menstruation begins and girls' bodies get ready for pregnancy, birthing, and nursing.

Adolescents don't grow gradually, they grow in spurts, physically, intellectually, socially, emotionally, and sexually. With each spurt there is a moment of disequilibrium. Between these times, teens are apt to regress as they face new challenges, such as experiencing a wet dream, asking for a first date, or managing a friend's rejection. The significance of these events may be much greater than teens let on. Moments of disequilibrium can be exhilarating, then painfully boring. Teenagers frequently require the safety of the family to express anger, "veg out" with younger siblings, withdraw in privacy, or, hopefully, have a conversation with a parent or other trusted adult.

Friends play an important role in the identity search. Friends decide what "we" wear, whom "we" talk to, and what "we" will do. As teens pull away from parental attachment, peer groups are a replacement. Teens become committed to their peers, stand up for them, and worry about them. Within the safety of peer groups, they begin to form their own ideas and opinions about self and relationships. They also discover a sense of belonging and confidence through interdependence.

During the adolescent years, some parents wish, *"Faster!"*; *"Let's get this over with!"*; *"Where is the child we used to know?"* Parental disapproval of the teen's "new ways" helps him to feel separate, older, and more independent. Family ideals are not lost forever, just long enough for the teen to claim them for himself, by himself.

The family, as well as the community, must be the anchor for the unsteady teen whose positive characteristics are over-ridden by mood swings, argumentativeness, and resentment. It can take seemingly endless patience and understanding for a parent to be enthusiastic for the adolescent and his culture. The rude and grating rock music is a way of expressing sexuality without being sexually active. The telephone and computer on-line services are ways to be close to friends while remaining in the safety of family; they also link teens to the outside world when they are in need of escaping from family. Teens often enjoy writing poetry and stories—this is another safe way for them to express their feelings when they don't feel ready for the real world. They are practicing. Masturbation, less common with girls than with boys, teaches both genders about their sexuality and that they have control over sexual excitement. This may help create self-control when they feel tempted to be sexually active with the opposite sex.

For an adolescent to grow into a creative, contributing adult, interdependent with family and society, is a big task to accomplish in the relatively short space of the teen years. Teenagers need successes to gain confidence and self-esteem. Those who experience challenging wilderness training or other outdoor adventures report a tremendous sense of achievement. Typical of the comments heard: *"I not only learned about our environment, but it was the most mentally and physically rigorous adventure I ever experienced; it pushed us all to be our best."* Another: *"It did a lot for my self-esteem. I know now I can accomplish things I never thought I could."* Self-esteem is based on overcoming challenging obstacles, mentally, physically, emotionally, and socially. We must allow our teens to face obstacles within the boundaries of a safe environment.

In a world where violence, drugs and alcohol, teen pregnancy, sexually transmitted diseases, and other high-risk influences appear to dominate, parents need to continue "parenthood" despite the fast-approaching end of "childhood." You are needed throughout adolescence for the maturation process to evolve, to provide opportunities for your teen to become the most courageous, creative, responsible, respectful, and caring adult possible. *Positive Parenting Your Teens* addresses the concerns facing teens and parents today. As parents we need to know that, with our help, when the most challenging situations must be confronted, our teens are capable and resilient, and will finish "standing up."

2

THE POSITIVE PARENTING PHILOSOPHY

Our basic philosophy is culled from the works of Alfred Adler, Rudolf Dreikurs, Peter Blos, and D. W. Winnicott, to name only a few. We have designed a unique format for sharing our expertise with parents and teens, based on both our professional and our personal experiences. We recognize that teens are capable of making adult decisions and need to participate in resolving conflicts and setting rules and to contribute ideas. We also recognize that teenagers need the support and proper guidance that positive parents can best provide. When you're concerned about your adolescent, the following principles will help keep you from falling back into old, less helpful parenting styles.

Love and accept unconditionally. No other age group tests limits more. You will undoubtedly look at your daughter at some point and say, *"I can't believe that is our daughter."* It is often very hard as a parent to give the message, *"I love you,"* when you don't like her hair, her clothes, her friends, or how she spends her time. However, experts feel that gang activity begins with the need to feel significant. We want our children to hear loud and clear, *"You are significant to us."* Unconditional love says, *"You are special, and my love is based not on what you do but because you are you,"* and, *"No matter what you do, I will always love you."*

Foster accountability. This principle is closely associated with that of unconditional love. Parental love requires teaching responsibility. Setting limits is another way to say, *"I ask you to be responsible for your actions. Everyone makes mistakes and learns from them. You are capable of reconciling or repairing what you have undone."* For example, if you receive a call that your teen has shoplifted, he will need to own up to the behavior and make restitution. By communicating this, you send the message of strength: *"I trust that you can handle this. You are able to solve your own problems."*

Keep a positive attitude. Notice what she does right whenever you can. Adopt the philosophy that mistakes happen and we all learn from them. Looking for what is wrong focuses on blame. Parents need to model, and teach, ways in which to look for solutions. He may have broken curfew, but the car is intact and all the kids are safe. Every situation has something good about it. Build on that. Parents who have learned to use this attitude have seen wonderful changes in their relationships with their teenagers. (See "Encouragement" in Tools of the Trade, p. 21.)

Maintain mutual respect. This is not about control or manipulation. Rather than think, *"How can I make her do this?"* hold the attitude, *"I want to know what you are feeling and I want you to know what I'm feeling. It's imperative that we respect each other's viewpoints. I respect you and I respect myself."* This kind of thinking helps you determine what you will do, not what you will force her to do. This is not about reward, punishment, or control. It is about building a bond so that reason and respect can prevail.

Respect uniqueness. Treat each person and each situation individually. There is no one recipe. Your teen's self-esteem is changing rapidly in many areas: emotionally, physically, mentally, and socially. Yet his rate of change will not be identical to any other teen's. For example, one young teen was ready for more difficult mathematics and science because his abstract thinking developed early. He was bored and avoided classes until his parents moved him to a more challenging school. Some teens handle social situations more maturely than do others. Some handle dating and friendships more easily than do others. Be sensitive to environmental influences when resolving concerns. Some teens are more sensitive to family disruption than are others. A move to a new school or neighborhood may be very difficult for one teen, while another will adjust easily.

Base your positive parenting decisions on who your teen is and what he is experiencing today. Your moments of panic at his age may not be his. Your strengths may not necessarily be hers. You may have loved a particular summer camp and want your teen to experience it as you did. Even if the camp still exists, your teen may not choose it. You may have to let go of your dreams in order for your teen to have his.

Model what you want to see and hear. Even though your teen may seem to reject what you do, he is watching and learning. Your words have influence, and your actions set an example. The following skills are important for healthy development. When you model these, you set an example and teach at the same time.

- Communicate in a way that is not critical or demanding, making sure that your body language, your facial expression, and your tone of voice are in keeping with the words you choose. It is said that body language makes up three-quarters of what is "said" to a teen. When your body language is tense and your face shows anger, your words will tell it no differently. Your tone of voice is the second most important aspect of communicating with your teen. Demanding, yelling, or using a scolding tone falls on deaf ears and invites rebellion. Your words will be heard better if you use a friendly tone of voice to accompany comfortable body language. If you feel out of control it is best to first take a break. (See "Take a break" in Tools of the Trade, p. 20.)
- Show self-discipline. Because you are teaching cause and effect and demonstrating self-control, you must understand your

emotions. For example, your teen misses curfew and you get angry. You say things you are sorry for later and you threaten consequences that are unreasonable to follow through with. You feared for his safety because you love him. Yet, instead of understanding and sharing your deep concern and disciplining with good judgment, your anger controlled you. As you learn to understand your feelings and to parent with self-control, your teen will learn the same.

• Make choices that are consistent with your values. For example, if you take your teen to a movie and sneak him in as under twelve because he is small, you're teaching him that it is okay to cheat, just a little. But when you talk with him about the R-rated movie and ask his opinions and share your ideas, you model your values and help him to develop his.

• Be responsible for your actions. Because you love her, you will ask her to be responsible for hers. If she has to make retribution for irresponsible behavior, show her, through your behavior, that she will feel better when it is completed; she will feel worthwhile and valued. When you make an agreement, be consistent with follow-through. Do not rescue or overprotect, as in finishing her homework for her, or writing phony excuses for PE. To build good character, she must be held responsible for her actions. You help by setting the example.

Emphasize that the family is a team. The old, *"You will do this because I said so!"* does not work with today's teens. Quite possibly, it never worked. A cooperative approach will prepare him for the real world and encourage him to handle more and more responsibility. He needs to know that he is capable of making a decision that may affect others as well as himself. He needs to feel he is a part of a whole and that he has some control over what happens both to him and to others. He needs to feel that he belongs and is needed. Even if a particular task would be easier and more expedient to do yourself, let go and give your teen the opportunity for growth.

Take care of and understand yourself. You will be challenged every day by your teen. Sometimes learning about a teen's poor judgment, such as a shoplifting episode or a speeding violation, will knock the confidence from you. Sometimes what she says to you may cut to the core: *"Mom, remember not to talk when my friends are in the car,"* or, *"You aren't going out wearing that, are you?"* Turn such hurtful comments into learning opportunities; *"What would I say that could be so awful?" "What do you think would be a better outfit?"* Listen thoughtfully. She is awkwardly trying to find out who she is and what she will endorse. This may include hurtfully rejecting parts of you at certain times. Be curious about her remarks about you; you will be less apt to let them bother you this way. You will be able to remain open and handle all trouble spots much better if you keep up your energy and work on your own self-esteem.

- Reject old messages. The "perfect parent" is a myth and is quite different from being a "responsible parent." A teen needs a good enough parent, not an A-plus parent. "I can't make mistakes" is a myth. Admit your mistakes, and your teen will learn from them as well.
- Keep up your physical self. Raising teens takes energy! Make sure you exercise regularly and eat healthfully. Get your needed sleep and relaxation. Your young middle-aged body is changing, just as your teen's is. When you feel physically able, insensitive remarks will not get you down.
- Enhance your social life. Develop and strengthen friendships that support you. Parent groups can be very helpful. Take time to keep up with old friends and to cultivate new ones. Don't ignore family ties.
- Understand your own emotional needs. Your emotions are constantly changing, and they affect your parenting decisions. The stress of balancing work, family, and other obligations is extremely difficult. Mom is often facing hormonal replacement therapy at the same time her teen experiences the rush of hormonal development. Both may face terrific mood swings, and this can be difficult. When you identify and begin

to understand your own feelings, you may discover some good coping strategies: a soothing bath at the end of a long day, a heartfelt discussion with your best friend, a candlelight dinner with your spouse, time to yourself with a good book, or a long walk with your loyal dog. These will help you to remain calm and handle the teen years more confidently.

- Stimulate your intellectual and spiritual growth. Parents must be better informed than the soaps on television. Your curiosity and love for learning not only provide a good source for modeling, but they give you self-satisfaction as well. Keeping up with current teen issues by reading and attending lectures will provide self-protection! Participating in a stimulating hobby; attending church, art exhibits, concerts, plays, and cultural events; and exploring ideas for vacations are all ways to keep your mind active and alert.

Out of Apples? Understanding Personal Relationships by Lee Schnebly (Tucson: Fisher Books, 1988) is a short, light book on personal self-esteem.

3

TOOLS OF THE TRADE

These tools help teens and parents develop and maintain an atmosphere of open communication and cooperation. If you implement them, you'll discover that you and your teen may not be so very far apart and will enjoy adolescence together.

Tool 1: Listening. Your teenager needs to be able to talk to you, or some other trusted adult, without fear that he will be judged. Remember, when he wants to talk, he just wants to talk. Your response has everything to do with how much and what he will share with you. One of the most common complaints we hear from teens is, *"My parents don't listen to me."* Listening means accepting that anything your teen wants to tell you is significant and important to him, whether or not you agree with it. Your opinions are not important or wanted at this moment; what matters is that he is choosing to talk to you. Be interested and receptive, and thank him for sharing with you.

Reflective listening is used to validate what he has said and to help him think. Sincerely reflect the feeling that you believe underlies his words. *"It seems you're really upset with your grade. You are angry with your teacher."* If you have a burning desire to offer your opinion, ask, *"Jenny, would you like to know what I think?"* If she says yes, choose your words kindly. If she says no, respect her wishes. Most times you will have another opportunity, even if the issue comes up in a roundabout way, perhaps days or weeks later.

For more information on this topic, read *Raising Kids Who Can* by Betty Lou Bettner, Ph.D., and Amy Lew, Ph.D. (New York: HarperCollins, 1992).

Tool 2: Use fewer words. Another complaint we hear often is, *"My mom is always in my face."* She may perceive you as always nagging, directing, or lecturing. Learn to say what you mean and mean what you say. In other words, say it once and follow through. Leave notes. When you speak, use fewer words and make them neutral in tone. For example, if your son has forgotten to turn off the stove, say, *"Bill, the burner."* Don't get sucked in to begging or bribing, angry outbursts, or sulking. Teens often anticipate what you will say and "hook you" for the sake of argument. Arguing can become chronic and is unsatisfactory for all. Changing communication styles starts with the parent, not the teen.

Tool 3: Problem solving. Never attempt to resolve a problem in the heat of the moment. Have a good talk once you both have calmed down.

- Listen to your teen and reflect his feelings: *"It sounds as though you're tired of the same chore."* He'll be more cooperative if you empathize with his feelings.
- Share your feelings, with as few words as possible: *"I hear you, and at the same time I'm frustrated. The work needs to be done."*
- Think of ideas together: *"I'd like your input on this."* Any ideas are valid. Some families like to write the ideas down.
- Agree on a solution. Make sure you both have the same understanding. Prevent, *"You didn't tell me that."* Avoid using *"Do you understand?"* Instead, say, *"Tell me your understanding of . . ."*
- Contracts can be useful: *"Just so we understand each other, let's write up an agreement and both sign it."*

Tool 4: Family meetings. Family meetings foster communication and cooperation, even though some concerns will not be resolved. Issues are at least expressed, both sides are heard, ideas are valued, and there is opportunity for consensus. By rewording hurtful comments among siblings, parents foster mutual respect. The agenda needs to be balanced between fun and serious issues. Family meetings are also wonderful opportunities to plan family trips and outings.

Some issues need to be resolved privately. For example, a family rule such as "no boyfriends in bedrooms" may be decided at a family meeting, but if the rule is broken, parents and teen should resolve the consequences alone, to avoid embarrassment in front of siblings.

Some families choose to run an informal meeting, while others do better when the meeting is more structured. In any case, plan ahead, giving ample time for everyone to adjust their schedules. A weekly meeting is recommended.

- Post an agenda anyone may add to during the week.
- Ideally, everyone participates. Giving allowances at the end of the family meeting encourages attendance.
- Do not allow outside interruptions. Unplug the phones if necessary.
- If possible, allow each family member a chance to serve as chairperson.
- Stick to a few simple rules: Only one person talks at a time; no interruptions; invite thoughts and ideas; don't interrogate; you have the right to pass or remain silent; and so on.
- Cover old business as well as new at each meeting.
- Review individual schedules for the week. A calendar of weekly events is helpful.
- Perhaps the most important item—remember that humor and planning family fun are crucial.

Raising Kids Who Can, by Betty Lou Bettner, Ph.D., and Amy Lew, Ph.D. (New York: HarperCollins, 1992), is a short, helpful book on running successful family meetings.

Tool 5. Act confused. When your teen flips out, when emotions seem to fly out of nowhere, when there is a sudden lack of cooperation—act confused. *"I don't get it"*; *"I don't understand. I only asked you to set the table and you threw the napkins across the room. What's going on?"*; *"What do you mean, you didn't think it would matter if you just took two when you paid for only one?"* Even when you think you understand, you need to act confused until he explains his behavior. Explaining allows him to get in touch with his feelings and to think about the consequences of his actions. This puts him on the path to self-control, which is so important to healthy self-esteem. When you are not the policeman, he will think and make good decisions on his own. It is a wonderful technique to help your teen be responsible for his behavior. Acting confused is a tool that allows an alternative to blaming, thus avoiding angry denials and confrontations.

Tool 6: Setting limits and teaching accountability. In order to help your teen become responsible for his actions, you must avoid being overly strict or overly permissive. Teens want and need limits, but the limits you set must allow room for your teen to have new experiences. Limits should be discussed between parent and teen, with the consequences agreed to ahead of time. This will help you to be a proactive parent rather than a reactive one.

Your goal is to teach your teen to make responsible choices. When she makes a poor choice, follow-through is crucial. For example: *"Suzy, your safety is important to me. The movie gets out at nine-thirty, which leaves plenty of time for you to get a Coke with your friends and get home by eleven tonight."* Then: *"Suzy, you're an hour late and you didn't call. I was really worried. You mean a lot to me. You chose to stay out late, and that means you also have chosen not to go out next Friday night."* She may have decided previously that this is what she wanted to do. Calmly support her decision.

Punishment sets a teen up to believe, *"If I don't get caught, I can do it."* A parent's overreaction removes the teen's responsibility for his action and does not encourage self-control. Try to avoid the pitfall of thinking that your teen should suffer for his wrongdoing. The consequence should be respectful and logical.

When a teen is left to determine her own rules or when you cave in to her whims and leave rules up to her *"because you have such good judgment,"* she is, in effect, abandoned. She may assume that you don't care what she does. Another pitfall is bribing or rewarding your teenager in order to gain his cooperation. This encourages him to regulate his behavior only when he believes he will be rewarded. An attitude of *"I'll only cooperate when I can get something for it"* is not conducive to learning to be a responsible person.

For more on this topic, read *Parents, Teens, and Boundaries; How to Draw the Line* by Jane Bluestein, Ph.D. (Florida: Health Communications, 1993).

Tool 7: Take a break. No one makes wise decisions or helpful statements in the heat of the moment. *"I need some space. You do, too. We'll talk about it later."* You are not running away from the problem if you talk about it later. After you and your teen have had time to wrestle with the problem, you will be ready to solve it together. This "time to think about it" can be one of the most useful of all tools, as your teen worries about what will happen next. He may not admit it, but he cares very much what you think and what your next move will be.

Tool 8: Stay calm. When what you really want is to scream, and to say things you may later regret, see how cool you can pretend to be. This is modeling self-control. If you "lose it" too often, your teen will believe that you are not a "together" parent. Responding respectfully, especially in the heat of the battle, is vital. It teaches skills that will benefit her in all aspects of her life. A calm response will be especially difficult if your own parents overreacted. You will need to learn self-control.

Tool 9: Give choices. Teenagers need to practice taking control of their lives. When offered real choices, your teen will feel empowered. He has graduated from when he was two and could choose between the red pants or the blue ones to choices that carry greater importance, such as whether to continue playing the flute or to give it up for varsity soccer. When a teen demonstrates responsibility by choosing to leave an unchaperoned party, she shows self-control and can be entrusted with more freedom. Help this process happen by including her in significant family decisions.

Tool 10: Special time. When was the last time you did something positive and meaningful with your teen, just for fun? Such occasions become scarce as your teen is drawn into doing things with his increasingly important groups of friends. When you allow your teen to drift too far away, he may feel that you don't care anymore. Find the energy and focus on him so that he knows that he's more important than your next phone call or committee meeting. If he doesn't seem overjoyed to be with you, don't feel rejected; hang in there, and in time your effort will be appreciated.

Tool 11: Encouragement. Teens need your help to believe "I can do it!" Becoming an adult is challenging and scary. Think back to your first day on the job, when you didn't know the protocol and moved carefully until you were tuned in to the way things work. Your teen is figuring out the rules around her, sometimes on a daily basis. Some are so sensitive to peer pressure that they are constantly exhausted. Your home can be the safety net where she knows that she is unconditionally loved and appreciated. She needs to hear that you have faith in her ability. You need to empower her to think positively, to give her best.

Tool 12: Humor. Laughter is good for everyone. Humor defuses potential power struggles. For example, your teen says, *"Mom, you're always on my back to do my laundry. It should be my deal!"* The humorous response might be, delivered with a smile, *"I think so, too, but I can already smell the mildew from the towels heaped on your floor. It's hard to wash out, so it may become the family perfume."* This may not get the towels picked up, but it will ease the way for your next comment: *"You need to wash and dry the towels today."*

Never use humor at someone else's expense. Humor and sarcasm are close cousins, and the tone of voice makes all the difference. What may seem funny to you may hurt your teen's feelings. Sensitive teens will take almost any remark personally.

Tool 13: Parent networking. A parent network is a small group of parents who meet to discuss topics pertinent to the decisions they are facing at home with their teen. One mom said, *"Parent networking is as important as family meetings are for us at home. We are busy working parents, and this is an efficient way to connect us to our teen and his world."* A dad said, *"Now when we hear, 'But Dad, everyone else gets to . . . ,' we know truly how other parents feel. I feel more confident sticking to our rules and decisions."*

A group can begin easily. One started with five parents inviting three friends each to come for coffee. One parent took the lead. *"We are not a parent patrol. We are not a group of parents gathering to gossip about our kids. We will refrain from sharing names and personal details. We are here to share concerns and questions."* These guidelines are important.

One group discussed what to expect regarding the Homecoming Semi-Formal Dance. *"I learned that fourteen other parents didn't want to rent limousines. We discussed expenses: dinner, pictures, tux rentals, and so forth. I learned other kids were pressing for a coed overnight party, too."*

It is an advantage to invite parents who have teens just a bit older than yours so that you learn some of the traditions and loopholes they have experienced. One mom said her daughter's graduation was so "smooth" because of the senior class parent network. *"We listened to parents share last year's graduation experiences. I felt so much better prepared."*

You may feel awkward trying to start a parent network meeting. Have courage. Begin with baby steps; start discussing this concept with a few trusted friends. You will be surprised at how many other parents are looking for this same support. In our fast-paced, mobile society, parents of teens are often not well-connected to other families. Networking creates community. This is a modern, helpful tool for parenting in the 1990s.

4

HOW THE ENTRIES
ARE ORGANIZED

This book tackles more than one hundred of the most common concerns of teens and their parents, in alphabetical order.

Quotes. Each topic begins with illustrative comments that indicate the perceptions of both parent and teen, and makes the entry interesting and helpful. Your concern may not exactly match the example given, but read on. We present our information with the hope that you will resolve your own situation creatively and effectively.

Understanding the Situation. Since every teen is unique, there is no single solution for any one concern. In this section of the book we intend to provide as much pertinent information as possible in order to be effective. It isn't enough to parent with skills from the '60s or '70s. The 1990s present new issues; the situations are not the same for your teen as they were for you. For example, today sex can kill. A joint is stronger and more addictive than when you may have used. Colleges are looking for high SAT scores, great grades, athletic achievement, and more. The situations are not the same for a parent either. A parent may lose his home in a legal suit over offering a teen alcohol. We face raising our children at the same time as we care for our aging parents. There are more single parents, and more two-parent households in which both parents must work outside of the home to make ends meet. College expenses are high. We all have a responsibility to learn as much as possible about what teens and parents are facing.

What to Say and Do. All parents appreciate learning new ways to react to a new problem, such as their teen coming in two hours past curfew, or to an old, familiar situation, such as sibling fighting. These sections offer strategies and suggestions for choosing the right course of action. All suggestions have been used and recommended by parents or others who enjoy working with teens.

Preventive Tips. Many problems may be prevented from recurring, at least with the same magnitude. You will see some tips repeated from time to time, such as "take time to listen," "encourage community volunteering," or "give your teen a diary and teach the value of recording her thoughts and feelings." There is no main plan to follow when choosing a preventive tip, and many tips are very specific to the topic. As with the What to Say and Do suggestions, these tips have been found very useful by parents and others who like working with teens. We sometimes offer recommended readings related to the topic. There is a full list of further resources on p. 393.

When to Seek Help. This section will be useful for the times when you may want or need outside support, both for your teen and for you. There comes a time when we all need added resources, be it from a book, a friend, an understanding sibling or parent, a clergyman, a teacher, or a professional therapist. Parent support groups are terrific. Parents often ask, *"What's normal and what isn't? How do I know if he spends too much time alone in his room? He hasn't talked to us in weeks. Is this normal teen moodiness?"* It is often very difficult for a parent to ask for help. We offer ways to seek help from those who know your teen and can give needed perspective. We will also look at how to find professionals who are responsible and sensitive to the special needs of adolescents and their families.

See Also. Often, this is the last section in the entry. It refers you to other appropriate entries that may give you further insight.

ACNE

*"Suddenly Pete's face is breaking out. I hope he doesn't get
big pockmarks like his father."*
*"No way! I can't leave the house with all these zits. What
will people think?"*

UNDERSTANDING THE SITUATION

Your young teen's first pimple, sometimes before junior high,
is an unwelcome surprise. In many ways it can cause worry, as
can other early signs of puberty. Unfortunately, for many teens,
acne is a seemingly endless, mortifying battle.

When teens feel different from their peers, they are self-
conscious and miserable. Pimples are the worst! Some teens are
certain that they are "out of it" because of their acne. They feel
humiliated and can become depressed over severe acne. They
may dread going to school, and school performance may suffer.
A negative body image is a big blow to the ego! Self-esteem is
at risk, even over a pimple.

WHAT TO SAY AND DO

Acne is alarming to a self-conscious teen. Stay calm, and empathize, perhaps by sharing a little about your experiences. She
may be quite emotional, and she needs your calm, caring attitude. *"Lisa, I know you feel like one big zit and that everyone
will notice. I remember when I had pimples. It's frustrating, to say
the least. I truly don't think others noticed as much as I did. Kids
your age are mostly concerned about themselves."* Or you may
offer, *"Katy, pimples are an indication that you are growing into*

an adult. It is a sign we could even celebrate. Your hormones are kicking in. Hurray, hurray."

Help her to realize that there is plenty more to life. *"Ginger, it is true that pimples are hard to bear, but luckily you are also a wonderful baby-sitter, have a great sense of humor, and sing beautifully. Zits are a nuisance, but don't let them control you or your happiness!"*

Gather information. *"Joey, pimples are frustrating. Many teens get them, some worse than others. The zits will come and go. I know you want to pop them, but that won't get rid of the problem—in fact, it may make it worse."* Teach him. Knowledge that he may be able to improve the problem through careful skin care is a great motivator for self-care in all regards. See a dermatologist before putting a lot of money into over-the-counter products. Your teen also needs to know that sometimes nothing keeps acne away completely. Dermatologists may recommend an antibiotic.

Following are some basic guidelines for your teen.

1. Never pop a pimple. You may spread the infection.
2. Hot-soak the area at night before bed.
3. Keep your hands away from your face. Try not to lean on your hands in class or when studying.
4. Eat healthfully: include fruits, vegetables, and eight glasses of water in your diet each day.

Discuss soaps and skin cleansers with your physician if your teenager has a serious skin condition. She may recommend a dermatologist.

Emphasize her inner strengths, not makeup: *"Your face lights up when you're with your friends"*; *"Your bright blue eyes are so expressive."*

Don't laugh at her when she is most upset; treating it lightly, when possible, is helpful. *"Honey, I bet there will be five hundred other pimples at the dance tonight"*; *"Nick, if I had a dollar for every zit I've had in my lifetime I could buy you the car of your dreams."* Few young teens maintain good hygiene without their parents' help. Offer good foods, direct him toward good exercise, and suggest a cleansing program. Then, back off. Your job is to lovingly and firmly guide without nagging.

PREVENTIVE TIPS

To keep a bad pimple from becoming an emergency, such as on prom night or on picture day, help your teen plan ahead. If she (or he) has learned how to apply cover-up, she won't feel as horrified.

More than ever, your teen needs to hear what he is doing well. Try to focus on things other than how he looks. Tell him, *"Michael, you really organized that well—good thinking!"*; *"The soccer game was terrific. You're an important team player, and your legs are strong and fast"*; *"I like having the guys here. You have nice friends"*; *"The artwork is bright and cheery. You have a lot of talent."* There are so many ways you can encourage your teen to feel good about himself and help him to keep his mind off his appearance.

WHEN TO SEEK HELP

If you notice that your teen is overly concerned about her skin condition, take her to a dermatologist. Let a professional determine the care and give reassurance.

The good news is that most teens outgrow acne and learn to cope along the way. An occasional pimple is common and can generally be controlled with over-the-counter products. However, some serious skin conditions result in deep infections. This may start as late as nineteen or even older. Find a dermatologist who is knowledgeable about and sensitive to teen acne. If your teen doesn't like the dermatologist you choose, find another. The last thing your insecure, vulnerable teen needs is to feel intimidated. Acne can be painful and cause terrible self-consciousness. Do not put this off. Your teen needs your help to get through this difficult condition, which sometimes takes years to clear up.

See also: Hygiene

ADOPTION

"My adopted son is going through a terrible, angry time. Suddenly he seems lost, and he's challenging us like never before."

"You don't understand me. If you were my real mom, it wouldn't be like this."

UNDERSTANDING THE SITUATION

All teens need to create a new identity for themselves, leaving parts of the younger child behind and developing new, adult parts. We observe their mood swings and turmoil. Adopted children have some additional issues. For example, thirteen-year-old Sally spends an inordinate amount of time in the bathroom getting ready for school. She has worried about never fitting in with her family. Now she worries, *"Why would you have wanted to adopt a black baby?"* and, *"Do you still love me now that I'm older and have pimples and am not cute anymore?"* These questions deserve attention. Adopted children need to confront identity issues during adolescence just as birth children do, but it need not be more problematic when sensitively managed. Each situation is unique; early or late adoption will trigger quite different feelings and behaviors.

Adopted children have varying amounts of information about their parentage. Some birth parents are known. Others, such as those adopted from overseas orphanages, have only a picture of the orphanage. Information for others is sealed until age eighteen. Adolescence is a critical time for many adoptees to inquire about their family of origin.

Adopted teens often question, *"Do I look like my mother or my father? What would I be like if I were being raised by them? Do I have siblings? My birth mother was pregnant at fifteen; will I be, too?"* These questions can be complicated for adopted children. Often, as they approach age eleven or twelve, some basic information about themselves becomes important. When she reaches this age, you may see some behavioral problems as she begins to struggle with adoption issues. Sometimes the anxiety is displayed as anger. For most, this stage passes quickly. Your teen needs you to listen to her concerns and to keep the rules and expectations clear so that she feels safe and well grounded.

Adopted teens may feel an unevenness with their siblings and how they are treated by their parents and grandparents. She may not look like her adopted family. He may feel he's asked to do chores more than his natural sibling, who is good at the same sports as Dad, and he may be right. Some parents are not as tough on their adopted children as on their natural ones. Teens often associate these comparisons with being different.

As you attempt to adjust to your adopted teen's normal separation from you, you may experience feelings of loss and a crisis of your own. Many parents waited so long for a baby that they are not ready for them to grow up. Likewise, adopted children, having been separated from their birth parents and now facing separation from their adopted parents, may be fraught with heavy, mixed emotions. This deserves careful consideration.

WHAT TO SAY AND DO

Parent your adopted teen just as you would if he were your natural born. Do you worry that he may leave? Positive feelings are stronger than biologic ties. Listen to your teen. Try to understand his world. Be honest and forthright. Help him to feel good about his life. Help him to be accountable so that he can maintain his integrity.

Some teens have a great need to seek information about their origins. Don't hesitate to help when needed. However, timing is important. Never push your teen to find her origin; she may be content and not need it at this time. The searching must be at the pace of your teen. It is her search. If she is ready, she will follow through. If she is not, she will probably let it drop. It is imperative that these fits and starts be allowed to happen. It is a process that may take years or may never happen.

When needed, reinforce different ethnic backgrounds and recognize your family as an interracial one. Help your adoptive teen to cope with discrimination and to respond to thoughtless prejudiced comments. Don't patronize. Differences can be celebrated.

PREVENTIVE TIPS

When hurt by your adopted teen's negative attitude toward you, hold on to your conviction that you were the best person for him when you adopted him and you still are. As you feel increasingly challenged, you may need a support system. Contact friends, clergy, or a professional therapist to reaffirm your sense of worth.

An adolescent who knows she was born to young teen parents may need to be reassured that this does not mean that the same will happen to her. It is very important to talk about this in a matter-of-fact way. Assume that she does not want to become pregnant before she has completed her education and is married. Assume that she will need guidance about birth control. Unfortunately, many repeat their birth parents' past, largely because it is often the only thing they know about their origins, and because they have frequently been told that their birth parents were good people. Many recent adoptees have far more information about their birth parents, and this can help you to avoid repeating the past. *"She wanted to go to business college to be a legal secretary,"* and other bits of information allow a broader understanding of this unknown woman beyond the early pregnancy.

Some adoptees look forward to age eighteen, when they can legally look up their birth parents. Many fears and questions surface during the process. Counseling can be very helpful.

For more information on this topic, read *Being Adopted: The Life-Long Search for Self* by David M. Brodzinsky, Marshall D. Henig, and Robin Marantz Henig (New York: Anchor Books, 1992); and *How to Raise an Adopted Child: A Guide to Help Your*

Child Flourish from Infancy Through Adolescence by Judith Schaffer and Christina Lindstrom (Copestone Press, 1991).

WHEN TO SEEK HELP

Adopted teens have a great need to find identities and sometimes latch on to alcohol and other drugs, violence, gang activity, and other high-risk behaviors. Do not be naive to what needs these identities may fulfill. Seek help from a school counselor or other professional.

General anxiety is common when the adopted teen decides to look for his natural parents. Adoptive parents may feel this as well. Discuss these feelings with your teen, and keep in mind that professional help can be very useful. Most cities have support groups that help in the search.

See also: Body Image

ALCOHOL AND OTHER DRUGS

*"I have to stop her. How can I control this situation? I feel
   like locking her up in her closet."*
*"They don't understand. I know what I'm doing. They
   can ground me, but they can't stop me from using."*

UNDERSTANDING THE SITUATION

We have put alcohol and other drugs together because alcohol is the United States' drug of choice and is extremely dangerous when used by teenagers. Because it is a commonly accepted drug, you may not be as upset when your teen comes home drunk as you would be if she were high on another drug.

However, there is no question that alcohol is as harmful as any other drug to a teen who knows no moderation. Alcohol and many other drugs are inexpensive and frighteningly available to our youth. Marijuana and alcohol are common "gateway drugs" for teens and are often used interchangeably: if one is not available, the other will do. Both produce the desired effect—mood alteration. As a result, multiple drug use is the rule for today's teens. Your response needs to be consistent for all substances.

Professionals in the field, school-based educational programs, and Alcoholics Anonymous consider alcohol at least as damaging as pot, cocaine, and speed. This reflects our better understanding about the effects of alcohol on youth. Chemical substances are illegal and dangerous to teens. Because addiction is now considered a disease, rather than, as in the past, a moral issue, it has become easier to seek help. Most medical plans cover some form of treatment. However, prevention is the key.

Not infrequently, tobacco is included when addictive drugs are discussed. However, we have opted to treat smoking separately, despite the fact that tobacco is one of the most addictive substances. Its effects may not include drunkenness or impaired judgment, but we must concede that smoking may be closely linked to future use of other harmful substances.

Today the pressure on kids to use substances is enormous. It's especially important that you understand the ramifications of chemical use and abuse. Adolescence is a major period of physical and psychological development, and use during this period can cause irreparable physical and psychological damage. Due to their developing bodies, teens can become addicted quickly.

Emotionally, chemicals interfere with learning to manage life's ups and downs. Too often, alcohol and other drugs are used to ease uncomfortable situations and become a solution for coping with life stresses. They allow teens to avoid working through the pain of difficult relationships or events in their lives. They mask the real job needed to solve social problems.

Few teens who drink and take drugs realize or heed the risks.

Adolescence is a period of perceived indestructibility, and risk taking is part of life. Combine risky behavior with the way chemicals interfere with decision making, problem solving, and resolving conflicts, and trouble ensues. "Am I sober enough to drive?" The statistics suggest that more than ninety thousand teenagers a year get the answer wrong. Date rape and other violent behaviors are common when substances are involved. However, these crimes frequently do not get reported. A significant number of sexual assaults happen before age seventeen, most involving alcohol or other drugs.

Teens start using drugs for many reasons. It makes them feel like adults. It's against the law, which makes it enticing. Life feels a whole lot easier: *"I feel more comfortable in a group when I have a few drinks"*; *"I really fit in with the gang when I get high like they do"*; *"School isn't as boring when I get high"*; *"Drugs make me so in touch with myself. Nothing else matters; I can even stand my dad yelling."*

Children of alcoholic parents see drinking as a way of life. The addictive process is the same as for other drugs that have mood-altering effects. The using teen learns to cope with the anxiety of social situations by drinking a beer or two. Using does *not* help them to develop the interactive social skills they need in the adult world. Heavy-using adults are often emotionally stunted at the age at which they began drinking.

When police and other adults have a lax attitude about teen alcohol use, teens get mixed messages. When a high-school team makes the finals, parents and other fans turn a blind eye to the drinking during the celebrations. The winning high-school crew passes beers from boat to boat despite strict drinking regulations. The law is too flexible, and it is not easy to toe the line. All these enabling behaviors reinforce use.

Advertising depicts drinking as sexy and part of the good life. Movies and television ads are full of false glamour. Some TV networks that target teens literally push drug use through the drug-culture music they promote. The images of the fashion world with models dressed in rags, and the music world with

teen pop musicians with disheveled hair, suggest the glorifica-
tion of drug culture. Our impressionable teens could benefit
from songs sung about the hero and heroine teenagers who get
themselves off of heroin. Unfortunately, there are few songs
about the ugly side of drug use.

Teen drug abuse has four levels, from experimentation to
dependency.

Experimentation is the beginning. The first try gives an unfa-
miliar high. Some are frightened, don't like the euphoric mood
change, and stop.

The next phase is social use. Alcohol and other drugs are used
at specific times, such as parties.

The third phase is regular use. The teen is preoccupied with
drug use, hides it from others, and denies its importance to
himself. Old friends give up on him, and new, using friends
take their place. He loses his self-respect, and school becomes
unimportant.

The dependency stage is last. Characterized by loss of control of
use, blackouts, and paranoid thinking, using helps the teen to
feel "normal."

Different stages of abuse require different parental action. At
stage one, experimentation, state your values and hold him
accountable. If experimenting was an adventure, ask what he
feels about it and discuss what he will do next time. Stage two,
the social stage, indicates that drugs are beginning to be a way
of life. Accountability plus intervention with professional help
is warranted. In-patient rehabilitation is often considered with
stage three and definitely with stage four.

Today, as new forms of drugs become popular, medical awareness of their effects advances daily. It is clearly a very different
world from when you were raised. Twenty-five years ago, a
seventeen-year-old friend experimented with alcohol. Today, she

experiments at fourteen, and she uses marijuana laced with LSD, or even heroin. The ramifications are serious and dangerous.

The following are commonly used drugs. For some teens, one hit can have disastrous effects. There is too wide a range of reactions to condone any use.

- Alcohol and marijuana cause relaxation of inhibitions, poor coordination, sleepiness, and depression. Marijuana can have hallucinogenic effects as well. These are the most frequently used drugs among teens. Used by more than half of all teens before they are sixteen, these drugs can cause impairment in physical function, poor judgment resulting in date rape or other unwanted sexual activity, and car wrecks or other accidents. Use leads to the destruction of brain cells. Unlike alcohol, marijuana does not dilute with water and stays in the body for more than a week. Many use it daily, and it becomes a self-medicating, or maintenance, drug, which is easily hidden.
- Cocaine is usually snorted, which gives a brief feeling of euphoria and a strong desire for another high. Cocaine also causes depression, nervousness, and agitated behavior. Frequent users enjoy the ritual of preparing the cocaine to be sniffed.
- Crack is a purified form of cocaine that is smoked and is extremely potent, dangerous, and highly addictive. It is inexpensive and easily available.
- Heroin, once the last drug of choice because of its nasty, addictive effects, is now available in a new powder form, which is cheap and, unfortunately, easy to use. It can be sniffed or smoked in this form and is as addictive as the old, injectable form. It has been popularized by adolescent rock culture and is an increasing favorite among teens.
- Inhalant drugs are used mainly by teens who have difficulty getting other types. They include fumes from glues, paints, hair spray, petroleum products, and other chemical substances. Inhalants give a silly moment and if used regularly cause dangerous side effects and permanent damage to growing bodies.
- LSD and other hallucinogenic drugs, such as peyote and

psilocybin mushrooms, are usually smoked or eaten and cause the user to experience hallucinations. "Bad trips" can last hours and may require careful supervision so that the user doesn't hurt himself in uncontrollable panic. These are dangerous drugs, even though they are not addictive.

- PCP, or angel dust, usually "laced" on cigarettes or marijuana joints, is a hallucinogen that causes extremely bizarre behavior and damages body cells. It can totally disconnect the user from reality, sometimes permanently. It was developed as an anesthetic, but that use has been discontinued due to its extremely dangerous side effects.

- "Speed," or amphetamines, is swallowed in pill form; "crystal meth," in powder form, is snorted or injected. This stimulant drug gives the user so much energy that she might not be able to sleep for days at a time. It decreases appetite and can cause extreme anxiety and hypertension, as it affects the central nervous system. It is very dangerous and addictive.

Teens who have learning problems are at high risk for alcohol or other drug use. They often drop out of the competitive academic world directly into the less painful world of self-medication. They need adult help to find activities where they can experience the highs of success rather than the highs of drugs. High-risk teens exhibit a history of behavioral and school problems, sensation seeking, some aggressiveness, and a general lack of responsibility regarding rules, friendships, and society. For some, drugs numb the pain of a family crisis, death, divorce, and other troubles.

Teens who are pulling good grades, are popular, and are on the student council or involved in team sports, may appear to have it all together. However, some take drugs just the same, to relieve the pressure they feel to succeed or to avoid appearing not "with it."

WHAT TO SAY AND DO

Follow a simple routine when she gets home from a night out. Have her check in with you for a short conversation or a kiss good night so that you know she is home. Such a small task may prevent experimentation. *"No, thanks. My mom will be able to tell, and then I won't be allowed to do anything with you ever again."*

Don't panic over first-time use. Confront him, and make your expectations clear, but understand that many experiment and never touch the substance again. One boy told his parents, *"I learned how to look and act like I was drinking, but I really don't like it, so I fake it. You don't have to worry about me."*

Teens use drugs to defy or to rebel against their parents and society. Generally this is a peer issue as well as an individual one. If you suspect that your teen is socially experimenting with any drug—glue, diet pills that contain amphetamine (speed), marijuana, or alcohol—your first concern is for her safety. Stay calm. Many parents seek professional guidance at this point. Confront her: *"I know you're using because I know what I smell."* Friends' parents should be notified, and it is effective to discuss a common plan. Handled properly, this incident could be a godsend, an opportunity to address something that might have remained hidden. You have weathered other storms; you will get through this one, too.

Learn the typical symptoms. Do not be naive. Chemical dependency does not go away by itself. If you have a child involved at any age, you need to become as informed as possible so that you can confront him in a direct and unemotional manner. Stay abreast of your teen's peer groups and activities.

Know what to look for: changes in personality; changes in friendships; dropping out of sports or other extracurricular activities; declining grades; bloodshot eyes; increased or decreased amounts of sleep; the smell of alcohol or pot; a lack of concern or callousness about school and other responsibilities; alcohol- and drug-related messages on T-shirts; talk of partying; a negative attitude toward authority figures; increased or decreased eating; complaints of headaches or stomachaches; changes in weight, wardrobe, and overall appearance; strange phone calls at odd hours; extreme mood changes. Watch for drug paraphernalia such as packets of rolling papers, clips for holding marijuana butts, pipes, small spoons or mirrors for cocaine, scales, cigarette lighters, and syringes.

If you worry about drugs, observe your teen's spending habits. If she is buying drugs, she will be low on money. If she is selling drugs, she will have money and purchases she can't account for.

If you suspect use of alcohol or other drugs, confront him with a statement. Avoid asking, *"Are you using?"* A question invites denial. Instead, say, *"Jim, I know that I smelled pot last night when you came in. We need to talk. I'm concerned about your safety and what's happening to you."*

When she says, *"Mom, I promise I won't use again,"* or tries to talk her way to innocence: *"Mom, you're being ridiculous. I'm keeping that for a friend,"* her manipulation pressures you, since you obviously want to be able to trust her. Typically, however, users continue to use. In many cases, a turnaround is possible only when the teen experiences some painful or difficult consequences related to the drug use. Your firm response will create discomfort. Ignore her whining and promising, follow your instinct, and firmly tell her, *"Intentions are great, but I need more. You will not be allowed to drive until I'm sure you can be responsible. If after three months you've proven to us that you're not using any drugs or alcohol, you can begin to earn back your driving privileges. I love you too much to risk your getting hurt."* She may cry in frustration, yell, and tell you that you're the meanest mother in the world. Stay firm and consistent. Giving in to her begging fosters irresponsibility, insults her, and indicates that you don't feel she is capable of quitting.

Don't wait for school policy to set limits—be proactive. One mother let her son know loud and clear that if he used, she would no longer allow him to play varsity football. His team had a questionable track record for staying clean.

Discuss strategies to refuse substances.

• Convey that you understand the pressures he faces: *"I know you're under pressure to drink and sometimes do drugs."*

- Discuss saying no: *"It's difficult to say no. When friends pressure you, you may be tempted. That's normal. I'd like to know that you feel you could say, 'No way.' "* Reflect on a previous positive situation: *"Remember when you were training for cross-country? If someone had tried to give you a cigarette you would have said, 'No way.' "* Role-play saying no.
- Discuss the concept of loneliness: *"Loneliness is one of the biggest reasons teens use. Kids will do almost anything to avoid being rejected."* Help him understand that his friends are not good friends if he has to use drugs to fit in with them.

Call the parents of your teen's friend to discuss your rules and expectations. Many teens cleverly stay overnight with a friend whose parents are very lax about curfew and keeping track of their whereabouts. Share your concerns: *"Regan, I know that Mark's parents have different rules than we do, but we expect you to follow our agreement whenever you stay there. The same consequences apply if we learn you're using even though you're at someone else's house."* Your teen may object, but your follow-through is very important. It says that you really do care. The message is clear.

Sign a contract with your daughter in which she agrees to call you for a ride home if needed. *"Sarah, we love you and want you to be safe. Rather than ride with someone who's been using, please call us."* This works only when parents agree to refrain from lecturing. If your teen has called more than twice, be concerned. Discuss this at an appropriate time and decide if this problem requires closer attention or intervention.

If you suspect drug use, take action immediately. *"This is of great concern to us. I'm very worried about your health and safety, so I'm making an appointment with a drug counselor. This is beyond my expertise. If the evaluation shows there's no problem, I'll jump for joy."* She will get the message that you really care. Most teens feel shocked and embarrassed when they have to face a drug counselor. This gives the responsibility for defining drug use to the counselor and the teen. Most teens will go along with a parent's plan if it is strongly and firmly presented. You need to remember how you got him to the dentist when he was young: you said matter-of-factly, *"You may not like it, but it's got to be done."*

PREVENTIVE TIPS

A wise high-school principal reminded parents two or three times a year that teens need limits and should not be left at home without adult supervision. A few friends in an empty house is an invitation for dangerous experimentation and has the potential to develop into a situation that can get out of control, even if the teen doesn't want it to.

Examine your own drug and alcohol use. Your behavior and attitudes influence your children. Drinking too much sends a dangerous message. You may be surprised at how aware your children are of your alcohol use. Checking out his perceptions can be very interesting and enlightening. *"Ben, what do you think about my drinking habits?"* You may be embarrassed. He may know more than you are comfortable with.

Many parents offer a small, token glass of wine to their teen as a toast on a special occasion with the family. When introduced as celebration, and in such moderation, the message to the teen is, *"You are growing up, we love including you."*

Be proactive. If your teen's school does not have a strong program for prevention of substance abuse, start one. The elementary school may have had a program, but that's not enough. Use an informative approach rather than scare tactics. One high school held an event called "party patrol." The students heard the forum during the day at assembly; then it was repeated at night for parents. One seventeen-year-old boy commented on how surprised he was to hear that marijuana stays in the body a long time. If he smoked one joint a week, the pot would always be in his system. He was even more surprised to learn that marijuana has terrible effects on brain cells and the reproductive organs. This boy made the decision not to smoke pot, ever, and to drink only on rare occasions.

Don't minimize the temptations younger teens face. Experimenting with inhalants and alcohol begins early, and it is imperative that education begin prior to junior high. Many high-school seniors reflect on junior high as a time of wild experimentation. *"We had drinking parties in eighth grade. It was easy to fool our parents because they had no idea we might be interested at our age. We fooled around then a lot more than we do now."* Support school programs focused on prevention of substance abuse.

Do not serve her friends. It is illegal, even in your own home. If she has a party at your house, do not let her guests leave the house and come back in, having "found" a source in the driveway. Underage drinking is illegal. You are putting your entire family at risk. Some states hold parents liable if a teen drinks and drives and is in an accident. You are also sending the message to your teen that having a good time with friends requires alcohol.

As hard as it may be when you feel that trust has been broken, your continued warmth and affection is extremely important, as well as communication of your values. Remember, plenty of kids will experiment but still desperately need to stay connected emotionally. Your attachment will help him quit after the experimental stage. If he is angry and isolated because of his parents' severe reaction, he may use to spite them and numb the pain.

Teens are less likely to rebel with drugs and alcohol if parents attempt direct communication with them about their use. Let your teen know that you are aware of the pressure she faces with her peers. Empathize with her and share your faith and trust in her. Share your feelings and values clearly.

Discuss family members who may have had problems with alcohol or other drugs. Explain that it may be genetic: *"Aunt Sue never finished college because she was hooked on drugs and alcohol, and Grandpa was an alcoholic. It runs in families. The people in our family do not tolerate alcohol well. We don't have enough of the enzyme in the liver that gets rid of alcohol. It may only take one drink to lose control."*

Explain your understanding of how drug dependency occurs. *"Will, I'd like to share some information I've read about alcohol and other drugs. Would you be willing to discuss this with me? It may not be new to you."* If his answer is no, at least he will know that you care. If it is yes, share the following.

1. Kids generally try beer, or whatever they can find, the first time for the taste and to see what it feels like to be high.
2. Next, a group of friends gets together without parental supervision to party and drink. There may be some other substances around, such as marijuana, or even harder drugs, such as crack. When kids get together to party, it is sometimes hard to be different, not to follow the crowd. It is important not to let peer pressure control what your teen does.
3. Social drinking can lead to heavier involvement. Kids decide they have more fun when they feel high. Because their normal inhibitions and sense of responsibility are loosened up, they may not think about what will happen when substances are mixed and can become very seriously ill. These teens need help.
4. The next two stages are addiction and dependency. These kids will go to any extreme to get their drugs or alcohol. They wake up in the morning figuring a way to get a drink or a drug. They become both physically and mentally dependent. Addiction is a disease and requires professional help and in-patient hospitalization. Having a drug addiction is the opposite of becoming emancipated. It is going from parental control to drug control.

When you are an active parent within your teen's school community and are familiar with his friends and with the curriculum on drug prevention, you can discuss pertinent information. Since teens like to feel the expert, use questions to gain information. *"John, what do you know about the dangers of intoxication? What did they tell you in the DARE program?"* Many opportunities lend themselves to discussion. Watching a news report of a tragic drunk-driving incident in which a child or a teen is killed can open a conversation.

Vulnerable, insecure teens can gain a greater sense of inner worth and strength when they are given the chance to help younger children or the physically challenged in swim programs, day care, summer camps, hospitals, and other community programs. The experiences had when volunteering in the community are far more effective than any parents' warnings or lectures about safety or values.

For more information on this topic, read *Teen Addiction: A Book of Hope for the Parents, Teachers, and Counselors of Chemically Dependent Adolescents* by Marti Heuer (New York: Ballantine Books, 1994); and *How to Tell if Your Kids Are Using Drugs* by Timothy Dimoff and Steve Carper (New York: Facts on File, Inc., 1992).

WHEN TO SEEK HELP

You worry and feel guilty when your teen is using drugs and behaving irresponsibly. You lose sleep, feel embarrassed with friends and relatives, and fear leaving him alone in the house. You may have to miss work because of appointments with counselors. The disease affects whole families, and parents have little or no control. Your teen needs to get to a point where he can say he wants help. Unfortunately, the old saying, "You can lead a horse to water but you can't make him drink," often applies here. This is the time to consult a professional substance-abuse counselor to help you assess the seriousness of the situation. Do not wait. Get help before he hits bottom, marked by flunking out of school, trouble with the law, and so on.

Timing is crucial. A crisis such as being arrested for drunk driving or for possession of drug paraphernalia may do it. Take advantage of this crisis. Your teen is now obviously aware of her problem and can no longer hide it from you. Be ready. Have a consultation ahead of time and make a plan in advance with the counselor or agency.

If treatment is recommended, support it and be involved. Learn how the family can become a family again. It will help everyone. Treatment is never over—it is a lifelong process.

Many Alcoholics Anonymous groups are geared for young people. Find one. Teens stop drinking and drugging when they are involved with others who are in recovery. This is AA's success. Your teen may want you to go with him at first. Family members may want to support him by attending Alateen and Al-Anon meetings. They are wonderful support groups for all.

See also: Counseling; Dating, Teens; Learning Problems; Parties; Smoking

---

ANGER

"I feel totally helpless when Roger flies off the handle and smashes things. What can a parent do? Nothing I do helps. It gets scary."

"I can't stand it! No one thinks about me. I never get to do what I want! I get so mad I feel like exploding!"

UNDERSTANDING THE SITUATION

Violence is common in our homes, in our schools, and on our streets. No wonder you panic when your teen yells or hits the walls. Often it is a vicious cycle: He gets angry, you get angrier. Where will it lead? Expressing anger may be normal, but when is it too much?

Behaviors you observed when you were a child are likely to be what you and your family struggle with now. One woman claimed that when her mother was angry, she would clam up, hold in her feelings, and withdraw from the family. This woman is now a parent, and having learned from her mother to hide her feelings, she suffers from depression, stomach ulcers, and occasional violent outbursts at family members over unimportant issues. Depression, eating disorders, and suicide are among the results of anger turned inward.

A father remembers, *"We hid when Dad got mad, especially*

when he was drunk. He threw whatever got in his way, be it a frying pan or my mother." These are poor ways to cope with life's all-too-common stresses.

Historically, anger has been misunderstood, but it is now the subject of significant research in leading universities. It is currently believed that inappropriate outbursts are a secondary expression of other emotions, such as embarrassment, a feeling of lack of control or of being wronged, and a host of other personal hurts or feelings of inadequacy. For example, Tom was embarrassed when a "friend" poked fun at his beardless face in front of his peers. Unable to brush off the comment, Tom punched his harasser in the face. The fight that followed resulted in his being sent home from school, thereby missing an algebra exam. Frustrated, he took his anger out on his family. Such reactions are common with teens. Most have not learned how to identify, understand, or moderate their feelings, and so act inappropriately. The safest people for teens to dump on are siblings and parents.

Help your teen recognize his patterns of angry behavior. Does it come after being teased by a sibling, after a rejection by a friend, or after losing a game? Has winning or being right become his ultimate symbol of success? Without it, does he feel worthless and become hostile? School may be difficult—sitting and concentrating for long periods, not understanding, and being frustrated by poor grades and failures. Many teens compare themselves to successful older siblings and feel inadequate: *"I've let my parents down, and I'm unlovable and miserable."* The alternative for some is to turn the anger inward. Poor anger management can be life-threatening. An angry teen is not happy when he is out of control, and deep down, he wants to improve.

Experts state that emotional control is necessary for healthy self-esteem. All teens experience anger, but it must not be all-consuming. Wouldn't it be wonderful if we could convey to our teens that anger is real and is okay, and that it is possible to decide how we want to be angry—that it does not have to control us? We know that the more we understand about our anger, the more responsible we are in expressing it. Your job is to help your teen understand the feelings beneath her angry outbursts. Teach her to understand that her actions are a result of bad feelings that can be dealt with differently. This is a process of maturing. She can learn to soothe herself before losing control and to use words to express her feelings.

WHAT TO SAY AND DO

Household rules provide a safe outlet for every member of the family.

1. Do not hurt others verbally, emotionally, or physically.
2. Do not hurt yourself.
3. Do not ruin your property or another's.
4. Work on finding solutions to problems rather than on blaming.

It is impossible to be a sweet parent all the time. You can and do have angry feelings toward your teen, especially when he disrupts your life and disappoints you. Your most important job is to handle your anger responsibly; demonstrate the action you want your teen to use. When something he does makes you angry, tell him. *"Adam, I'm furious at _____. I need a time-out; then we'll discuss this."* Vent somehow, somewhere, but not at him. Take a shower or a run, call a good friend, vacuum, water the yard—whatever will help you cool off and stay objective. When you are calm, say, *"I feel _____ when you _____ because _____, so what I need is _____."*

When your teen says something like, *"I hate Rebecca. She makes me so mad,"* reflect her feeling: *"Zoe, you're really furious at Rebecca."* If her feeling is hard to define, say, with true concern, *"Oh?"* She needs you to listen sincerely. Later, ask, *"Zoe, would you like to learn something interesting about anger?"* To encourage her to discuss this, be sure not to make it sound like a critical lecture: *"No one can make you angry. You choose to be angry because you feel hurt, embarrassed, wronged, and so forth. You can never make anyone do what you want them to do, but you can decide what you will do. When*

Rebecca embarrassed you, you couldn't make her stop. Rather than stand there being teased, you might decide to leave. Just quietly walk away. Then Rebecca will have no one to torment, and you can find something to do or someone else to be with so that you feel better. What else do you think you could do to avoid feeling so helpless and frustrated?" This isn't the approach you will use every time she is angry, but you'll have similar opportunities throughout her adolescent years.

When your teen is hostile, stay calm. Anger creates more anger. Act bewildered. "Whoa! Wait a minute. I'm really confused. What's going on?" Give him time to answer. Then, listen. This technique generates calm and encourages reflection.

Your teen needs to know that you love him *and* you expect him to be responsible for his actions. When Robert angrily kicked a hole in the door, he was expected to pay for its repair. When his mother cooled off, she said, lovingly, "You lost it, you fix it."

Parents need to learn to say, "I'm sorry." When you lose your temper, it is very empowering to admit the mistake to your teen. Say, "I'm sorry for _____." You are modeling taking responsibility for your own actions.

When helping your teen with anger control, share these hints.

1. What feeling did you have that triggered the anger?
2. Think about what you will get out of being angry. Apart from some satisfaction in slamming the back door or screaming at someone, being angry doesn't feel good for very long and tends to ruin the rest of the day.
3. Decide how long you want to be angry: "I'll need fifteen minutes; I'm pretty mad." (Those who have tried this sometimes laugh at how hard it is to stay angry for the length of time decided on.)
4. Brainstorm techniques for gaining control. Go running, kick a rock while taking a walk, stomp on an old cardboard box, talk to yourself alone in your room, play an instrument, sock a tether ball, write a letter telling the person off (you need not mail it). Punching pillows works for some, but it may escalate feelings of rage, which does not help in the long run.

5. Reward yourself after you have successfully defused a potentially explosive moment. You might paint a picture, take a warm bath, lie on your bed listening to music, talk to a good friend, watch a favorite TV show or go to a movie with a friend, window-shop, and so forth.

PREVENTIVE TIPS

Take the time necessary to teach your teen about anger. Say, *"Sam, tell me about a recent time when you were very angry."* Ask for another example. Then explain, *"The common thread running between both your examples is that you felt you had no control over the situation. We all get angry when we feel we have no control."* If Katy got angry when her sister teased her in front of others, say, *"When Cindy teased you, you felt embarrassed and cornered. You were angry because you couldn't make her stop."* Believe it or not, this information in itself may be quite helpful to your teen. You may overhear her on the phone passing it on to a friend.

Some teens worry about challenges away from home, from signing up for camp to leaving for college. Anger becomes a buffer. It is easier to leave those you love when you create some distance, and anger does just that. Through anger, she can believe she doesn't need you so much. Encourage your teen to feel capable of and excited by new experiences. Your pity or overprotectiveness is not helpful, nor are hurt feelings.

Your teen is feeling his own pressures. Your daily nagging or criticism is not helpful. Look for what he does right—there is always something. Save your concerns for a planned problem-solving time, such as the family meeting.

Your teen needs to feel control over her world. She needs to be involved with the decisions and responsibilities that affect her.

Express your anger honestly in appropriate places with people who can listen well. Perhaps you are frustrated or angry because she is not doing well. You know she tries her best, and you feel guilty for having these feelings. You need to share your disappointments safely with others so that they won't eat at you. Guilt is the unwelcome gift that keeps on giving. If you repress these feelings, they are likely to come out as hostile comments that can destroy your otherwise good relationship with your teen and eventually cause you to feel depressed. To deny conflicting emotions is not helpful to anyone in the family.

WHEN TO SEEK HELP

When anger becomes chronic, destructive, or dangerous, take it seriously. Explore the pressures your teen feels at home, at school, and elsewhere. Seek professional help, be it from a school counselor, doctor, therapist, or clergyman, to understand and make needed changes. It may require family counseling, it may not. You may be able to institute changes to increase her self-esteem, to help her feel capable and in better control. Sometimes chemical imbalances cause "short fuses" and a doctor may prescribe an appropriate medication.

If he is angry enough to be aggressive, to throw things or destroy property, and you fear what may happen next, you or someone else could be the object of his rage. Let him know that if he becomes a danger to himself or to others, you will call the police. He may test you. Call the police. It is very unpleasant and embarrassing, but the police are trained to deal with domestic disputes; de-escalation techniques and family disputes are part of their everyday work. They can draw that line for the out-of-control teen when the parent may not be able to.

See also: Depression; Learning Problems; Siblings; Stress

ANNOYING BEHAVIOR

"He's so embarrassing. I never know what to expect, especially in front of my friends. What others must think!"
"They have no sense of humor. Watch this—I'll really get her mad."

UNDERSTANDING THE SITUATION

One of the most irritating traits of adolescents is their compelling need to draw attention to themselves. Commonly used are bodily noises such as farting, belching, and knuckle cracking, and some get very creative with mouth noises or by cupping their hands against their chests or armpits to create a loud, deep honk. Some rudely interrupt a conversation in order to be included; some move about loudly in a group when they are told to be quiet. Some play the same song over and over, knowing it will irritate a tired parent. Ironically, the more irritation you show, the worse the actions will be. Your teen will try different behaviors as he seeks his identity, especially when he is with his friends. Don't overreact. Be kind and firm in letting him know what is acceptable. At the same time, keep a sense of humor and appreciate the creativity of this age group. As indicated by the brevity of this entry, this problem should be one of the lesser concerns for parents of teens. Treat it lightly and calmly and it will dissipate.

WHAT TO SAY AND DO

Unfortunately, this is one way kids find to be "in" with their peers. With a poker face, address the whole group, rather than single out one person. *"Hey, kids, please, not in our home. Thank you."*

Do the unexpected. If he expects that you will get mad, he'll be amazed when you respond lightly, *"Oh my, that was a good one. We should save it for America's Funniest Home Videos."* You may then have to say calmly, *"Enough's enough."*

Most annoying behavior is intended to get attention. Ignore it. Give no social gratification. If you are in public or in a private social situation, do not embarrass her. You may stop her with a simple, straightforward, *"Emma,"* or a knowing glance or a hand signal that indicates, *"Enough's enough."* If she still shows no sign of stopping, say, *"Please excuse yourself and come back when you can be polite."*

It's amazing just how influential your habits are. You might burp loudly after drinking a soda, but you wouldn't do it in public. Do not assume your young teen knows this. He's likely to repeat the burp loudly in school to get the other kids laughing.

You may feel that certain friends are bad influences. A subtle suggestion to make him think: *"Lory, you seem to be more obnoxious when you're around Jon. I don't notice the same behavior when you are with other friends. Which way do you like to be?"* Or: *"Lory, you seem to show off more when you're with Jim. Please show him how we act in our home, or he won't be welcome here."*

Do not use a scare tactic to get your teen to stop annoying behavior. For example, contrary to popular opinion, knuckle cracking does not injure knuckles. It is simply irritating to those who have to hear it.

PREVENTIVE TIPS

At a good talk time, build cooperation by doing the following.

Address how he might be feeling. For example: *"Larry, it seems as though you want everyone to notice you. Are you feeling left out these days?"*

State briefly how you and others feel. *"I feel embarrassed when you draw attention to yourself with your rudeness. I love you and I want you to feel good enough about yourself so that you don't need to seek attention with that kind of behavior. I expected it when you were younger, but now that you're fifteen I think it is time to move on."*

Ask him what he might do instead. *"Can you think of any ways to be noticed, have fun, and not be so disrespectful?"*

Follow up this conversation a week later. Notice his improvements. If there are none, other issues may be stifling his cooperation.

Make opportunities to have fun together. Hiking and other outdoor activities allow for time for telling jokes and loosening up. The more fun you have with your teen, the more likely she'll respect your limits and conform to your standards.

WHEN TO SEEK HELP

Some teens use attention-getting noises and gestures to annoy teachers, bring themselves into the limelight, and thus avoid classroom lessons. Usually such behavior relates to having trouble with schoolwork, which makes teens feel like failures. It might have something to do with a new setting, new school, or new teacher. Catching the problem early is important, before he loses too much ground and self-esteem. Have a conference with his teacher and his school counselor and set up a plan to get him tested and, if needed, tutored. Often, this solves the problem.

Other teens haven't learned how to interact with peers appropriately, relying on behavior more typical of elementary-school children. Attempts to make friends are rejected. Talk with his teachers to confirm your observations. He may be lonely. Seek professional help.

See also: Bullied; Depression; Friends, Left Out

ARGUING

"Trevor argues with almost everything I say."
"My mom always wants things to go her way. What about what I want?"

UNDERSTANDING THE SITUATION

Little compares to the tenacity of an arguing teenager. Many parents liken it to the toddler years, when "no" was the standard response to almost everything, though a teen is far stronger and much more creative. Your teen is learning new skills; he can now think more abstractly and is learning to deduce and arrange consequences. To engage in a power struggle is futile. You can't win. If he disagrees, he's big enough to disobey. A wise parent avoids those push-pull, no-win arguments. Arguing can become a habit, an aggressive style of gaining attention or power. Deflate the power struggles by refusing to get involved.

It may seem that she rudely challenges your every word and that every step must be negotiated. One father said, *"When he turned thirteen, I turned stupid."* This is typical. Ironically, as strong as she may act, her ego is in a formative state, and her sense of self is not as strong as she would like you to think. If you scold or punish harshly, she may back down, but her self-esteem will be diminished. If you often act controlling (*"She's not winning this one!"*) and insist she stop arguing, she may rebel to show control in another way. If you throw up your hands and give in, she feels she doesn't matter.

Good communication builds healthy self-esteem and teaches the value of dialogue. Listen, and patiently guide her toward constructive dialogue: *"Sally, you sound very angry. Could you say that with a nicer tone? I'd like to have a pleasant conversation with you."* She needs to learn to resolve conflicts when she's away from home, and home is a safe place for her to practice the important skills of negotiation and assertiveness. Finding the balance between arguing and negotiating will take practice for both of you.

WHAT TO SAY AND DO

Find a parenting group or a close and mature relative or good friend to talk with to help you keep your feet on the ground, especially if you are a single parent. Often, the teen living with a single parent feels more like a partner, able to make adult decisions.

If you're a single parent, learn to say, *"Andrea, I need some time to think about that."* Do not feel pressured to answer immediately, because you'll probably say, *"No,"* which invites a hassle. It does not leave room for you to have a change of heart and can give the message that you don't mean what you say.

At times you will want to change your mind about a previous decision. Sometimes an adolescent's arguments will make sense! Give her credit, and tell her why you decided to go along with her. It is also beneficial to her to hear why you disagree. *"Because I told you so"* does not work for today's teens.

After a decision is made, it is imperative that the discussion end. Leave him some time to consider the situation. You can defer more discussion to the family meeting or to a time when you have had a chance to reconsider. *"Rilie, you still feel very strongly about that. We can talk more about it in a week if you're still concerned."* Allowing for future negotiations is a prudent move. It also teaches patience and deflates the intensity of the moment.

Stay calm. Your tone of voice and body language are key. When one person is rudely demanding and unpleasant, the other person is likely to respond in kind, by triggering an argument. Your teen needs to figure out that when he presents his case in an appropriate manner, he increases his chance of winning the argument. Humor helps alter a potential power struggle: *"Jack, your tone of voice sounds like a Mack truck climbing a hill in reverse. How about putting it into first?"*

Encourage her assertiveness skills. Model and teach: *"I feel _____ about _____ because _____, therefore _____."* Aggressive people generally do not answer the, "because _____, therefore_____." Say, *"Heather, I'm upset because you weren't at Marnie's house as you said you would be. We want to know where you are. Therefore, to help us both, here's a form to fill out when you go out in the evening. It tells us where you'll be and the phone number there."*

When you need to say, *"No, that is nonnegotiable,"* give good, specific reasons.

Likewise, make specific compliments when he makes good choices. Notice when he thinks for himself. *"Val, that must have been a hard decision. I know you wanted to go to the movies with your friends. You chose the right thing to do. Bravo!"*

When you feel she is being disrespectful in an argument, tell her so. Do not be a doormat and give in. *"Helen, this is too heated. We both need a break. We'll discuss it later, when we cool off."* Then simply leave the room. If she follows in a rage, repeat that you are finished talking about it for now; then ignore her. This may make her madder yet.

Do not respond to her angry words with your anger. She is learning self-control. She needs to know that you love her and won't reject her when she pushes against you. Let go of the need to be right all the time. You are the adult, the parent: it is up to you to step out of the vicious circle and avoid the power struggle. Stay calm, and try, *"Janet, how could you say that more respectfully?"* or, *"Janet, I'll listen to you when you use a softer tone,"* or, *"Janet, I'll listen to you if you talk nicely to me, or we can discuss this another time. You choose."*

PREVENTIVE TIPS

When you are past the heat of the argument, help your teen with the problem-solving approach.

Identify his feeling. "Roy, I know you feel angry that we're the only parents who don't allow talking on the phone after nine at night."

Show you understand, even though you may not agree. "I know this must be hard for you. I remember my own dad yelling at me to get off the phone. Sometimes he'd rudely hang up on my friends."

State your concern. "Your father and I are tired and go to work early. You leave for school early. We all need the house to be quiet after nine o'clock."

Listen to him. If he is still feeling pressured by this expectation, brainstorm ideas together. Writing down the ideas shows your interest and concern.

Pick one or two ideas and agree to try them. "Okay, we agree that you may talk after nine if it's about schoolwork, provided that our phone doesn't ring." Arrange a time—three to seven days later—to evaluate the new arrangement.

Follow up.

If yours is a two-parent household, take a good look at your mode of communication. How do you and your spouse resolve conflict?

Arguing reflects how a teen feels about herself and life in general. Be a good listener. Use reflective listening. You need not feel that you must fix her angry or frustrated feelings, but your listening will be of great help.

WHEN TO SEEK HELP

If you feel that you've been locked into an arguing mode too long, and that every conversation is an angry one, let your teenager know what options are available. Make an appointment for you both to see a counselor to learn better communication skills. Admit your own responsibility. Do not blame him. Tell him that it's important: *"Sean, we're not able to resolve any conflict. This is very important. We both need help. It is not good for either one of us to argue all the time. It hurts."*

See also: Anger; Complaining; Chapter 3, Tools of the Trade, Problem solving

BEDROOMS

"We've always battled the mess in her room. Now she wants boys in there!"

"Even though I keep my grades up, practice my music, work my part-time job, balance the sports and friend-ships, my bedroom is always the rub. You don't have to live in my bedroom. I'll keep it the way I want."

UNDERSTANDING THE SITUATION

The bedroom is the eternal battleground for parent and child; sometimes it begins in early childhood and never lets up. Struggles with younger children over picking up toys and clothes translate to more clothes, bigger toys, athletic equipment, food and drinks, pets, schoolwork, and, last but not least, entertaining the questionable visitor. Teens go through "neatnik" stages and horribly messy stages, but when it comes to half-full bottles of soda, week-old sweaty T-shirts, wet towels, and not an inch of floor visible, you may lose it. Either way, your teen may be setting you up: *"If I keep my room a pigsty, my mom won't come in here,"* or, *"My pigsty will really bug her."*

A messy bedroom is just not worth a battle. Eventually, not because she fought with you but because she learned to like a sense of order, she'll have no problem keeping up her room. Other issues may be more important, such as whether you should allow boys in your daughter's room. Most of the bedroom hassles can be eliminated respectfully with house rules and consistency. Everyone does better when limits are clear and mutually agreed upon. Then, there are no sudden surprises. Be patient; time flies. One mother sat in her son's empty room after he'd left for college. *"It's so empty,"* she said sadly. *"I never thought I'd actually miss his piles of clothes and that messy hamster."*

WHAT TO SAY AND DO

A healthy philosophy is, *"Your room is yours and we respect your need for privacy. This is also our family home and needs respect from all of us."* Decide with your teen what things are not acceptable. Food may be okay with you, if it's cleaned up and the plates and utensils are returned to the kitchen. Decide what your bottom line is with your teen and be consistent with follow-through on your agreement.

Some parents are fairly relaxed about how tidy the room is on a daily basis—they've managed to give bedroom neatness a low priority. However, their expectations are clear. Their posted rules may look like this:

1. No food or drinks in the bedroom.
2. Clean up once a week. Vacuum, dust, laundry. (Saturday before soccer.)
3. No entertaining your "steady."

Your teen needs privacy. A younger sister must learn to knock and so must you. Your son or daughter has a lot to deal with when it comes to her changing body. Surprise entrances are not welcome, and it is important for the family to respect this. The bedroom is also a place to listen to favorite music, loud. Earphones are an easy solution when he wants to crank up the sound.

Sarcasm only builds resistance. It is not helpful to say, *"Your room looks like a pigsty. When did the bomb hit?"* Instead, comment on something positive; there's always something. At the family meeting or other good talk time, bring up the issue of establishing a routine that attempts to meet everyone's needs.

Take time to teach your teen how to do the cleaning and the laundry. Remember, never do for him what he can do for himself. Both boys and girls should take responsibility for washing and drying their clothes. This helps them think before throwing them in a heap on the floor. Once the agreement is made, back off, and don't expect perfection. Some well-meaning parents make an agreement with their teen saying their room is theirs. But, a week later, Mom is in her daughter's room rescuing wet towels and a new blouse. Whose responsibility is it? Who should face the consequences?

Do not nag. Ask, *"Melanie, what was our agreement this week about your room?"* Then: *"Great! I'll expect it to be done before you leave with your friends Saturday night."* If she hasn't cleaned her room by the agreed time, say, *"It seems you've decided not to go out with your friends."* If she leaves without keeping her end of the agreement, do not panic or chase her down. The next day, say calmly, *"Melanie, before you leave, you have a job to do."* If she's rebelling, something other than her room is probably on her mind. At a good talk time, try to find out what it is.

When teens share a room with siblings, boundaries become very important and must be respected. Gather all children together and discuss their individual wants and needs. Make agreements. Finish the discussion with a handshake. One girl put a strip of masking tape down the center of the room to define her space.

Some families use a professional housecleaner. Make an agreement with your teen. If his room is not picked up, it doesn't get vacuumed or dusted—he must do it himself. Or, everything goes on the bed in a pile. He will learn not to leave things in his room that he doesn't want touched or seen. Be firm and consistent. The trick is to avoid hassles that wear everyone down.

PREVENTIVE TIPS

Do not wait until an issue arises to discuss bedroom rules. One nervous mother felt that it was unwise to discuss the rule "no boys in the bedroom" when at age thirteen her daughter didn't seem to have thought about it. *"I don't want to give her any ideas."* Another mother countered, *"On the contrary, our house rule is: 'We don't entertain in our bedroom, and neither do the kids.' "* When parents are matter-of-fact and the rules are clear, fewer embarrassing situations occur.

A messy room is not necessarily a sign that your teen is sloppy or negligent. Some kids' rooms are in turmoil, yet they know right where everything is located. Many adults who keep very disorderly desks have the same organizational pattern. The way your child chooses to keep her room may be an indication of her organizational style.

See also: Arguing; Clothes; Rebelliousness; Siblings

BIRTHDAYS

"Sofia thinks she needs another birthday party. Wouldn't you think by age sixteen we could forget the party? And now I suppose she wants boys, too."

"I can't wait until my sixteenth birthday. I think my parents are going to give me a car."

UNDERSTANDING THE SITUATION

Most teens, young and old, look forward to their birthdays with just as much, or maybe more, excitement as they did when they were five. Their friends join in the planning six months prior, deciding on the guest list and the activities. Sometimes several parties must be planned to accommodate the church youth group, the soccer team, and school friends. It's no wonder that by the sixteenth birthday you're pretty tired of planning parties. You also may be concerned about the type of party it might turn into. You do not know all her friends as you once did. Will they drink? Will they smoke? Will they make out in dark corners?

During the teen years you may not be so intimately involved in all the events. Friends begin planning birthday events for their pals in junior high. At this age you may be asked to function merely as a mode of transportation or to provide the space for the party. It may be a struggle for your teen to find time to celebrate with the family. However, it is still very important, so don't give that up. Age sixteen is a time of coming of age, sanctioned by society as old enough to earn a driver's license. Do not underestimate it—this birthday is an important one. Her friends and relatives will want to acknowledge this one.

Birthdays do bring family hassles and teen disappointments. Expectations may far exceed reality. One girl envisioned her friends around a table at an expensive restaurant. This would have cost far more than her family could afford. Keep your lines of communication open, and focus on celebrating her being, her growing, and her maturing rather than on the material gifts.

WHAT TO SAY AND DO

Birthdays are a great time to express deeply felt values. Birthdays come and go, but the memories linger. We're raising our teens in a fast-paced, materialistic world. The most important gifts of all are kind, loving words. At a time when gift cards are "saying it all," write a poem or a note to say what you may take for granted she knows. *"You have been a member of our family for fourteen years and it has been a pleasure beyond our dreams that you are our daughter! We love you so much. Thank you for being you!"* This is a gift from the heart.

To emphasize that she is becoming more adult, give her something that is both traditional and special. Grandmother's locket on a thirteenth or sixteenth birthday says, *"You are now a responsible, mature person. Grandmother is smiling."* (Remember, mistakes happen. Should she lose the gift, you will *both* be crushed. Show understanding.)

Work with him, and remind him to compromise. When he moans, *"Mom, I want a bigger party than that!"* say, *"Jack, I can't see twenty-four teenagers in our house. How about a picnic with an organized baseball game?"* Or, *"I can't handle a party that size until we can be outdoors in the summer. How about inviting two good friends out to dinner and a movie and we'll have a summer party later."*

Birthday celebrations don't have to be coed. Invite her girl-friends to plan the party. Suggest to her best friend that she help plan your daughter's surprise party—you'll be pleased with the results. Teens are creative and take the work and worry out of planning and organizing. *"Ronnie, would you like to organize some of your girlfriends for a surprise breakfast for Tammy's fourteenth birthday? I'll be happy to drive. We'll work together."* When her friends can drive, they'll probably organize it all.

One of the true rubs comes when your teen forgets your birthday. You think, *"Why should I remember hers when she doesn't remember mine?"* You are the adult. Act your age! Plan your party, invite her, and don't make it a poor-me pity party!

PREVENTIVE TIPS

Do not feel rejected when he wants to invite only his friends, not the family. Some teens will spend their birthdays at camp or out of town with friends—something that you never dreamed would happen. Do not create guilt! Teens face conflicts: They have two groups to satisfy, family and friends. Discuss with him how he might satisfy relatives who want to celebrate with him and still have his party with his friends.

Look ahead to potential trouble spots and discuss her expectations. Big disappointments can ruin a birthday. Discuss her wish list. What present is she expecting? *"I'm sixteen, it's a great time to give me a car."* This is a good time to point out some realities. Discuss her party ideas. She may be expecting you to surprise her with a party. She may be counting on two dozen boys and girls watching videos all night. *"I'm practically an adult now."* Teens consider birthdays milestones, and you need to discuss what rules she thinks should change at home now that she's older.

Discuss your expectations. Big hassles occur around birthdays. Discuss the details of his party. If money is a factor, let him know; tell him what you can afford. If you feel thank-you notes are important, tell him before the party and ask him for a commitment to write them. (You might give him a pack of notepaper as part of his birthday present.)

See also: Friends, Choosing; Parties; Traditions

BODY ART

"My son wants to pierce his nose and tattoo his arms. Help!"
"It's my body. I should be able to make my own decisions.
  A nose ring would fit great with the shape of my nose;
  see, right here where it indents."

UNDERSTANDING THE SITUATION

It is hard for any parent to watch his son or daughter experiment with eye-catching body decor. The gamut runs from makeup to wild haircuts, possibly dyed or painted, to tattoos and pierced body parts. Unfortunately, the importance of body appearance is not only trumpeted every day through ads, television, movies, and so on; it is also age appropriate for teens to experiment with who they are and what they want to look like. The message, too often, is that bodies are more important than the whole person.

Traditionally, junior-high kids put on far too much makeup. One father said, *"They all looked like hookers."* His wife told him to stop over at the high school and have a look at what they would look like in a few short years. He did. High-school kids looked much tamer! Junior-high adolescents are "trying on" ideas and experimenting. Their mothers are not dressing them anymore. They are decorating themselves.

Body art, especially the loud, rebellious, way-out looks, is a way for your teen to say, *"I am special. Look at me!"* Most teens are interested in attention-getting styles. They are trying to please their peers, and a "uniform" is one way to do it. In other words, your teen is probably not unique. She may be saying the same thing that all her peers are saying to their parents: *"You are no longer in control of what I wear."*

Parents are concerned with health hazards, and rightly so. Recent studies indicate that body piercing and tattooing are significant causes of hepatitis, which can lead to liver failure and death. Other health hazards related to the use of dirty needles include HIV.

WHAT TO SAY AND DO

"No, you absolutely may not go out looking like that!" invites a power contest, and it generally doesn't work. As hard as it is to do, your letting go empowers your teen. It says, *"I trust you. I have faith in you."* Be honest about what you think of the experimental look, but emphasize that you trust she will learn what is right for herself. She needs to know that you believe she will make good choices about her body. She may try something and learn that it isn't for her. If you can bite your tongue and allow harmless experiments, she will make better decisions, and maybe even ask your advice, over bigger issues later.

When something seems unsafe, stay calm, but state your limits with good reasons. *"Because I said so"* is not enough. You may need to do your homework. For example, ask your physician for articles regarding adolescent tattooing. Showing an article to your son is a concrete, informational approach that says, *"You are capable."* This will go further to prevent rebellion than any emotional lecture on your fears for his safety. *"Nick, many articles say that tattooing is dangerous to your health. Hepatitis and HIV are major concerns. Having the tattoo removed is another process I want you to understand. Besides reading this, if you're still not convinced, I want you to talk with Dr. J."* Whether it concerns tattoos, makeup, hair, or clothes, consulting a respected authority figure other than Mom or Dad is often helpful.

Avoid acting shocked when you are approached with a new idea or look. Overreacting most likely will trigger her planned defense, and battle lines will be drawn. Instead, recognize her feelings. *"I notice you wearing more makeup lately. I know you are older."* Be honest, using *"I feel _____ about _____ because _____."* *"Molly, I don't like too much makeup on you because it hides that healthy, rosy complexion. I like the subtle, natural look."* Take time to teach her about makeup. Ask, *"Terra, would you be willing to have a facial with some friends and to learn proper skin care and makeup colors?"*

Hairstyling is a common way to show independence. Be honest, but let go. *"Ginny, I'm not wild about the new hair color. However, I'm not embarrassed for you."* Always try to find something positive to say: *"You have more courage than I did at your age."*

When interaction is positive, your teen will strive to seek your approval in the future. This helps keep the rebelliousness to a minimum. One girl worried about her mother's reaction to a new, wild spiked haircut and was surprised: *"Mom complimented me and acted truly impressed. I bragged about her to my friends. 'My mom was so cool! She actually likes my hair and couldn't stop touching the short ends.' "* Despite Mom's chagrin, she realized this wasn't a life-or-death matter. It paid off. This teen will continue to communicate openly with her mother.

PREVENTIVE TIPS

The family meeting is a safe arena for kids and parents to say what kinds of body art are acceptable and to establish general family standards. An older sister or brother may have an experience to share. The family may agree to some guidelines: *"It's okay to pierce your ears when you're ten. But you wait until sixteen if you want two holes in an ear."* Or, *"When you decide on a major change, we ask only that you plan, consider the pros and cons, and share that with us, so that your decision is based on good thinking and not on impulse."*

Body art is sold to teens through the media. Counter this appearance-based advertising at home by noticing the characteristics that make up the inner person: *"You have a great sense of humor"*; *"Your voice has such determination"*; *"You move so gracefully"*; *"You may be short, but you're assertive. You give dynamite debates."*

The media often lures with sexual innuendos. An ad might show a girl in tight-fitting jeans with a tattoo on the upper right of her bare back. The message is, *"With those jeans and that tattoo, I will be that sexy."* Ask hard questions such as, *"What are they selling in that ad? Is it a tattoo, tight jeans, or sex?"* This often leads to discussion about values. You may ask, *"What kind of message do you want to send to other people? What do you want other people to know about you? What kind of person are you?"*

Find times to talk together about short-term and long-term goals. Some body art is permanent. What might this mean in the future?

Some high schools have good career programs where representatives from the business community come to talk to teens about their work. This is an ideal time to discuss what is an acceptable look in the workplace.

WHEN TO SEEK HELP

Rebelling is often indicated by extremes in body decor. If grades drop, friends change, or she gives up her activities, in combination with an attention-getting look, seek counseling.

She may be confusing the importance of her appearance with her inner self.

Gang members wear clothing, hats, or handkerchiefs that identify their wearers' association. Parents are often the last to know what these are. If you are unsure about your teen's associations, you may want to consult school counselors or local police. If you discover that your teen belongs to a gang, you need to respond, but carefully.

See also: Body Image; Clothes; Gangs; Rebelliousness

BODY IMAGE

"Ken's so short, his brother calls him a wimp. He's not built like anyone else in the family. I'm afraid kids will tease him." Or, "I wish I had a better body to pass on to her." "I don't fit in my family. I must be adopted, since I don't look like anyone. Who am I, anyway?" Or, "I'm not going to have your thighs, am I, Mom?"

UNDERSTANDING THE SITUATION

One of the greatest issues teens face today concerns healthy self-esteem based on body image. Your teen's rapid growth makes life difficult as he compares himself to his peers. Girls generally develop sooner than boys, yet all differ. Those who begin to develop younger generally reach full development earlier. Physical changes can begin at age nine, on the early side, and may continue through the teen years. One thirteen-year-old said, *"I never know what I'm going to be looking at in the mirror. Every morning a new body, a new face, something weird is always popping out."* Your self-conscious teen may create a "bad hair day" over a pimple; one red bump feels like a face covered with acne; facial hair, especially disturbing to girls, may show up; and new curves mean that nothing will fit. Feelings are strong: *"Everyone is sure to notice."* You begin to worry because your son is so much smaller than other boys his age, and he complains about his skinny arms. His voice cracks, so he decides never to speak again. Perhaps your daughter's breasts have developed before you feel she is ready, and you worry that she will attract older boys too soon. Maybe your teen is suddenly putting on weight but not growing taller. Should you control her diet? You care about how she feels about herself, and you know how important a good self-image is.

Unfortunately, teens must cope with very different physiques just at the time when conforming is so important. This is universally difficult for the teen who develops either faster or slower than his friends. He may feel something is really wrong with him. He may be teased and laughed at, which can be devastating. Parents, teachers, and coaches must encourage these teens and supply activities and opportunities directed at their inner strengths. Physical development will eventually catch up.

In our mobile society, teens are usually identified by how they look rather than by the family they come from or their activities and talents. Girls are supposed to be tall, thin, and "buff," with beautiful hair; boys should be tall, handsome, strong, and buff. The clothes must be expensive, high-end name brands. Even the "granola" (earthy) look has become exclusive.

Your appearance is changing, too, and your issues can get tangled up with your teen's. Will she have to grow up with the same concerns about herself as you have? Will she have the family thighs? Do you have the patience to calm her worries about her body? Can she tell that you really do worry and find her pimples unattractive? Is it hard for you to be helpful when you worry about these same issues?

Mortified is the word that best defines the feelings teens have when they perceive themselves as inadequate or different. The lucky coincidence is that cognitive development is maturing, meaning that this former child, who took everything quite literally, can now think about different ways of seeing herself.

WHAT TO SAY AND DO

Emphasize her character rather than her appearance. Rather than comment on how pretty she is, or how much you like what she's wearing, say sincerely, *"Miranda, you're ready for the day. I like your style."* Remember, teens can sniff out insincerity every time.

Reassure her with your love as you concentrate on her inner qualities. *"You're a beautiful person"*; *"People will always seek you out because you're fun to be with and you have such a great sense of humor"*; *"You're a wonderful team player. You have strong legs and a powerful kick. Any team would be lucky to have you."*

Watch out for labels: *"He's our wimp"*; *"She's our beauty queen."* Nicknames such as *"Short stuff"* (your youngest), *"Dream boat"* (your daydreamer), or *"Mike"* (because you wanted her to be a boy) may seem endearing, but they could have negative connotations to your teen. Check out your teen's perceptions: *"Hillary, how do you feel when I call you 'Poky'?"* (She never did anything fast.) *"My little princess"* is a common nickname that she may interpret literally; girls raised with that label and treated accordingly can be mighty hard to live with.

Keep your negative issues about your body image to yourself. This does not mean you need to hide how you feel, but model positive self-talk and action, and, most important, accept yourself.

Some of your daughter's typical comments really cut to the core: *"Mom, you're not wearing that, are you?"* Or, *"Just don't get out of the car. I don't want anyone to see your hair like that."* These comments also reflect how she's feeling about herself—her looks are everything to her. Don't let it get to you; don't take it personally. This can be one of those times when a middle-aged mother feels her physical self-esteem plummeting, as new wrinkles and bulges appear. Humor her: *"What color would you like my hair to be, purple or gray?"*

Sympathize with her. Her concerns are deeply felt. *"Holly, you'll be growing and changing throughout your teen years, and at times you may feel very annoyed and unhappy with your appearance. This seems to be one of those times."* You cannot fix her feelings. Don't rush out to buy her a new outfit to soothe unhappy feelings. She will learn self-acceptance. Help her work through them: *"What do you need from me?"*

Some girls show physical changes as early as ten years old. If your daughter starts her period this early or develops early in other ways, Dad may need help in understanding his role. He needs to be encouraged to continue to be as loving and close as before.

It is hard not to compare your teen to others his age or even to her older siblings. Yet you need to consider that every teen has his own developmental time clock and genetic outcome. No two teens develop at the same rate, and some will continue changing throughout their young adult years.

Encourage positive thinking. To a negative comment such as, *"I'm just a punk runt,"* offer something positive: *"The best things come in small packages."*

Encourage her to take action. After years of worry, a teen with mild cerebral palsy decided her life was not going to be limited by her limp. Her physical limitations were a very small part of who she would be. One high-school gymnastics champion was eliminated from state competition because she was only four-feet-eight and had to move the uneven bars closer than regulations allowed. This was discriminatory. Despite feeling humiliated, she began to work for changes in the state regulations. She turned her embarrassment and disappointment into positive action.

Share family patterns of development with your teen. Boys who are late developers fear there is something wrong if they are small. It is important that you tell your son about relatives who also were late developers: *"Your uncle Jake remembers how embarrassed he was when his voice cracked in the middle of his high-school valedictorian speech. Ask him about it now and he'll laugh. That seems to be a characteristic in our family."*

PREVENTIVE TIPS

Your teen needs time to talk with you. Be available. Some teens prefer to chat at bedtime, usually with the light off. At these moments you can reinforce what you see "right" about him, and he can share his worries. Concentrate on his specific inner strengths. Ask questions that make him think. *"What are you good at? What do you do well?"*

Friends and relatives who enjoy family activities are important. Older, mature teens or adults who are close with your family will notice and support your teen's inner strengths and talents.

There is always another pond to swim in, where your teen can be a big fish. One tall, gangly teen who was not good in school sports found, to his surprise, that he excelled at biking. He was elected lead rider on his four-man team.

Give your teen a lockable diary in which to record her private thoughts and feelings and her activities. Reviewing it, she will be encouraged by her growth and changes in attitude.

Find new areas of interest. When teens set goals, experience new challenges, and overcome obstacles, it enhances their sense of self-satisfaction.

WHEN TO SEEK HELP

A teen who is self-conscious about his body image may become depressed or turn to regressive behaviors such as childlike dependency and/or withdrawal. For example, if your teen needs constant feedback about her appearance and she's devastated if compliments aren't profuse, it's likely that she's valuing only what others say about her rather than what she feels inside. She may need help building her inner strengths. As you feel her pain, you may find yourself on the verge of panic over her well-being. Be patient and give this time. The transition from innocence to awareness to acceptance can be a painful process. If you're concerned that your teen may be excessively worried or depressed, seek counseling.

See also: Acne; Body Art; Clothes; Depression; Overweight; Sex, Talking About; Sports

BULLIED

"Tim seems very anxious about a boy who is teasing and threatening him, and I don't know what to do. He won't tell me who it is."

"If I tell my mom I'm afraid, she'll tell other people, and then it'll get around. If that happens, it would be even worse!"

UNDERSTANDING THE SITUATION

Naturally, parents worry when their teen withdraws or is anxious about walking to school or even attending school. Sometimes being bullied is the cause. He may not tell you what is happening to him; he may even believe he deserves this bad treatment. Teens worry that if they tell on the bully, they will be branded a squealer, and that if the bully finds out, the situation may escalate. Victims are often embarrassed and afraid, so they keep silent. They will continue to hide the taunting if teachers and other students don't intervene to support the victim. The old, irresponsible adages *"Everyone has to learn to stand up for himself someday"* and *"All kids go through that stuff"* support the bully and his actions.

Victims believe they are "uncool" and feel despised by those they sometimes most admire. Smaller teens are picked on because they cannot protect themselves physically and are quick to submit. They are not cowards, they just don't know how to handle the situation. They are not used to taking charge and are caught off-guard, not knowing what to do or say to defend themselves.

Traditionally freshmen are humiliated by upperclassmen

through what is known as "hazing." This can mean a ninth-grader is forced to give his lunch to an upperclassman or is ordered to do a hundred push-ups in the main auditorium. Though this initiation process may be done without cruel intentions, too often it turns into a victimization of the younger student. Not wanting to buck tradition, the ninth-grader will accept the treatment.

Some victims actually taunt the bully in order to win attention, however negative or hurtful this may be. This unhealthy way of gaining recognition may stem from very low self-esteem and deserves intervention.

Gang-related bullying is not rare in inner-city schools and is very harmful. A strong, aggressive teen may threaten harm unless the victim pays him off with money. These potentially dangerous situations need to be carefully managed with the proper authorities.

If your teen is being bullied, take his fears seriously. He needs to know that you are really going to do something to protect him. Your follow-through says, *"I love you and you are worth protecting."*

WHAT TO SAY AND DO

If your teen confides that he is humiliated, hurt, or scared but begs you not to tell anyone, explain to him that safety must come first. Tell him the steps you will take to keep him safe and promise that you will not do anything without first discussing it with him.

You may want to encourage your teen to face the bully head-on. But do not encourage fighting, as this can lead to very hurtful consequences. Give your teen guidance: *"Drew, when Thomas tricked you into stealing the extra lunch, he put you in a bad position. If you had realized this and told the vice principal what happened, how could this have backfired? If you report an incident of taunting and humiliating, you might save someone else from being badly hurt."* Or, *"Drew, when you're harassed, withdraw calmly and tell an authority. Withdrawing is not losing or being a wimp. Reporting taunting and bullying may save someone from being badly hurt."*

You empower him by saying he could actually save someone else, and this is true.

Your teen has the right to walk to school and along the school hallways without being fearful, physically or emotionally. Tell the situation to the principal, the school counselor, the teachers, or whoever else is in a position to help stop the bullying. Victimizing is not acceptable. It is a crime and is punishable in the adult world. The old adage, "Sticks and stones may break your bones but names can never hurt you," does not apply.

When your teen tells you of a problem with a bully, listen. A typical—and unhelpful—response is, *"What did you do to make him pick on you? You must have done something."* Explaining why bullies act the way they do is helpful. *"Miles, this isn't about you. Sam feels important when he pushes others around. You happen to be the innocent victim. Belonging to the cool crowd is not always so cool. It is definitely uncool to be a mean person!"* Or, *"Margo, people don't pick on others when they feel good about themselves. Greta is insecure. She may even envy you because you get good grades. She's just putting you down to make herself feel better. But this does not excuse her. It is wrong to hurt others."*

Teach assertiveness skills. There can be no bully without a victim. *"Randy, Rick can't be a bully if there's no one to bully. If you tease him, you're asking for it. If you ignore him and he keeps bugging you, he may keep it up until you respond. How could you respond in a way that might make him stop? Could you look him in the eye and ask him why he doesn't pick on someone his own size? Beating you up is hardly a feat, since you're forty pounds lighter. Or say, 'Bug off!' Or, 'Aren't you tired of teasing me yet?' with a big voice. When you act confident, stand up straight instead of slinking away, he may leave you alone."*

All the above, perhaps coupled with good physical training such as martial arts, gymnastics, or wrestling, may boost his confidence, courage, and leadership skills.

PREVENTIVE TIPS

Encourage, encourage, encourage! Self-esteem is built within the family and is the single most important preventive factor. Take special moments with your teen to:

- Tell her that you love and respect her, that she is *"the best Amy"* in the world and that she is unique, very bright, helpful, and capable.
- Give her new, meaningful responsibilities and decision-making opportunities.
- Compliment her good thinking. Ask her opinions.
- Focus on what she does right.

If possible, make time to volunteer at school or on parent committees. One mother said that working in the school office once a week gave her an opportunity to become familiar with her daughter's peers, teachers, and other staff members. She learned about extracurricular activities that would interest her and introduce her to a new peer group. Learning more about the social dynamics of the school helped her to guide her daughter.

WHEN TO SEEK HELP

Sometimes those in authority do not take the action you expect. Remind them that during school hours they are legally responsible for your teen and that although you are willing to work with him, it is ultimately their responsibility to see that your child's environment is a safe one.

If your teen tells you he feels defeated or has no friends, acts anxious, and does not want to go to school, counseling is necessary. These are signs of giving up, and most likely you feel like doing the same. Get professional help.

Some social service agencies have groups to help teens learn how to make friends. Some school counselors may do the same with a "lunch bunch" group for adolescents who have few if any friends. If such a group is not available, help start one.

Other teens are suffering, too. Teaching them, in a safe place, how to make friends and defend themselves against bullies is surely a worthwhile activity.

See also: Bullying; Chapter 1, What Happens During the Teen Years; Gangs; Hanging Out; Shyness

---

BULLYING

"The principal told me that Derek is mean and is bullying other kids. I can't believe it."
"The kid's such a wimp. He deserves to get hurt. Maybe it'll toughen him up."

UNDERSTANDING THE SITUATION

Dismayingly, too many teenagers are bullied. It is often much more subtle in junior high and high school than in the younger age groups. It is a silent crime and it is extremely hurtful.

Bullying takes many forms. Girls give subtle put-downs and write mean notes containing personal attacks. Jealous girls are good at spreading rumors or backbiting: *"I can't believe you like Sandra. She's such a whore!"* Most bullying is verbal and experimental but very damaging. One junior-high girl said that many times girls are picked on if they are more developed than others. *"I know a lot of people who bully others because they have more money. Also people bully each other for not 'going with the group.' "* Teen boys are sometimes verbally abusive. They may coerce, blackmail, or even threaten to beat up their victim. Jabs in the ribs may be accompanied with a mean personal comment: *"You're a wimp and wimps deserve to be hurt!"*

Some kids resort to bullying to show off and create peer

excitement. *"I'm noticed when I create excitement and entertain."* As long as there are onlookers, the bully is reinforced by enthusiasm from the crowd. Some bullies love to control others: *"I'm superior. I'm the boss."* Behavior reflects how the teen feels about himself. If not addressed, it can lead to antisocial behavior, petty crime, and even to prison.

Many bullies come from excessively strict homes where emotional and physical punishment is the norm. Others are from permissive environments where there is a lot of nagging, no limits or routine, and a lack of privacy; as a result: *"Give it to me, it's my right!"* These kids are angry, and they find it is easy and satisfying to pick on someone smaller. Many teens who bully have been bullied themselves and are mimicking how they have been treated. Others are discouraged and bully to gain control but are not really proud of their acts. However, victimization is inexcusable under any circumstances.

WHAT TO SAY AND DO

When you get a report that your teen is causing trouble, he may flatly deny it: *"The kid is a wimp, I didn't do anything to hurt him. The principal is overreacting."* Or, *"He asked for it. He knows I hate his whiny little face in mine; I warned him."* Though you should always be your teen's advocate, listen to the school authorities. Go with your teen to meet with the proper school personnel. Many school disciplinarians meet with the bully and the bullied together to get both perspectives and to make each party accountable.

Bullies usually do not respond to polite hints. It takes a firm approach, clear limits and consequences— *"I'll call the police if I have to"*—and the threat of expulsion or community service. Police need to be notified if physical violence is involved and reasoning and detention have proved ineffective.

Some bullies cannot believe that it's not okay to abuse others, but you do your teen a disservice when you ignore his behavior. A clear message must be sent. Concern about how to approach him is reasonable. Instead of confronting him alone, talk to a school counselor. Many are excellent at befriending this age group. Often, shop teachers, coaches, or custodians are good at approaching troubled teens.

If your child is the bully, act promptly to help him develop a sense of empathy for his victim. Make comments like, *"How do you think he felt when you embarrassed him in front of all those kids?"*; *"Have you ever been in such a position? How did it feel to you?"* Wait for responses. Ask these questions frequently. Connect his answers with what in his life may have prompted the behavior. Did his estranged father hurt his feelings when he was younger? Is this a way for him to get back at others so he isn't the only one who feels hurt? Counseling with him and others in the family could be very helpful. He will be less likely to be hurtful to others if he can share his own pain.

Unfortunately, some "popular" teens keep their superior position by being mean to those less desirable, perhaps smaller, more studious, foreign, or otherwise "different." This is the most hurtful sort of snobbery. Address his feelings: *"Adam, you generally are quite a leader, you like that."* Point out the behavior and your feelings. *"Recently you gave Charlie a hard time because you were annoyed with him. Those actions are cruel and bullying. You're bound to work with others who annoy you. Life's like that. How could you handle a Charlie situation differently?"*

· Parents of a bully must take charge of their teen's inappropriate behavior and should try to help him turn his desire for leadership around. Point out that he might be liked more if he were nice to Charlie: *"Instead of being nasty, how about making it cool to make friends with the underdog?"* Being kind to everyone could be a very "cool" thing. His popularity could rise in the eyes of his peers. Such a solution may seem unrealistic, but it works often when groups of teens are challenged to depend on one another in gym class or other activities.

When you hear your teen bullying a sibling, stop him. Teach him to use his words in a nonhurtful, assertive way. *"Rich, how could you tell your sister in a different way that you are angry with her? In our family we use our words nicely to get what we* need. Try, 'When you _____, I feel _____ because _____, therefore _____."

Do not ever call or label your teen a "bully." You do not want to give her something she must live up to. If you give up on her, she'll give up on herself. To say, *"I love you,"* when you are discouraged may seem next to impossible, but she needs to feel your love, faith, and trust. Her behavior is not excusable, but that does not mean she is unlovable.

PREVENTIVE TIPS

Examine your parenting style. Is there an authority figure in your household who is abusive either physically or emotionally? If so, seek family counseling.

You may have to take a painful look at your style of interacting with others. How do you treat other adults or talk about them? Are you aware of their feelings? Do you phrase your comments carefully so they are not hurtful? Your teen is watching.

Communicate the value of respecting others. Choose a good talk time, and stay calm. Question rather than lecture. Poor responses will shut down possible discussion. Avoid: *"How could you ever . . . ?" "You should have known better. I'm surprised at you." "How thoughtless of you."* Helpful questions are not blaming or accusing: *"How do you want to be thought of—as someone to fear and distrust, someone who is mean? Or as a person who is looked up to, who is thoughtful to others, and who can be trusted and depended on? How would you feel if someone made you cry and then laughed at you?"*

The bully needs healthy self-esteem. Check out local scouting or youth community volunteer programs. Seek out an organized wilderness program that is experienced in working with teens. This may be expensive, but if a program can instill leadership and improve behavior, the money spent is well worth it. If the negative behavior worsens, it could cost you more in the long run.

WHEN TO SEEK HELP

If you receive reports of the use of a weapon, gang-related activities, or extreme physically or emotionally hurtful behavior, you have a responsibility to get help. Generally, a bully will have a difficult time keeping jobs and staying out of trouble throughout life. He needs treatment now, and he needs your support to find it. He may be raising a red flag, asking for help.

Bullies sometimes speak only bully language. Some need to be taken to court and forced by law to improve their behavior.

See also: Anger; Bullied; Chapter 1, What Happens During the Teen Years; Gangs; Hanging Out; Siblings

CHORES

"How do I make him do his chores? We all have our jobs, and we may hate them, but we must do them. He's so self-centered. He does just what he needs to do for himself."

"I'm sick of being told what to do. My parents ride me about everything. So what if the lawn goes an extra week without being mowed? I'm too busy."

UNDERSTANDING THE SITUATION

Motivating children of any age to do chores is a common problem. It would be far easier to hire someone or to do the work yourself. However, sad but true, that is not responsible parenting.

Your goal is to guide your teen, through proactive parenting, to become a "willing to pitch in" person, as well as a "noticing things that need doing" person. This is an interdependent person. If you have raised your child to work as part of the family team, to be a contributing member, an asset to the family, you will have an easier time. However, it is never too late to encourage doing chores and to compliment jobs well done!

When you adopt the philosophy that *"We are a team!"* you create an atmosphere of community. Your teen matures in character when she feels that you can count on her, that you feel she is intelligent, worthwhile, and needed. In return, she feels capable, trusted, and depended on, all of which build healthy self-esteem.

WHAT TO SAY AND DO

The parent always loses in a power struggle with a teen. Avoid win/lose confrontations. *"Yes, you will or else . . ."* is not a sensible attitude. Cooperation is built on understanding *"We are working together."* If he is defiant or manipulative (which all teens are at one time or another), you need to realize that these are touchy situations that can lead to alienation when not managed sensitively. You need to be flexible without becoming a doormat. A mature parent will find flexibility and logic in establishing consequences and letting something go once in a while.

Require that chores be completed. You are not doing your teen any favor by allowing him to let his responsibilities slide.

Together, make a list of all it takes to run the household. Chores can be negotiated and traded in your family meeting. All families tackle chores differently, depending on lifestyle, schedules, and individual preferences. The important thing is that you not avoid them.

A positive attitude is a must. What they see is what you'll get. Some families have "gang attack" on the chores on Saturday mornings, a social activity in which everyone contributes. When undertaken as a group, the jobs seem less distasteful. Decide on a family work time. Don't forget to take a break from yard cleanup or housework for hard-earned hamburgers, and treat yourselves later to a movie, a bike ride, a concert or a play, or just "vegging out."

Begin by making a list of what needs to be done. Ask your teen to help draw up the list.

Yard: mow, weed, rake
Porch: sweep, hose off
Garage: sweep, stack wood
Pets: feed, groom, clean up poop
Cars: Vacuum, wash
Kitchen: cook, empty and fill dishwasher, wash dirty pans and dishes, floors, countertops, refrigerator, oven, take out garbage
Bedroom: change sheets, vacuum, dust, laundry, straighten up
Bathroom: clean toilet, sink, tub/shower, floor
Living room: Vacuum, dust, empty ashes in fireplace

Are your expectations reasonable? Are you asking too much or too little? Learning organizational skills is a necessary part of your teen's development. Chores are never a top priority, and she will complain and truly feel put upon. Consistently, firmly, gently bring her back to the task: *"Maureen, you need to mow the lawn. I know you have a busy schedule this week, but the lawn is your commitment. Let's decide when you'll do it."* If she does a poor job, tell her kindly and firmly, *"Reen, you didn't trim the edges. The job is not finished. Please trim the edges."*

Deal with a defiant teen calmly. He may be in a power struggle with you over other matters, and winning his cooperation will take time and patience. Firmly say what you need: *"You can go to Jim's after you've fed the dog."* If he sneaks out anyway, quietly take care of the pet yourself. Don't let your pet starve. At a better time, say, *"Ryan, you're neglecting the job that you agreed to do. What's going on? This isn't like you. I know you love the dog. How can we make sure this is done tomorrow?"* Consistent, calm, loving, and firm discussions at good talk times, along with follow-through, will help create cooperation.

Nagging will only make her "parent deaf." Negotiate a written contract, including time commitments. When chores are not done on schedule, simply say, *"Letty, you have to wash the porch before you go to your friend's house."* Mean what you say, and don't be afraid to follow through. *"It seems you've decided not to go to your friend's."* This makes it clearly her choice and her responsibility.

Stay calm and do not engage in a battle over chores. Act a little bewildered: *"Chelsea, this isn't like you. I'm confused. What's going on? It's only the dishes; it takes fifteen minutes. What could be so important that you flip out like this?"* Your emotional teen needs these moments of understanding. She's probably worried about her math grade or is anxiously awaiting a VIP phone call.

Do not attach allowance to chores. You expect these jobs to be done because *"You belong to this family."* Extra jobs may be assigned when needed for extra money, or you can barter for a tank of gas. Pay the going rate for a job well done. Do not bribe. Be direct: *"Robert, I need my car washed. I'll pay you with a tank of gas."*

Don't be a nitpicker. Notice what your teen is doing right. No one grows on criticism. She has forgotten to wipe the counters, and you are annoyed: notice something she has done well. A little later, when you are having a good discussion, comment, *"Hailey, you took out the garbage, hooray! But what happened to the counters? Next time?"* You may be happily surprised when she does the counters next time.

When a chore is not done as agreed, avoid blaming. Instead, look for the solution. What are the needs of the situation? *"Heather, the laundry needs to be done before you go out tonight."*

PREVENTIVE TIPS

Family fun plays a large part in winning cooperation. Spend time together, both alone and with friends, on occasional weekend trips, camping, hiking, skiing, going out to dinner or the theater, and so on.

If possible, cancel your professional housecleaner and gardener and give these responsibilities to your family. Your teen will someday have to know how to do these common tasks, and this hands-on experience will serve her well.

If you want your teen's sheets changed, her bed made, or her shoes put away, be sure that yours are, too. Be a model. Also, to get around the boy-girl issues, have Dad do the dishes and make the beds sometimes, while Mom cleans the garage and washes the car.

To illustrate the concept of the family as a team, envision a wagon that represents the family. Each person is a wheel, needed to help move the wagon. What happens if one family member decides to be a tiny wheel, or if someone wants to control everyone and be the big wheel—or if someone decides to be a square wheel, really different and of no help at all? Your teen can relate to this concrete example.

WHEN TO SEEK HELP

A truly discouraged teen will not cooperate easily. Do not make the small issues into major battles. Cleaning bedrooms, vacuuming, and so on are small issues compared with alcohol or drug issues, learning problems, and depression. Even very well-adjusted teens moan and groan about chores. However, when life with your teen has become troublesome across the board, it may mean that he has emotionally "moved out" of the family. Talking with someone who knows you and your teen, such as a close friend, another parent, a school counselor, or a minister, may be helpful.

See also: Arguing; Bedrooms; Money; Mood Swings; Rebelliousness

CLOTHES

"He looks awful! His pants are so baggy they hang below his hips. I don't know how he can walk!"
"Mom won't get off my back. If I wore what she wanted, I'd look like a real geek."

UNDERSTANDING THE SITUATION

Big battles develop around clothing. You may feel truly embarrassed: *"That's not what I raised you to look like!"* Then, frustrated by your advice, with her confident opinion she says, *"I look just the way I want to look,"* adding, *"Get with it."* This reaction can make you angry and strike at your self-confidence: *"Where have I gone wrong?"* *"What will others think of him?"* *"What will people think of me as a parent?"* You may fear that his wardrobe indicates he's headed for trouble—clothes now, drugs next?

Your teen is dressing that way for several reasons: to get positive attention and acceptance from his peers, to be different from you and your generation, and to express his individuality.

Many parents let their children choose their clothes in elementary school and then mistakenly begin limiting choices in junior high. You can let her know what is appropriate and at the same time make her understand that you feel she is capable of choosing what she wears. Your message to her needs to convey trust and confidence; she needs encouragement, not criticism. One of the most helpful and difficult things is to stay objective. Ask yourself, *"What is her world like? What does this mean to her?"* How you react to the clothing situation often depends on how you answer these questions. She is trying on new identities, and clothing reflects these roles. Inside, she is terribly unsure about how she looks to others—even to you. When parents back off, the responsibility becomes the teen's. She'll learn much sooner what feels right and what is appropriate for her.

This does not mean you should ignore what she wears. She may interpret that as lack of caring. Don't bribe, threaten, or punish. If she's timid and acquiesces, she won't develop the confidence to make her own decisions and to think for herself when you're not there. Strictness—*"Young lady, you won't leave this house in that getup. Try it and you're grounded!"*—may promote worse behavior. A layered look with baggy clothes on your thirteen-year-old may seem fine when compared with purple spiked hair, tattoos, or strings of earrings.

WHAT TO SAY AND DO

A younger teen may need stronger guidelines. Suggest appropriate attire for school, social or religious functions, outdoor activities, or a visit to Grandma's. You may shop together, though the selection should be hers. Most teens prefer to shop for clothes with friends.

Be honest and direct. If you are worried, say so. Even a capable, intelligent sixteen-year-old lacks experience. *"Carol, your outfit could be very misleading to your date. Those tight short shorts and your midriff showing are seductive. Your date may expect more than you intend. Please consider dressing more appropriately."*

Family guidelines reflect values and may become family standards, to be discussed at mealtimes and agreed to at the family meeting. "Our family" is a helpful concept when it reflects structure and flexibility. Do not be the type of parent who sets all rules. Being a part of "our family" helps your teen find her identity as she tries out all sorts of new things, be it curfews, religions, or clothing styles. Guidelines such as, *"In our family, black leather miniskirts and black-purple lipstick are reserved for Halloween,"* help her make decisions within her peer group. One teen confided, *"It is easier for me to say, 'I can't get away with wearing that in my family.'"*

Tell her how you feel: *"I'd rather you didn't wear that."* Don't go to war over it. We all understand that teens dress weirdly. If we don't resist, the trend will usually wear off. In the meantime, you can say, *"James, I'm not used to your new look, and I may not ever be. But I love you just the same."*

Get in touch with what you're feeling, whether it's concern, frustration, or anger. Does she look like a druggie? Does the way she looks reflect how good a parent you are? Once you identify and understand your feelings, you may be able to communicate more effectively. *"Mary, I love you, and I would rather you didn't wear those shorts to school. To me, they're too short and suggestive, and I think they send the wrong message about you. It's much better to attract others with your smile and enthusiasm."*

Think ahead, and give a warning to avoid a battle. With a sense of humor, say, *"Joe, we're having dinner with Grandma tonight. Please try to pick an outfit that won't send her into shock."* You are staying light and at the same time delivering a message of respect and consideration for others, which is something teens can forget as they grapple with other emotional issues. If your teen seems not to like your sense of humor, remember that we all have a hard time laughing at ourselves when we don't feel self-confident. You may have more success making yourself the brunt of the joke: *"I'm amazed that those shoes stay on your feet with no laces. I can just see myself wearing those and trying to run for the bus."* You can laugh together about that scene.

Even though you may not be happy with his attire, find something positive to notice—there's always something. *"I like that color green on you. It complements your eyes."* Keep your comments short, and make sure they're sincere. That way, he'll begin to understand how much you love and trust him.

PREVENTIVE TIPS

Some high schools have good career programs where representatives from the business community come to talk to teens about their work. This is an ideal time to discuss what is acceptable attire in the workplace.

If you're interested in what's "in" with her crowd, ask her at a good talk time. When she sees that you're sincerely interested, she may begin asking for your opinion about how she looks. If you are troubled about the way she dresses, you will be able to discuss this much better if you have had some positive interactions as well.

Have fun together looking at clothes, and use the opportunity to express your values. How do you feel about designer clothes? How do you feel about quality versus quantity? If you pay for the clothes, is she allowed to decide what items to buy? Often, both boys and girls enjoy shopping at thrift shops and looking for great buys. Attend fashion shows together. Window-shop or thumb through catalogs together.

When you pass a store window and you feel she's receptive—ideally at a moment when clothing is not an issue—discuss how she might dress to her best interest. Thoughtful questions stimulate good thinking, which will help her in her search for identity. Say, *"Jeannie, what you wear makes a statement to others; it tells them about you. Some girls want their bodies noticed and dress in tight shirts and short skirts. What is important to you, or about you, that you'd like others to know?"* Even if you get only a grunt or a shrug, you have encouraged her to think. *"When you go for a job interview, conforming to the company's dress code may help you to get, or to keep, the job."* Keep your remarks short and simple. Help her to understand that opinions do count, especially first impressions, and that how she presents herself gives her greater control in many situations. She has choices.

WHEN TO SEEK HELP

If your teen's clothing has become a big problem for you, ask yourself, *"Are there other areas of concern? Is her schoolwork still important to her? Have her grades dropped? Is she attending classes? Has she begun to hang out with a new crowd that I consider marginal and possibly on drugs?"* Usually, it is not just the clothing that presents a problem—it is other issues in concert with the clothing that make it appear a symbol of more serious things. Talk to his teachers and school counselor about your concerns.

You may know a teen who wears highly seductive clothing and is overly flirtatious. This sometimes indicates that the teen has been sexually abused. These kids sometimes act out with provocative and unusually seductive and sexualized behavior. Your awareness could be of great help to such a teen, who may need to work through her past abuse before she can form healthy relationships with the opposite sex. Counseling is highly recommended.

See also: Alcohol and Other Drugs; Body Art; Clothing Allowance; Gangs; Rebelliousness

CLOTHING ALLOWANCE

"I'm tired of her hounding me for more clothes. I buy them, and then she leaves them on the floor, in the closet, or she loans them to her friends."

"My mom is always ragging on me about being responsible for my clothes. I always have to ask for money and justify what I want to buy. I wish I could just buy my own clothes."

UNDERSTANDING THE SITUATION

A clothing allowance may help you and your teen to resolve common clothes-buying hassles. Your teen is rapidly changing, and body image is of great concern. Outgrowing a pair of jeans when they've been worn only a few times is not unusual, as she may grow four inches in six months. His clothes reflect how he feels and who he is currently identifying with. Trading, borrowing, and buying clothes is in. Teens feel that change is important, and parents feel that spending is out of control.

Whether your teen is ready for, and successful with, a clothing allowance is determined by her interest, not her age. Start the plan with small steps, and learn what works for you both by trial and error. Determine your goals. Hers may be to get more clothes, or to be more independent and free of parental control. Your goal may be for her to learn the value of money. These goals are different but do not need to oppose each other. Both are important and, with good communication, can be reached. Be sure to define what you expect her to be responsible for. This is a separate money matter from her general allowance.

You will want to establish a budget according to what you can afford. Together, record her clothing needs for the next twelve months. Reviewing past bills will help. Identify the items that you will continue to buy, such as the more expensive outerwear, sports uniforms and equipment, and so forth.

Success will vary with each individual. Liz's mother's goal was to establish a clothing allowance to stop the arguing over buying more clothes she couldn't afford. Liz, age fourteen, took three months to decide that she didn't want to be on a clothing allowance. She wasn't ready for it. However, she did develop an appreciation for the family budget and stopped whining about buying more clothes. This brief experience satisfied them both. For other families, this might have been just the beginning of a very workable ongoing plan.

Teens' spending habits vary. Should your teen have a credit card with a clothing allowance? Should you give cash monthly or weekly? Katy and Lisa are sisters. Katy, seventeen, uses her parents' credit card, stays within her budget, and tracks her spending better than when she had cash in her pocket. However, her sixteen-year-old sister, Lisa, did better with cash. The credit card was much too tempting for her, and her spending went out of control.

A clothing allowance will work only if there is mutual

respect and flexibility. If you initiate the plan with a rigid, excessively strict attitude and are unwilling to bend or give in to unexpected circumstances, you will discourage your teen from wanting to try. If you are the type of parent who alternately rescues when your teen falls behind and then yells and lectures because of all the mistakes made, you and your teen will soon lose all respect for the plan. Your job is to structure the clothing allowance with your teen. Help her understand that this allowance is a privilege and requires a good deal of responsibility. When designed with respect, the expectations, the rules, and the consequences will be clear before the program begins. There will be very difficult times when your teen makes mistakes. You will need to determine what constitutes rescuing and enabling irresponsible behavior and what is helpful support, teaching your teen that we learn from our mistakes.

This program can teach saving for and valuing possessions and pride in personal responsibility for clothes—wonderful life lessons that will be invaluable when your teen leaves home for college or work. It teaches responsibility for spending, and it can ease the tension that occurs when a teen rejects clothes bought for him by a parent. It can also increase self-confidence and pride, especially when it is started with young teens. Basically, a clothing allowance is a demarcation time of switching control from parent to teen.

Your teen will need your ongoing attention and assistance to make this budget work. He will err, and there will be moments of great frustration for you both. Keep in mind that this is a process of learning and growing and that it takes hard work. When your teen makes a mistake, do not penalize him or show any resentment. Instead, encourage him to be creative in thinking of ways to earn money to add to the allowance. This is one more way to help him recognize his abilities. Keep the faith.

WHAT TO SAY AND DO

Use the family meeting to set up and evaluate clothing allowances and other money issues. These valuable life lessons need to be treated as business. This also may motivate a reluctant teen who doesn't want to go to the family meeting otherwise.

If your younger teen shows interest and maturity, he may want to be given a clothing allowance. Plan for success. Give less money and less responsibility at first, until he demonstrates that he can handle more. Evaluate the program frequently at the family meeting. By doing so, you can lessen the chance for failure when you are just getting started.

Parents and teens have met with success when the clothing allowance and the regular allowance are kept separate, at least initially. This seems to give the teen a "time for learning." The many facets of budgeting can seem overwhelming, and this is a way to simplify while your teen learns a very hefty lesson.

Before setting up the clothing allowance, hold a family meeting. Your success lies in the clarity of your communication. You need to decide what you can afford, and she needs to analyze what she will need. Refer to recent records when available so that she sees what has been spent on clothes in the past.

Eliminate the possibility for surprises. *"But, Dad, you said you would buy . . ."* is a common problem. Teens try to split parents at every turn. Make sure you are on the same wavelength. If not foreseen and addressed, such issues may destroy your good intentions. Once an amount is determined, check her perception of what is expected.

Discuss possible scenarios when setting up a budget. This will help illustrate consequences without having to lecture. *"Scott, say you buy the expensive name-brand sweatshirt with all your clothing savings. What will you do when you have no money for pants or shirts? It wouldn't be fair to you or me for me to bail you out."*

Don't rescue. Empower your teen to learn to save for the denim jacket he's been craving. Occasionally, you may loan him the money—for instance, if it is on sale and you want him to learn to take advantage of good bargains. He may also learn that what he really wants is very different from what he really needs, and decide to forgo the jacket.

Many teens loan clothing to their friends, and it is not uncommon for items to get lost. Do not rescue. Do not lecture. If she nags or complains, give her an understanding look. She may be willing to problem solve with you. Say, *"Anna, I'm sorry Kathy lost your skirt."* She may reply, *"I could wear my red one instead. Or I could buy another one. Maybe I could ask her to pay for it. What do you think?"* Do not say, *"I told you so."* You can bet she has learned something from this.

PREVENTIVE TIPS

When you're considering a purchase for yourself or others in the family, discuss it with your teen. The more he observes how you weigh the pros and cons and understand the difference between needs and wants, the more he will learn to do so as well. You must model good thinking, restraint, and reasoning.

Take the time to ask for your teen's opinion: *"Sarah, which do you think is most practical for me?"* She will feel more capable when she feels you depend on her judgment and will do better with her own choices, and you will benefit from her good ideas as well.

See also: Body Image; Jobs; Money

COLLEGE

"We're so worried about Tom. He is not taking the college application process very seriously. He may not go any-where."

"I wish Mom and Dad would lay off the college thing. I'll get my applications in. They need to get off my back. It's all they talk about. You'd think they want to get rid of me!"

UNDERSTANDING THE SITUATION

It is no wonder that when the topic How to Help Your Teen Get into College is discussed at high-school parent night, parents show up in droves. You know how important a college education is. You want your teen to have the same or better advantages than you did. College is also a tangible symbol of success of the teen, of the parents, and even of the high school. No wonder teens feel pressured. Kids are taking the SATs two, three, and four times, and some are spending hundreds of dollars for extra lessons. You can help ease the pressure on your teen by being careful that she isn't measuring her success by your approval but rather by what is best for her.

Whose choice is it, and what will it be? Whose goal is it? Some parents start by choosing the proper preschool that will lead to the proper elementary school that will ensure admission to the proper upper schools, in order to have the teen graduate from the same college as his father and grandfather did. Where does this leave room for the teen who needs to take a break from school, perhaps to work and travel? Where does this leave the teen who may do best at a local community college? Many college students are struggling over which major to pursue. Some take five or six years to get through.

Your teen needs your support, your ear, and your guidance. He needs to know how much money you are able to provide for his schooling and what amount he will have to provide himself. The final decisions should be his. When the commitment is his, he will take full responsibility for it, whether it is right or wrong. Remember, a wrong decision can still be a good learning experience.

College planning is loaded with pressures. Teens who are fortunate to have little financial restriction tour the country visiting a number of colleges, then spend months filling out costly applications and worrying over being accepted by the best. Ask yourself, *"Is my success measured by which college my teen gets into? Is my teen's self-worth measured by the college scholarships awarded?"* Teens compare themselves to one another, and so do parents. The process is not easy or fair; a friend who gets straight A's may not be accepted while another with lower grades and a good football record does. Rejections can be confusing and painful. Financial concerns may dictate whether college is a choice, and, if so, which colleges. Grade point averages as well as test scores are significant factors.

Going to one of the best colleges in the country does not guarantee success or lifelong happiness. College does provide a wonderful opportunity to face many new, character-building life challenges. Many teens do very well at local colleges, while others are ready and eager to take off on their own, some far from home.

Your teen will need you not only through this period of complicated decision making but for the preparation for departure from home (the letting-go process), as well as for the growing pains of the years ahead. As peer groups diversify and best friends begin to go their own separate ways, following their unique personal strengths and interests, parents continue to be a very much needed presence.

WHAT TO SAY AND DO

Good decisions are based on proper information. Help your teen set her goals and then gather the relevant information.

Be positive. If she is college-bound, it is healthy to stress that there are plenty of "right" colleges for your teen, there is no one perfect college, and there is always room for change down the road. Many students transfer from one college to another after one or two years. For example, Molly was in a small, liberal arts college. In her sophomore year she decided to major in a science and transferred to her state university, which had more lab equipment and an excellent reputation in her area of interest.

The SAT exams and the expensive practice courses are an early and major consideration. Encourage your teen to talk with his school's college counselor or a private college counselor, as well as the educational company giving the SAT course. Talking with older students who have completed the process will also be helpful.

The process of selection may begin as early as the spring of the junior year. Make sure your plans are financially viable. Tell your teen how much you have saved and what you can afford each year. This discussion will have a direct impact on college selection and future opportunities. For example: *"If you choose this college, we will not be able to help you with a car."*

If possible, visit colleges around the country. Suggest a weekend visit to spend time on campus, stay in the dorms, and experience campus life. Her future won't seem quite so uncertain, and the break from old ties will be easier.

College counselors have a great deal of information, including videos that colleges provide. Discuss your teen's long-range goals and preferences. Ask: *"Do you want a big school or a small one? Class sizes of thirty or five hundred? Do you want to go far from home? Do you want a big-city school or a smaller college community? What courses interest you?"*

Teens compare their college choices with those of their

friends. You can help her to separate and to make sound individual decisions based on what's best for her. Some teens have a more difficult time letting go than others. This often manifests as angry outbursts, impatience, or moodiness. It may be hard, but healthy, for your teen to break off a steady dating relationship. Listen. Understand how difficult this is. When you are positive, she will be, too.

PREVENTIVE TIPS

Let go of your dreams and wishes and trust that your young adult knows best. You have given her eighteen years of guidance, and now she needs to have a chance at realizing her dreams. Listen to her. She will have an innate sense of what is right for her. Becoming a good friend to your teenager is one of your lifelong goals. This could be the beginning of a new relationship.

Dreams are very important. Whether or not they are fulfilled, only time will tell. Support her dream any way you can. Be glad she has a dream greater than the next party or the latest boyfriend.

Admit your sadness at watching your child grow up and leave home. This time, known as "empty nest syndrome," can be difficult for everyone in the family. When you identify your feelings about this major event, and seek support from other parents or professionals, you may find that you treat your teen with more confidence and trust. A parent who hasn't dealt with his personal feelings may unconsciously put added pressure on his teen.

Many teens are quite irritable throughout the senior year. By the time the college application process is finished, the kids are ready to leave and the parents are ready to let them go. Don't lose faith in your teen; choosing a college is a major process. As she is preparing to leave home, she must separate; she will return.

SEEKING HELP

This is probably the biggest decision your teen has ever faced. He may show signs of temporary depression, sleeplessness, or excessive irritability. He needs good counsel to help calm his fears and make decisions. College counselors can be found locally through private business, high schools, community colleges, and four-year colleges. Take advantage of whatever is offered to help.

See also: Grades and Homework; Leaving Home; Losses and Grief; Stress

COMPLAINING

"My daughter complains and whines excessively."
"This is totally stupid. I don't even know why I have to be here. I'm bored. Why did you even bring me here?" Or, "Our house is so dumb. I wish I were Samantha. Her mom is cool and Samantha gets anything she wants."

UNDERSTANDING THE SITUATION

Constant complaining can be very annoying, especially when it occurs in front of your adult friends. Some teens whine and grouse more than others. Siblings often compare themselves to one another. To them, life feels unfair. All the sudden changes with her body, her friends, and so forth are just not fair! Your teen probably isn't consciously calculating, "How difficult can I be today?" but you may feel that he is. Intense, sensitive children are likely to be more irritable during the emotional surges and physical changes of adolescence. And you are likely to take the brunt of it. He may blame the world for his frustrations, but he feels safe taking them out on you.

He also may be unpredictable, feeling insecure, fluctuating from close to distant, cranky to clingy, not daring to meet the world head-on. Usually, complainers are very unsure of themselves and have low self-esteem: *"Am I worth as much as my sister Jane or my friend Pete?"* He wants you to commiserate about life and to listen to how he feels mistreated.

He may whine and fuss to the point where you feel sick and tired of him. When you nag him to stop, he is likely to continue or even increase the whining to get attention. When you get frustrated with him and push him away because he's a pain in the neck, you are sending the message, *"You are not worthy."* This communicates that you don't trust him to do a good job by himself and reinforces his need for your support.

As hard as it may be, do not join the pity party. The complaining will lessen over time, if handled well. Work on building his self-esteem and encouraging him to handle his responsibilities. This takes volumes of patience and encouragement from the person he complains to the most.

WHAT TO SAY AND DO

Pay little attention to the complaining and be very specific about positive behavior: *"Nat, you have such good ideas. I think you're ready to solve these problems pretty much on your own."* It is important for him to hear that you think he is capable. If he's a complainer, he probably has a poor sense of his capabilities. Never use the word *complaining* to a teen when you are trying to offer positive reinforcement.

Be a positive role model: *"The glass is not half-empty. It appears half-full to me."* Any positive attitude you convey to your teen now is likely to become an important part of his value system later.

Respond by reflecting your teen's feeling: *"Sandy, you sound frustrated."* Reply to the complaint with a question: *"What do you need from me?"* or, *"What are you going to do about that?"*

Questions pass the responsibility back to her so that she'll think about what she needs.

Complainers typically blame bad feelings or outcomes on someone or something else. Help her identify her feelings by putting a name to the emotion: *"Andrea, I know you feel disappointed."* Here's the hard part—sympathize, show understanding: *"I know it's hard."* Give her a perspective on areas in which she does well: *"You do so many things so well in baseball. Hitting isn't the only skill needed to play the game. You caught a very difficult line drive and got it back to the pitcher pronto."* Leave the "but" out of your dialogue. It's not helpful to say, *"But life goes on and so must you,"* or *"But life's just not fair."* Sarcasm (*"Oh, aren't you Mr. Happy today!"*) and negative labels (*"You're a real pill lately!"*) are not helpful.

Encourage him to find a solution to the problem rather than to blame others. He needs to assume responsibility for his feelings and actions. The little "Eeyore" in all of us can hold us back from reaching our full potential. Say, *"Bob, I don't know that the teacher is being unfair. I do know that you felt you did a good job on this paper and she gave you a low mark. I feel you should talk to her, ask her what she liked and what she didn't like. Perhaps she'll let you rewrite the paper."* Once you have listened, back off. Say only once, *"I've listened, and we've brainstormed ideas. Let me know what you decide to do."* Or, *"I know you can handle this. I'll be eager to hear how it goes."*

The next step is the *big* one. How do you get past the feeling that you should solve your teen's problem? It's safe to assume that he will have problems when you can't be there for him. Give him time to come up with his own ideas and choose the one he thinks he can carry out. A few ideas from you won't hurt, but he needs to know it is his choice. Then you can congratulate him for solving his problem.

When eating, exercise, and sleeping schedules are disrupted, crabbiness is the outcome. When she's grouchy, point out that it may be a result of staying up all night at that slumber party. Help her plan ahead to handle her feelings when she comes home: *"Trisha, when you come home, Aunt Shelly and Uncle Tim will be here, so you'll have to keep functioning. I know you may have a hard time because you'll be short on sleep, but I know you'll keep it together while they're here. You can take a nap later."* Or, help with limits: *"Marcia, the family rule is one overnight a weekend."* Or, *"You have soccer tryouts tomorrow. How will you play your best if you go to the party?"* Give options: *"You could go to the early part of the party and come home at nine o'clock."*

Teens are noted for their unkind comments. Help her to understand the difference between "put-downs" and "put-ups." *"April, when kids want to make themselves look good to others, they often give put-downs. Put-downs are comments that feel like a slug in the stomach: 'You couldn't get a good grade even if the teacher gave you all the answers.' In our family, we work on put-ups. We encourage each other with positive comments. When someone gives you a put-down, say, 'Ouch, that hurts.' Don't accept it."*

Check out your teen's perceptions of various situations. Often, teens observe situations accurately but interpret poorly. For example, Julie's sister, Irene, was graduating from high school. Julie couldn't help but notice the gala celebration—the new dress, the gifts, the phone calls, and the parties for Irene. Julie assumed that her parents cared more about Irene. She felt that life was unfair, and ardent complaining was the outcome. Faced with this scenario, you might say, *"Julie, you seem very unhappy lately. I can tell by the way you get upset so easily."* Use fantasy. *"I bet you wish you were graduating."* Offer a question to help her rethink her perception: *"Julie, what do you like about Irene's graduation and what would you want to change for your own?"*

Do the unexpected; lighten up and, without hurtful sarcasm, use a sense of humor. Tell her once that you have heard enough: *"Claire, I've listened and listened and listened, and I can't listen anymore. My ears are beginning to frizzle and my brain is tuning out."* If you must, walk away with a poker face.

PREVENTIVE TIPS

Some things in life are not fair and some we have no control over. This is a life lesson. Post a copy of the Serenity Prayer (author unknown) on the refrigerator. This is used by AA and many other self-help programs.

> Grant me the serenity to accept the things I cannot change
> The courage to change the things I can
> And the wisdom to know the difference.

When complaining is strong and a solution is impossible, direct him to read the poem.

Complaining is sometimes the result when a teen is so self-centered that he feels his way is the only way. Listening, brainstorming, and consideration are parts of successful leadership. At a good talk time, ask questions relating to what it takes to be a strong leader.

- Is there ever more than one way to solve a problem?
- What would happen if the entire cast wanted to direct the play?
- What's the best way to get someone to listen and understand what you have to say?

Model a positive attitude. Watch your own reaction style. Demonstrate seeking solutions to problems rather than complaining or blaming.

Have a secret word or a hand signal that means, *"You are using a hurtful voice again,"* that you can use when you observe this behavior.

At a good talk time, suggest ideas for getting out of funks: *"While you work through a feeling you want to complain about, you could take a walk, read a book, or write a letter."*

WHEN TO SEEK HELP

When complaining begins to sound like hopelessness, be a good listener and observer. If your teen verbalizes giving up: *"Life isn't worth living; nobody cares; I don't even care,"* these are red flags. If, in addition to these comments, you feel like giving up on your teen: *"I've had it; I don't know what else I can do,"* you both need counseling. Discouragement can be a warning sign for depression. Listen to it and act on it. Get help.

See also: Arguing; Chapter 1, What Happens During the Teen Years; Depression; Mood Swings

COMPUTER

"He spends every free minute on the computer. This seems so antisocial. And what's worse is that he avoids his chores, insisting he's too busy."
"She's always on my back. I wish she'd leave me alone!"

UNDERSTANDING THE SITUATION

The home computer is rapidly becoming more available to families throughout the world. This opens wonderful, expansive opportunities for our teens, enabling them to access a multitude of resources worldwide. Families connected with private on-line companies have access to E-mail and can write to friends and relatives who are also connected. Kids have "Web pals" around the world. Parents at work connect with their children at home or at school. Computer software allows teens to write themes, do research or graphics, make large posters or overheads, and complete other homework assignments. Cameras and scanners make it possible to transfer almost anything imaginable to the computer. Computer games have hit our country by storm. The good news is that they can challenge the imagination, improve concentration and hand-eye coordination, and spark new computer skills. The bad news is that these games can become addictive, and some are becoming increasingly violent. At this time there is no "Web-wide" rating system such as the video and movie industries have.

The field is growing and changing rapidly, and this creates some problems. A teen who understands the many facets of the computer—the Internet, its connection with TV, E-mail, video games, and so forth—is generally far ahead of a busy parent. Parents boast, *"My son has taught me everything I know about my computer."* You can't keep up with what your teen understands and is using, but you must not be naive either.

The Internet is a wide-open highway, connecting your home computer to virtually every other computer in the world. Few rules exist at this time. No government agency controls what your teen may plug in to. The Internet is especially scary for parents who read headlines such as "Thirteen-year-old Is Abducted by Internet Love Date," knowing that your own teen is spending hours exploring Web pages, bulletin boards, and chat rooms. One computer science teacher talked about his alarming experience with his third- and fourth-grade students. To research the name of their school, they typed in the name; the computer's first response was to show a woman, who was using the same name, selling pornography. The teacher was shocked. One concerned father of a seventeen-year-old son lamented that his son's computer abilities were far more advanced than he could begin to understand. His son was connecting with people over the Internet and then meeting them in person. This has obvious risks.

Anyone can put anything on the Internet. Content is not regulated by anything but "free speech." Sometimes the message "Only for people over the age of seventeen" warns of "adult only" material. But such messages may function as an invitation for your teen rather than as a warning.

Parents share many concerns about the use of the computer. Working parents, knowing their teens are unsupervised at home, worry about what they may be learning from unknown sources. Complaints are commonly heard that chores and responsibilities are ignored or replaced by video games and computer time. What has happened to "more worthwhile" activities such as reading, doing homework, playing sports, or practicing music?

Wary parents are concerned that excessive time on-line could become dangerous or addictive to their children.

Positive parents keep the lines of communication open with interest, trust, and curiosity. The most important lessons a parent can convey regarding this rapidly changing technology is the importance of ethics, or in computer terms, "Netiquette." It is imperative that parents continue learning and understanding this complex technology; it's here to stay. Be a proactive parent, do not let the computer run your household. Once trust is established and parents relax, they are repeatedly amazed at the exceptional talents of their teen. He can teach you a whole new vocabulary. Have you heard of "keyboard plaque"*? How about a "cobweb site"**?

WHAT TO SAY AND DO

Hold a family meeting to discuss and establish the rules about using the computer. When leading this discussion, pose questions to create ethical thinking and involvement. *"What rules will make it possible for you to get your chores and responsibilities done and have computer time as well?"* *"What will we do if chores aren't done and grades drop?"* *"What rules do we need to minimize fighting over computer and TV use?"* An effective method is to use a sign-up sheet and allow an hour at a time, unless otherwise arranged. *"What areas on the Web site are not permissible on our family computer?"* Here you will need to educate yourself as to what to avoid. Your teen can help you do this, and you'll both learn. Some areas are rated. Your computer software may allow you to block undesirable information. This is not a well-developed system at this time. However, a knowledgeable teen can easily learn how to unblock an area.

It is best to win cooperation with the understanding that the poor-rated material is off-limits to your family, and together discuss the reasons.

*Keyboard plaque is grunge stuck in the keyboard.
**A cobweb site is an outdated Web page.

Discuss why the use of chat rooms, chat lines, flirt rooms, and private areas on the Internet are all potentially unhealthy and dangerous. Sexual topics, gimmicks asking for credit card numbers, and other unguarded manipulative correspondence happens. "Do not enter" is a good rule for any family. Another must is never to give credit card numbers, phone numbers, addresses, or passwords over the computer.

PREVENTIVE TIPS

Keep the computer and television in family areas. When kids have their own electronics in their own rooms, they will disappear; out of sight, out of mind.

Stay interested and ask that your teen teach you what he knows. This is one area where many kids truly are more capable than their parents.

Be a good model. When your teen sees you reading, exercising, or engrossed in a favorite hobby rather than watching hours of television or playing computer games, she will probably follow suit.

For more information on this topic, read *Online Kids: A Young Surfer's Guide to Cyberspace* by Preston Gralla (New York: John Wiley and Sons, Inc., 1996).

WHEN TO SEEK HELP

Counselors are seeing teens, as well as adults, who have become obsessive/compulsive with computer use. The computer can get in the way of normal social development. Similarly to an alcoholic who takes a drink rather than confront a new social situation, a teen may spend excessive time focused on video games or computer on-line services rather than participate in a healthy, well-rounded lifestyle. Address this concern with him. School counselors, coaches, and teachers may be able to interest him in other activities and expand his experiences.

See also: Friends, Left Out; Siblings; Telephone; Television; Trust; Values

COUNSELING

"My daughter is pacing the floor at night. She says she hates herself, she can't sleep, and she's scared about these feelings. How do I find help?"

"My mom said she talked to someone who can help me feel better. I guess that's okay." Or, *"I'm not crazy. I can talk with my friends."*

UNDERSTANDING THE SITUATION

If you and your teen are having continued difficulty interacting, and if you are worried about his well-being, you will be wise to seek help. Deciding that you and your teen need outside help is a huge step toward healing. Today, counseling is good preventive medicine. Just as you regularly have physical and dental checkups, counseling can help keep a family balanced and functioning well. The decision is very difficult, but once it is made, you will feel hopeful. How to begin the search for a good professional is the daunting part. You struggle with questions such as, *"How do I begin? Which one of us should go, me or my daughter, or all of us? How do I get her there? How do I know what kind of therapist to look for? How do I know if the one I find will be good? I've heard some horror stories about lots of money spent for nothing."*

You may feel you have failed at the one job you care about the most; you may feel embarrassed and vulnerable—and you may not want to admit to a stranger that you have these thoughts. All these feelings are valid. It is imperative that you do not blame yourself. You are seeking a solution to a problem that others have experienced. There is a professional out there trained to help you and your teen. Go for it!

Good therapy is a uniquely rewarding, growing experience. It helps to eliminate blockages that keep us from feeling capable and makes it possible to reach our true potential. Whether it is family or individual counseling, therapy helps us identify important underlying beliefs or feelings. For example, Jenny, age thirteen, was having angry outbursts. She was easily frustrated and broke things. Friends shunned her, she wasn't invited to family functions, and she often was scolded at home. Dad sought counseling for himself and for Jenny. With individual counseling, Jenny got in touch with a deep feeling of hurt and rejection. When her mother left the family, she had begun to feel worthless. Jenny now saw the connection: *"I was hurt—I hurt others—they rejected me—I hurt more."* She learned to alter her underlying belief to, *"This was not my fault. I am lovable and worthwhile."* Dad realized that when Jenny had a temper tantrum, he flared and sent her off to her room, and Jenny then avoided him. This was how his father had handled him. Ironically, both Jenny and Dad wanted love, and both felt rejected. Dad learned appropriate responses to her anger, and life improved for both of them.

An adolescent's struggle for independence needs to be respected. Sometimes a skilled family therapist can succeed well in including the teen as part of the family therapy. However, some teens prefer private therapy, separate from their parents and siblings. Your teen must feel comfortable and be able to trust her therapist with sensitive feelings and ideas. This bond is called a therapeutic alliance. The therapist is not a friend; there are no reciprocal friendship responsibilities.

All types of therapy share a common theme of support. Counselors provide you with new ways to view and respond to your problems. The type of professional is not as important as the match between the individual and the therapist. Finding a good counselor, social worker, psychiatrist, or psychologist may take some work on your part, but the benefits will be well worth it. The following guidelines may make your search easier.

WHAT TO SAY AND DO

There are three ways to go when considering who needs counseling. You may choose individual counseling (for any one member of the family), marital, or family. If the problem is a family issue—for instance, a great deal of sibling fighting—a therapist trained in family dynamics should be considered. Generally, you will conduct the initial search and interviews with the professionals to decide what direction to take.

Although your teen may want to be seen alone, the counselor may prefer to see him as part of the family, or to have a combination of private and family sessions. This will depend on the diagnosis, the severity of the problem, and the preference of the teen and the therapist. For example, an isolated, depressed teen may need time to develop trust by sharing feelings with the counselor before sharing them with the family.

Ask your teen whether he would prefer to see a man or a woman. Don't pry. It is his therapy, his confidential time. If he wants to share it, that's up to him.

Many teens don't want to see a professional. It is unnerving when parents voice extreme concern. Try a more positive tone: *"Melissa, would you like to have more fun?"* Most teens will say yes. *"I know someone you can talk to, who will listen to you, take your ideas seriously, and help make it possible for you to have more fun, and for Dad and me to learn ways to be more helpful."*

Not everyone listed in the phone book is qualified. Talk to friends, school counselors, your family physician, your minister, or respected nonprofit agencies. Local universities that offer degrees in social work, counseling, or psychology can be invaluable resources. Try to find at least three names to choose from. You may need to call your insurance representative to check your insurance coverage.

Usually, your first contact with a prospective counselor is the telephone. The therapist will ask you questions, and you should have questions ready for her: *"How much experience have you had working with adolescents? What is your training in this area? Do you receive ongoing clinical consultation? Are you state licensed?"* Answers to these questions are as important as, *"What do you charge, and do you take insurance?"* To indicate how she would work with your teen, ask, *"What is your approach to adolescent anxiety, depression, drug dependency, and so forth? What is your approach to family issues? Do you recommend the use of medications?"* After asking these questions of at least three therapists, you should have some idea of which one you want to work with. These initial phone contacts may take ten to fifteen minutes and should be free.

During the first session you can ask questions such as, *"How do you set goals? What are your standards for confidentiality?"*

The first visit is usually considered a consultation and should help you decide if therapy is needed or desirable. Did the therapist listen to concerns and understand them? Were his comments thoughtful and considerate? He is not there to "fix" your problems, but you should feel "connected." Trust your intuition, especially if your feelings are negative.

If other family members are involved, decide together if you'd like to continue. Not everyone may like the therapist, yet everyone may be willing to work with her. Your positive attitude will make a difference to the others: *"This could be helpful!"*

Therapy usually works best when sessions are held at least weekly. Whether he is treating you or your teen individually or as a family, the therapist should not forget your issues or confuse them with others', nor should he talk about himself excessively or seek an outside friendship with you. He should treat you with care, respect, and dignity, and encourage you in finding your own solutions. He should make sense to you. If he does not, ask for clarification.

Therapists may suggest a referral. For example, if medication is recommended, you will be directed to a psychiatrist. Medication works better when paired with counseling.

Well into your therapy, ask yourself, *"Am I progressing? Am I being treated with respect? Am I sharing openly and becoming aware of new ways to interact? Am I recognizing issues and concerns and feeling confident that things are progressing? Am I sleeping, eating, or concentrating better? Am I able to see how to avoid old pitfalls?"* Effective therapy is very hard work. It touches on sensitive core issues; it won't always be comfortable. Hang in there, and review your goals periodically. You will do fine.

PREVENTIVE TIPS

Don't let the stigma of seeing a "shrink" stop you from seeking help. Your attitude will make all the difference. Parents often take out their stress on their children, sending messages of guilt and shame without realizing it. Counseling can teach you how to be positive and feel good and do the same for those you love the most.

If you know a teen who needs counseling but does not have supportive parents, you may direct her to a minister, school counselor, or reputable nonprofit organization. Teens can also seek help on their own, even with no money. Some teens have been known to use their own allowance. Parental involvement is not always possible, especially if physical or sexual abuse is involved.

CURFEWS

"He insists that we're the only parents who demand a curfew. He says we don't trust him and that using a curfew is treating him like a baby."
"She doesn't listen to reason. Sometimes it is impossible to get home when she says I should be."

UNDERSTANDING THE SITUATION

Fighting over curfews is all too common. Traditionally, there was a rigid rule, something like, *"Be home by nine o'clock on school nights, eleven on weekends."* In the strictest of households, even if a dance ended at midnight, the curfew was still eleven o'clock. A teen who was even ten minutes late could expect to be grounded for a month. Even if she wanted to come home early, she wouldn't, as it would mean to her that her parent had "won." Some remember bad accidents happening while racing to meet curfew.

The opposite is the permissive approach—anything goes. Parents may be too stressed to deal with curfew, perhaps confused about how it should work and easily talked out of it, or they may believe their teen is ready to assume his own schedule. In this case, a teen may feel no one cares, learn a disregard for limits, and get into trouble. Neither the overly strict nor the overly permissive approach works with teens and perhaps never has.

These are the final years in which you can help your child to feel capable. Curfews provide a nurturing structure. They work best when you invite your teen to make the rules with you and discuss the consequences of breaking them. We all have rules to live by. Consider the expanding-corral theory: You expand the fencing as she grows. A curfew helps young teens learn responsibility and accountability. It allows them to experience a good time within reasonable limits. Because teens mature at different rates, the rules must be tailored to the individual. Be flexible and willing to negotiate. If you maintain an attitude of trust and faith, you will see her grow into a responsible adult who is accountable to others. Be patient. There will be many slipups along the way.

WHAT TO SAY AND DO

Most parents cannot sleep until they know their child is home, safe in bed. One father said, *"Twelve is our agreed curfew. I don't sleep until I know you are in."* This rule was the same for both of his teenagers unless an exception was negotiated in advance. If the kids were fifteen minutes late once in a while, Dad let it go. If lateness became a pattern, he decided, he would ask them to be in that much earlier the following night out. Heavy-duty punishments are counterproductive when good judgment and common sense are being taught.

Tell your teen to call if she is going to be late. She needs to know that you trust her to do this. She knows you worry about her. You don't want her racing dangerously to get home by curfew. If she fears the punishment for breaking curfew, she may not call even in a dangerous situation.

You and your partner need to discuss how curfews were handled in your teen years and how, given your different experiences and attitudes, you want to parent your teen. Ideally, divorced parents should agree on the same rules at both homes. Often, teens will play one parent against the other in order to get the best deal for themselves. This leads to heartache for all.

If your teen shows good judgment, let him propose a reasonable curfew. Younger teens especially can benefit from sign-out sheets. This lets you obtain information without nagging. When you are not at home, use the same system for letting him know where you are. The practice of informing family members of the whereabouts of others shows respect and courtesy.

FAMILY SIGN-OUT SHEET

1. I, _____, am going to _____.
   (Phone number, if applicable) _____
2. I am with _____. Phone _____
3. I will be home at _____.
Initials _____ Date _____ Time _____

Allow your teen some flexibility. He won't always know how the evening will end up. If he is pressured into giving details, he may fabricate to get you off his back. He shouldn't have to report his every move, and you shouldn't act like a policeman or have him wake up the household with a phone call at midnight because he will be a few minutes late. A curfew works best as a guide. Fifteen minutes late is very different from three hours late. Take the fifteen minutes, even if chronic, as success. Technically, the curfew is working!

Planning is a learned skill. Take time to teach this important habit just as a coach would: *"Hank, you have a baseball game at ten o'clock tomorrow morning. What do you think is a reasonable time to get in tonight?"* It's his call. If he gets in later, there are two consequences: His game may suffer; and the following night he could be grounded or lose his car privileges. Consequences can be effective when used wisely to make a point. When over-used, they can become a battleground.

Allow room for mistakes. Let him find his way with guide-lines, not barbed-wire fences. Your teen wants you to respect and trust him. Don't lecture him; he knows he has messed up. Sometimes silence is best. The next week when he says he plans to go out, remind him that he was late a week ago and you expect he will make it in on time this week.

What about that last-minute phone call at 1:00 A.M. ex-plaining he has had too much to drink and is going to stay at Fred's? It may be startling, but it is responsible. Take it as such. The next day, congratulate him for his good judgment. Then, at a good talk time, address the drinking: *"Joe, thank you for calling last night. You used excellent judgment not driving home."* Use *"I feel _____ about _____ because _____, therefore _____."* Say, *"I hope drinking isn't a common activity, because it isn't good for you and it's against the law. If I see it as a pattern, we'll have to discuss the consequences."* Letting go is very hard. Realize that you will have some very difficult moments; as your teen experiments with newfound freedom and makes decisions on his own, he will make mistakes.

PREVENTIVE TIPS

Families with both girls and boys often have double stan-dards. The girls usually have the earlier curfew because parents traditionally worry more about them than about their sons. One solution is to involve teens in setting their own curfews. Circumstances rather than gender should determine curfew times.

When coaches or other leaders of teen activities ask the kids to keep a healthy routine, kids generally comply. Try to follow their lead.

Share a plan with your younger teen before curfew is an issue. Explain the concept of the expanding corral: *"Each time you show responsible behavior, we feel we can give you more freedom. By the time you're eighteen, you will be moving out and setting your own curfew."*

Discuss curfews at the family meeting. Explain why it is a tough issue. Parents worry about alcohol and drug experimentation, sex, parties, and the like. As one father put it, " *'Stuff' happens after midnight."* However, worry is nonproductive. Communicate exactly how you feel. Listen to your teen, and ask her to problem solve with you. The most satisfactory arrangements between parents and teens result when teens are allowed to state what they feel is reasonable.

Some communities impose legal curfews on teens. Both parent and teen may be fined if the teen is out past a certain hour. Such communities hope to reduce car thefts, gang activity, vandalism, alcohol and drug abuse, and teen pregnancies.

Teens argue that their friends' rules are different. Talk with the other parents. Some high schools have a parent support group and collaborate on curfews. However, do not feel pressured to change your rules just because other parents have different ones. Yours have to make sense to you.

See also: Alcohol and Other Drugs; Arguing; Dating, Teens; Leaving Home; Chapter 3, Tools of the Trade, Parent networking

DATING, PARENTS

"Dating is awkward enough at my age, let alone in front of my sixteen-year-old. What should my rules be?"

"Mom doesn't even listen to me anymore; she doesn't know I exist. She's so into dating Rick, she wouldn't even know if I wasn't here. She tells me not to have sex, but what do you think they do all night in her room?"

UNDERSTANDING THE SITUATION

The muddle is not whether a parent should date, but how to do it sensitively. Parenting your teenager is complicated enough, and your dating complicates it further. It is downright uncomfortable at times. Single parents need adult friendships and activities beyond work and children, but balancing it all can be tremendously stressful.

A stressed parent often becomes more self-centered and lacks the energy to focus on her teen. This can lead to over-permissiveness. You may think, *"He's resourceful and will be okay no matter what I do or say."* Your teen still needs your time.

When single parents date, their values are on the line and their characters are challenged. It is not easy. Hard questions follow: *"What if they don't like him?" "When should I introduce the kids to him?" "How intimate should I be when my children are around?" "What should I tell her if she asks if we're having sex?" "Do I take trips with him?" "Should I share my dating troubles with her?"*

No parent faces the same situation and certainly no parent needs to hear, *"Do it this way or else you'll screw up."* However, if dating is important to you, the responsible question is, *"How can this work best for all?"* While teenagers are living in the house, it is wise to think about their development and which parenting principles are important. One mother put her romantic life on hold: *"I've sequenced my life for now. For the next four years, I'm not looking for a relationship—it takes too much energy and time. I'll get Caitlin, my last, through high school; then maybe I'll have the energy to start dating. It is not a big thing for me now. I have a career and I have friends, and I'm content."* Another parent reported, *"I do have a man friend. We spend our alone time together at his apartment. We both feel that we have everything to gain by getting to know each other better and him getting to know my children long before we introduce our intimacy."*

Teens are discovering dating and sex. When you, too, are dating, your experiences parallel theirs. Inadvertently, you might become "peers." Avoid comparisons! Avoid competition! There are big differences that need to be clearly communicated and understood in order to provide a healthy social atmosphere for both of you. Your teen may need to gain experience with the opposite sex, but she is not necessarily ready to settle down and have a permanent, sexual relationship. One older teen admitted that when he was sixteen, he felt a need to prove that he could be sexually active: *"Maybe like my mom was."* It is impossible to hide the obvious, and teens will act out what they sense is going on around them. Most parents do not invite their new dating companions to stay overnight, especially early in the relationship.

WHAT TO SAY AND DO

Don't dump your dating troubles on your teen. Talk with a good friend, a support group, or a counselor. As a single parent, you need to understand how important this is. Your teen needs you to be his listener, the mature one.

Talk about the differences: *"You're fifteen and I'm thirty-seven. Our dating worlds are very different. You will have experiences that I had at your age, not the same issues as I have now. I'm always eager to listen and help you when you need me."*

See if she is anxious or worried about your behavior and intentions: *"How do you feel about my dating?" "Is there anything you would like to discuss with me about my dating?" "How does it feel to have men other than Dad around the house?"* Good communication may spare you both a lot of resentment and hard feelings. Do not let your teen's opinions stop you from dating. Your decision to do so will probably be challenged over and over. Reflect her feelings: *"It seems that you don't want me to date Bill."* Listen and stay calm. Try to understand her concern without anger and resentment. Ask, *"How do you feel when Bill is around the house? How about when he's here on weekends and for meals? Please tell me. I can take it."* Or, *"I like to be with my friends because they lift my spirits. I think I can be a better mom when I have a balance in my life, and friends are part of that balance."* Be firm and reassuring: *"I appreciate your concerns. Thank you for sharing with me. I love you and I will always consider your needs as well as mine."*

Make time with your teen a priority. He needs you to "be there" emotionally when he wants to talk. The excitement of dating may pull you away from home more than you intended. Abandonment is a common adolescent concern when new attachments are introduced. Your teen needs to know where he stands in relation to your new partner.

Complicating matters is your teen's loyalty to her other parent and the resulting conflicted feelings toward your new friend. One mother who had not dated since her husband's death, when the children were small, was shocked by their overt hostility at the very idea of her dating. These teens were not prepared to replace the ideal of their father. The notion of their mother being with another man was unthinkable. There needs to be plenty of discussion. Sometimes when families experience death or divorce, counseling may help with the move into new stages of life.

PREVENTIVE TIPS

Including your teenager on outings with your date is great, but it is no substitute for one-on-one time with either person.

Family meetings are extremely helpful to discuss and establish understanding about both teen dating and parent dating. The more this can be openly discussed, the better. This is a good, neutral arena in which to voice concerns and to problem solve.

Never discuss intimacies with your children. They do not want to hear about your sexual issues, nor should they have to. Teens tend to deny their parents' sexuality, and to push this side could result in their sexual acting out.

For more information on this topic, read *Growing Up Again: Parenting Ourselves, Parenting Our Children* by Jean Illsley Clark (San Fransisco: Harper/Hazelton, 1989).

WHEN TO SEEK HELP

Issues from a former marriage, such as the hope that Mom and Dad will get back together or the feeling that "Mom belongs to me," may need to be worked through, even if years later. Watch for warning signs of anger or depression and seek family counseling if needed.

See also: Dating, Teens; Divorce; Losses and Grief; Rebelliousness; Stepparents

DATING, TEENS

Younger Teens

"I understand that Monica is going steady, but I never see the boy. She's always with a group of her friends."
"I really love Keith. This is forever."

UNDERSTANDING THE SITUATION

"Going," otherwise known as "going steady" or "going out," is a commonly sought arrangement among young teens. Some can't wait to be like their older siblings. These kids feel that parties and dating should magically begin with junior high. Yet, no two kids develop at the same rate, and most boys develop later than girls. However, generally, "going steady" in junior high means seeing each other at school, having phone conversations, and, at most, getting together outside of school with peers. For the most part, it's quite harmless. But when a junior-high teen—boy or girl—is going steady with a high schooler, you need to "listen up." Keep your lines of communication open, and be an aware parent, not a naive one. Teens several years older are at a different stage, with demands for intimacy that are premature for the young teen who does not have the experience or perspective to say no.

For some kids, the phone never stops ringing. The preteen's job is to begin experimenting with telephone conversations that range from friends setting up group dates, to talking with a special boy or girl, to becoming a boyfriend or a girlfriend. Going steady, breaking up, and going with another boy can all be arranged over the telephone, sometimes within just a few hours.

Don't assume you know what she is experiencing. Her world is very different from yours at that age. For example, if your first steady relationship ended in disaster, you may be horrified when your thirteen-year-old daughter tells you she is going steady. Unconsciously, our children play out our worries; we may even set them up, expecting them to do and feel the same way. Your teenager needs to be allowed to experience life in her way.

Most parents would rather not deal with their adolescents' going-steady issues. Early teens seem too young to get hooked on one person for any length of time. Yet, it is important developmentally for the young teen to learn about himself with others and to experience different friendships. Going steady, for some young teens who are ready, involves learning life lessons: how to attract the opposite sex, how to converse, how to act, how to break up without hurting someone's feelings, how to manage rejections, and so on. Don't panic. Keep the lines of communication open, and maintain your faith and trust. Your young teen will grow through these experiences and be better prepared to face what lies ahead.

WHAT TO SAY AND DO

Be calm. You need to be a good, caring listener and to be not too emotionally involved. It isn't helpful to "fall in love" with your young teen's "being in love." Parents who rush to invite the boyfriend to dinner, suggest movie dates, and arrange invitations to family gatherings may be promoting something quite premature and inappropriate.

She needs you to take her seriously. It is not helpful to tease her about each new "crush." These relationships may appear to you as puppy love, but to your teen these are big deals.

Discussions about relationships need to be ongoing. Explain your values and ideas: *"I know that with every person you get to know, you will learn a lot about yourself."* Or, *"Going steady is special as long as it doesn't become a dependency. That means that over a period of time you start to feel 'I can't be without him.' Or that you let him tell you what to do, what to wear, or how to act. You need to continue being you."*

Don't be afraid to make nonnegotiable rules, but try to offer some compromise. For instance, if your young teen is going steady with an older boy, the danger is that she will be unable to stand up for her beliefs. Be matter-of-fact: *"Mandy, going steady is okay, but we don't want you going out with older boys. You cannot go out in Richard's car. Richard is welcome to come to our home anytime and join you and your friends."*

Parents of young teens who are interacting with the opposite sex for the first time have a wonderful opportunity to set the stage for safe, healthy coed activities. When they want to have a party, instead of the usual, *"Already? You're too young,"* together plan activities such as volleyball and a picnic in the backyard, or in winter a skating or sledding party. These activities take time and energy, but they are far preferable to a day at the movies without a chaperon.

If you are a single parent and dating, life can get complicated. You and your teen may be both dating, but your situation must not be compared with your teen's. Your young teen is at an experimental stage and will fall in and out of love many times. You are an adult and your private life needs to be kept to yourself. Teens do not benefit from hearing about a parent's sexual life. Be discreet. Read the preceding entry, "Dating, Parents." Teens are close observers, but they may not correctly interpret what they see. Be a helpful role model for your young teen.

The section below will be helpful for parents of younger teens as well. Much of the information applies to all teenagers.

Older Teens

"Sasha's been seeing a new boy. I'm so uncomfortable because I don't know him and he doesn't go to her school. Kids date kids from all over the place. The norm is so different today."

"My parents are all freaked out about me going out with Jason. I'm old enough; they gotta let go."

UNDERSTANDING THE SITUATION

Realizing that your "little girl" is starting to date (actually going to a movie with one boy, and possibly riding in his car) may be disturbing. It is not easy for either parent or teen the first time she asks to go out with a boy. Take a deep breath and give yourself a minute to deal with the maze of parental fears.

Dating will trigger many mixed emotions. Your experiences may have been bumbling and uncomfortable. If your parents freaked, you may, too. One father noted that his first daughter had no interest in boys until her junior year in high school, but boys began hanging around his younger daughter in eighth grade. Dad installed a sensory device outside because Derek, a boy who fancied the younger daughter, lived three houses away. He called it the "Derek Detector." The lights came on when anybody entered the yard!

It's hard enough for a teen to deal with new, surging emotions and sexual feelings without having his parents fall to pieces. You will make things easier for both of you if you can separate your experiences and realize that his will be very different from yours. Remember, in this generation, boys and girls often are "just friends." You need to be a stable, listening parent who is there consistently for your teen.

Some girls are attracted to boys earlier than others and seek out older boys, as their male peers generally develop later. Don't be too quick to judge. You may be distressed to see how another parent handles her daughter's dating: *"She's much too young to ride alone with a boy in his car"*; *"Can you imagine, her dates are allowed in her bedroom?"* and so forth. Wait until it happens to you. Nothing is easy when it comes to parenting a newly dating teen.

Generally, teens today travel in groups. If a boy likes a girl, he tells his friends, they tell her friends, and a time is arranged to meet casually at a movie or mall or to talk on the phone. There is often an element of surprise: *"He called!"* Does this sound familiar? It is not very different from when you were her age. You may also be confronted with a very upset teen who has been hurt by rejection. These are character-building, real-life experiences. Help your teen to cope with his pain, his jealousies, and the multitude of other emotions he's going through.

Your teen's world is much different from the one you grew up in. Kids are so much more mobile now and are exposed to a wide range of values and attitudes. Both boys and girls compete widely in sports; more kids travel in foreign-exchange programs; church youth programs are increasingly popular. Do not make the mistake of assuming you know what she is experiencing. It may feel as though you are losing control. Attend the high-school parent talks and listen to what the counselors say. Read or listen to your local news. Be informed. Show interest in her friends and her activities. Dating rules need to be established together. She will beg for more rights, and she will be right when she tells you that some of her friends' parents are extremely permissive. At times it will be hard to know which limits and expectations are best. Work together with her, with her friends' parents, and with her school community. Some rules will be nonnegotiable (no drinking and driving), while others have some flexibility. Be ready to let go as she proves she is responsible. Be sure you give good, specific reasons when you deny a privilege. Be loving and very consistent. It's vital to convey your faith and trust in your teen.

WHAT TO SAY AND DO

If any issues in this section are new or uncomfortable for you, learn more about them. Talk with other parents and your friends. Your daughter is learning a lot from health classes. Ask her what she knows—you'll be surprised. Treat your teen with the respect you would a good friend. Ask, *"What do you know about drinking and dating?"* *"In health class, do you talk about the difference between good, healthy, romantic love as compared to not-so-healthy, possessive love? Tell me more."* And don't forget the familiar *"What would you do if . . . ?"* questions.

Rather than "don't" rules such as *"don't smoke, don't have sex, don't kiss on a first date,"* tell her what you feel is permissible. Compliment her: *"It's great that Jeff called you! I hope you have a good time."* When she comes to you for comfort, such as after breaking up or being turned down, take her concerns seriously, for they are real and deeply felt. Help her regain her self-esteem and give her hope: *"You have wonderful friends and will continue to have wonderful friends. You're loyal and fair, and you're learning that some others are not. Time heals, though it feels terrible right now. I know you can handle this. You and Jerry will probably be friends again someday. But these painful incidents just happen sometimes. I know—it hurts!"* Do not try to take away the hurt; just "be" with her for a while. You know it will pass. She has to learn this.

Share some boundary-setting skills for her relationships. These are important for both boys and girls, whether or not they are dating. *"Jennifer, establishing where your comfort level or line is with drinking, sex, and other things that go on in dating is an important skill that all teens must learn."* (You may want to give specific, personal examples with these ideas.)

1. When you date someone, you should always be able to express your opinions. Your opinions should be respected, even if your date doesn't agree with them. He should not tease you, mock you, or criticize your ideas.

2. You should feel free to change your mind, without fear of feeling dumb or being laughed at or teased.

3. Your needs are as important as his. When you date, you look for someone who listens to your ideas and can compromise.

4. You don't need to take responsibility for your date's behavior. You are an individual with individual rights and responsibilities, and so is he. Do not be embarrassed for him, but do decide what kind of person you want to be with.

5. Don't allow physical (shoving, pushing, hitting), sexual (forcing you into petting, and so on), or emotional abuse (name calling, threatening, teasing, put-downs).

6. You have a right to stop dating someone and begin dating someone else without being threatened. Relationships should make you feel good, increase your self-confidence, and be interesting. One grandmother said, *"If the relationship is getting better, that's wonderful, stick with it. If the relationship is getting bad or uncomfortable, get out. If the relationship is just going along, is kind of flat, beware!"*

Discussion with trusted persons can be a helpful way for you to gain perspective, but the responsibility and the decisions are your teen's.

Boys who like to date younger girls may do so in order to dominate the relationship. In small-community high schools it can be difficult for parents to prevent this, but in general, a fourteen-year-old should not date a seventeen-year-old.

Dating will eventually involve the issue of driving. *"How old should my daughter be to date a boy who has a car?"* As one mother said to her three-year-old, *"Don't climb up anything you can't get down from by yourself."* The same explanation applies to a fifteen-year-old who wants to date someone who is old enough to drive. *"Kari, until you've had your license with a clear driving record for six months, you may not date anyone who drives. I want you to always be able to drive yourself home if you need to."* The same holds true for a boy who wants to date an older girl.

Your teen may not be interested in dating. She may be shy or be more interested in sports or other activities. Don't rush her. Assure her that this is normal: *"In time you may have an interest in dating. Not everyone has the same interests at the same time."*

Your teen may feel left out and uncomfortable talking about this with peers. Ask, *"Conner, would you like to talk about dating?"* Wait for a yes before you go on. Rather than lecture, you may want to brainstorm together. Questions are helpful, too.

Peer pressure is always an influence in regard to dating. Kids taunt, *"What did you get from her last night?" "You can't mean you're still a virgin?"* Much of the bravado is false and the boasting untrue, and your teen will begin to see this with your help. The teaser is often taking out his own feelings of discomfort.

The family meeting is a good forum for discussing dating rules. The younger-teen siblings will benefit from this, as the rules will affect them later.

Curfew contracts can be helpful, too: *"I'm with _____. I'll be at _____. I'll be home at _____."*

PREVENTIVE TIPS

Help your teen stay on course with long-range goals and interests. Sports, music, schoolwork, important friends, and other wholesome activity should not become drowned out by the excitement over dating. Limits must be clearly agreed on; you need to be consistent and lovingly firm to help your teen stay on track.

Your library may carry helpful videotapes that you can view together with your teen. One good one is *Dating Violence: The Hidden Secret* (1993, Taylor and Zitner, 25 minutes). This tape is useful for all teens and parents because it is well presented, descriptive, and educational for any dating relationship. Some of the videos available are intended to scare teens; obviously, these are not helpful.

Arrange for a qualified teen counselor to speak about dating to the student body, the PTA, and the faculty. Adults as well as teens need to discuss today's new issues.

Parking on country roads, camping in the woods, hanging out in malls, and the like are all popular pastimes but are not recommended. It is much healthier to encourage activities that involve interests other than sex, such as a game of tennis or pool, or skiing or biking. These activities are fun and use up a lot of energy.

Discuss with your teen the dangers of drugging or drinking on dates. Boundaries get very weak. One high-school health class had a recent graduate come in and share how, on his first date as a college freshman, he got drunk and had sex. He wasn't proud of this and warned the high schoolers not to drink on a date.

Discuss what to do if date abuse happens. Ask, *"Mike, if you felt you or a friend was in an abusive relationship, what would you do? Many teens won't tell a teacher, parent, or any other adult. But it's important to tell. A trusted adult will help, and will keep your secret as well."*

Your teen sees many stereotypes on television and in movies. Point out that it is uncool when the man needs to be in charge and gets away with having many partners. Discuss the girl who is compliant, devious, beautiful, and feels she has to have a boyfriend to have status.

Today's teens often remain friends after they break up. *"We're better friends than a dating couple, so we are still going to the game together."* This was probably not the norm when you were in high school, when it was considered cool to hate your ex-girlfriend. Teens now are able to establish relationships of different intensities in what appears to be a fairly mature way.

Your teen may identify with a trusted older sibling, cousin, or friend and be able to benefit from discussions about dating and the opposite sex. Encourage and arrange such conversations.

WHEN TO SEEK HELP

If your daughter is preoccupied with dressing provocatively and her whole life appears directed toward attracting male attention, especially older males, talk with a teen counselor. She may be confused about how relationships begin and continue.

Studies show that too many teen dating relationships today include some emotional, physical, or sexual violence. Parents often don't know this and don't like hearing it, yet it happens. Both boys and girls can abuse, but boys generally abuse more frequently. This dangerous behavior, which is against the law, is prevalent at all socioeconomic levels. Most girls won't tell an adult, and few tell their peers. Some teens assume that power imbalance is the norm: girls submit, guys control, girls entice, guys can't help it. Abusive attention can feel flattering at first. But if a relationship begins to include possessiveness, jealousy, fear, anger, or making excuses for the other's hurtful behavior, a serious problem could be developing. If you know or suspect that your teen is dating someone who is affecting her self-esteem negatively, seek help. The earlier you do so, the better the odds that both teens will have healthier relationships in the future.

This may be the first time a teen questions his sexuality. As hormones kick in, he may find that he is aroused by boys, not girls (perhaps in the locker room). This can be a devastating discovery and cause great pain and confusion. This teen needs a trusted counselor, parent, or friend with whom to share these concerns. If your teen approaches you about it, try to stay calm. Your teen may not be able to help himself. You may need to find a counselor to help you both decide whether it is a "stage" or the early signs of homosexuality.

Your community may have good resources for help and information about current dating issues: youth services, domestic violence hot lines, women's counseling centers, and school and other counselors. Don't hesitate to call the police in an emergency.

See also: Chapter 3, Tools of the Trade, Parent networking; Curfews; Driving; Friends, Choosing; Going Steady; Homosexuality; Jealousy; Parties; Sex, Talking About

DEPRESSION

"My son seems so sad and morose; he doesn't want to interact with the family anymore. He's withdrawn and isn't even practicing his guitar anymore. He now says he 'didn't like it anyway.' This is not like him."
"I wish she would bug off. I just want to be alone."

UNDERSTANDING THE SITUATION

By nature, teens are dramatic, emotional, and somewhat susceptible to depression. Hormones are kicking in and can cause extreme mood swings as teens respond to and cope with life. They have little experience at moderating their reactions to their heightened and sometimes overwhelming feelings. They are apt to change their minds about decisions they've made, and they worry about how they look. A teen may rock out at a party, having the time of her life, and wake up the next morning feeling anxious or guilty about how she acted. Teens worry about being popular, being smart and successful in school, being athletic, being cool, macho, sexy, pretty, thin, and most anything else that concerns "belonging." These are normal concerns that are difficult but can usually be adequately managed.

Depression is different. The onset of teen depression may be so subtle that you don't notice it until you are presented with a sequence of concerns. Your son is unable to get up in the morning; he isn't sleeping well; his interests seem to have diminished; and he doesn't do much with friends anymore. He's not eating well; he seems very sad and cries at small things; he's very touchy. Most worrisome, his whole demeanor has changed since he broke up with his girlfriend. Once a good student, he has let his schoolwork go. *"He seems like a stranger. He's not getting over it. Would he try to kill himself? Is he going to need medication? Will he be so sick he'll need to be hospitalized like Aunt Florence? How do I find help for him? His father says he'll 'snap out of it' and doesn't want a 'shrink,' but I don't agree."*

Depression is like feeling stuck at the bottom of a pit where no one can hear you or see your pain. The top of the pit seems unreachable. Depressed people feel worthless, guilty, sad, and unlovable, and their feelings of hopelessness and helplessness are overwhelming. These extremely painful emotions are often masked by withdrawing, using alcohol or other drugs, developing eating disorders, suffering from sleeping disorders, or taking dangerous risks. Suicidal feelings are not uncommon. Depression isn't an adults-only condition; it is common among adolescents and children. It may underlie many adolescent misbehaviors.

There are several forms of depression to be aware of. Brief depression is most often a response to some situation where an adjustment, followed by acceptance, must be made before a more normal mood can reappear. During this period the teen may find himself reacting to a specific loss more seriously than expected. He finds himself daydreaming and feeling very sad and morose, often expressing himself angrily as he sorts out the emotional wound. It is usually manageable within the family, taking from a couple of weeks to several months to resolve. These mild types of depression usually respond to offers of comfort, distractions, and changes in the world around him that help to resolve his sad feelings. He improves when he comes to grips with the problem, perhaps finding a solution such as realizing that there are other nice girls besides the one who just jilted him.

More severe depression is like an exaggerated form of adolescent sadness that seriously affects a teen's normal activities. It can develop into a life-threatening illness. The teen's response to losses, hardship, or chronic anxiety is hopelessness. She has withdrawn from interest in school and even her friends' offers of movies and other social opportunities. It seems that she has lost her self-worth, and you worry about her lack of interest in life. Severe depression can also be caused by alcohol or other drug abuse, other psychiatric disorders, genetic factors, or a combination of several of these. Whatever the cause, if signs of hopelessness, helplessness, and loss of interest or pleasure in life are apparent and persist for several weeks, you need to consult professionals. You need to act to help your teen. A combination of antidepressant medication and counseling is almost always recommended and is very effective. Hospitalization is reserved for when suicide concerns are also severe and part of the depression.

Teens with a genetic predisposition to depression are lucky to be living in today's world. Modern medicine is able to restore balance to the body's necessary biochemicals that get out of balance with severe depression. Many families have felt great relief upon realizing that the grandfather who was always losing jobs, had a hard time keeping relationships, and once was hospitalized may have been dealing with a genetic or "chemical imbalance" depression all his life. It wasn't his fault, and it is not your teen's fault. This is a medical condition that can be successfully treated. For your teen, knowledge of family history is useful information in order to seek treatment early and correctly identify the depression.

Depressed teens are unable take part in "normal" teen activities; thus they are unable to accomplish developmental milestones. It makes no social distinctions. Kids may reject their friends, give up sports, drink or use other drugs, and withdraw to their room. They can become perfectionists in their schoolwork or compulsive with sports. Some become involved with sexual promiscuity or risky or even life-threatening behavior. Depression is thought to be suppressed anger. Some kids become quiet and withdrawn, while others are overtly angry.

Causes for depression are complex, usually are multiple, and are not well understood. A few examples follow:

Amy, age fourteen, was a "princess" at home. Her mother did her laundry, put away her clothes, cooked for her, and even did some of her homework. Amy felt, *"I'm significant when others are serving me."* Depression appeared in junior high school. None of Amy's friends wanted to do what she expected, even when she cried and sulked, which worked at home.

Barbara was troubled by small disappointments in junior high school. She worried about the child she baby-sat and about the callous waste of school paper that was not recycled. She became obsessed with her personal hygiene as well as that of others. She washed her hands many times a day. Soon her anxiety became incapacitating and she felt she could not go to school. This behavior reminded her mother of her own depressed sister.

Cindy's subconscious message was to be a pleaser: *"What can I do for others?"* Historically, this was the woman's role. She learned to put her own needs last in order to please others. Cindy's boyfriend took advantage of this and they had unprotected sex. Cindy got pregnant at age sixteen. Depression followed.

David felt, *"I'm important when I'm the best."* He was a straight-A student and played three varsity sports. Depression hit when he moved from a small high school to a large one where the competition was greater. The world became a very intimidating place for David when he could no longer be in control. His feelings of inadequacy depressed him. He became suicidal.

William grew up feeling he couldn't live up to his older brother. He never felt he could be as successful. After his brother left for college, he began binge drinking.

It is not unusual for college freshmen, away from home supports for the first time, to show signs of depression. New friends, a new school, difficult courses, and social expectations can be a jolt to the older teen who has never before had to manage such changes without family support.

Some teens are more sensitive, caring, concerned, or anxious than others, just like adults. Teens lack the experience to manage the situations that now overwhelm them. Later, they will have the maturity to cope. They all need to be loved, appreciated, and directed to express their feelings in positive and constructive ways. You will hurt and worry. Yet, more than ever, your teen must feel that you believe in her, that you have confidence that she will work through this because she's a very capable person.

WHAT TO SAY AND DO

Is this a passing phase, or is your teen truly depressed? Changes such as altered eating habits, sleeping too little or too much, pacing the floor at night, irritability, withdrawing from friends and activities, or giving up on schoolwork may indicate that your teen is depressed. Hopelessness, helplessness, and lack of interest in life or the capacity to feel pleasure are major signs of depression. Talk with his school counselor or favorite teachers to get their perspective.

Listen and be there. Try to be honest with yourself: Are you pulling back from her? Are you giving her a chance to talk? Are you truly listening to what's going on in her mind without judging or criticizing? Your body language needs to be relaxed and your tone sincere and caring. This can be difficult, especially if she is hostile and angry. She may be disrespectful in order to hurt you as she hurts. In order to love her and be there for her, which she needs so badly, you may have to bear the pain, cool down, take deep breaths, and listen. You may need some space (go to the bathroom and wash your face, or take a walk) in order to regain your energy and patience and to use your listening skills.

Communicate to her specifically what you have observed. She needs your feedback. She may not be able to recognize what is obvious to those around her. *"Shawn, I've noticed recently that you're not playing basketball after school, you're not eating well, that you seem sad and cry sometimes. I hear you pacing the floor at night and see you barely getting up for school. You seem depressed. Can you tell me what's happening to you?"* If your teen rejects your reaching out, say, *"If you feel like talking I'd like to be there for you. I may not be the right person to talk with, but perhaps we can find someone who does understand. I have a feeling that I sometimes push you too hard and am not always a good listener. I will try to only listen and not tell you what I think."*

Are you afraid you might be labeled a bad parent? That hits the core! Your child may need you very badly at this point in her life. Backing away now is not the thing to do. Overreacting can be equally disquieting to your teen. You may need to talk to a professional about your feelings of failure, guilt, fear, or anger. At this point you may think, *"I don't have time for it all, and besides, it costs a lot of money to get treatment. Maybe it'll go away—she'll get better next week. All kids go through this stuff."* Denial is dangerous. Your responsibility is to act in the best interests of your child. You need to take control. Depression is very serious. The reality is that she is not doing well and needs your help, now.

Approaching a resistant teen is difficult. He may be angry, but underneath he feels hurt and afraid. He may fear the stigma of going to a therapist, and so may you. He needs you to empower him. Think of his strengths and reflect with him on past experiences that show his abilities: *"James, you're such a capable person. I really believe that, but I don't believe you feel that way about yourself now. Last year when you conquered the ropes course at school, you showed such courage. You have such determination— your hockey coach will tell anyone that. Your friends really like and trust you. I want you to feel all your strengths as truly as I do. I've made an appointment with a counselor who I think will help you begin to believe in yourself again and help me to understand and support you through this low period."*

Rely on your counselor and your teen to determine what type of counseling would be most useful now as well as later in the therapy process. Your teen may start with seeing someone alone through the immediate crisis and then find that family counseling is recommended. Tell him, *"Ray, we need to see a family counselor to help all of us. You need to know it is not your fault. All of us are involved. We all care about each other and we all need to find new ways to interact."*

PREVENTIVE TIPS

You can help your teen to learn helpful skills for managing life competently.

Do not associate your teen's self-worth with his grades or any label such as *"our star athlete," "the brain of our family," "our comedian,"* and so forth. If he fails at one of those, he needs a strong inner self to rely on, so that he doesn't feel, *"I'm not worthwhile unless I am the best at . . ."* He needs to know he is valued for many other reasons as well. Tell him, *"I love you because you are you, unlike anyone else."*

Compliment your teen very specifically on what she did that you liked, even if it is her weekly job. Rather than, *"Karen, great job,"* say, *"Karen, I really appreciate your sweeping out the garage. It's been a long time since it looked so clean. Thank you."* Notice what is right and be specific. Then she may be more willing to listen when you want to correct something important.

Do not base your love for her on what she does. Tell her you love her anytime, not just when she's done something to deserve it. When she wins the swim race, don't say, *"I love you so much because you are the fastest on the team."* She must believe that you love her no matter how well she does.

Your perspective and your supportive comments are invaluable to your teen's self-concept. Body image is one of the most sensitive areas of low self-esteem among teens. Girls are concerned that they are too flat-chested or too big-breasted, and boys are concerned that their thin arms will never be as big and strong as their ideal. They live in constant fear that someone will reveal their shortcomings. You can help. Listen carefully when he makes comments about himself. Do not agree when he puts himself down—instead, encourage positive self-talk. Emphasize the inner self rather than appearance. Say, *"Gary, you seem unhappy with your body. Have you noticed how everyone is changing at very different rates? Don't give up on yourself; you're growing and changing too. The boys in our family did most of their growing after sixteen. Help yourself by being patient and noticing what's right with you. Your voice is so strong and deep and it's stopped squeaking. You still have the greatest grin and sense of humor! Everyone likes that."* Or, *"Janie, your friends have always liked you because you're fun to be with. People trust your ideas, and you're a very thoughtful girl. The size of your hips has nothing to do with whether people like you or not. There will always be a few hurtful, teasing remarks from some kids, but those kids have problems of their own and take them out inappropriately on others. Ignore them if you can, so they get no satisfaction from hurting you."*

Disorganization can lead to anxiety and sleeplessness and is a setup for poor performance, which can lead to depression. Discuss stress management with your teen. Many need to learn strategies to stay focused on their tasks. Weekly organizers, a wall calendar, a chart with daily reminders, and sometimes permission to take personal time, time with self, are often helpful.

Your teen needs your undivided, personal attention, though she may not ask for it. Make time during the week to play cards or a board game, bake cookies, work on craft projects, or go out to dinner. Be prepared to overcome everyday interruptions to make time for your teen. She may make you think she can handle everything on her own, but most teens need interested, caring adults, especially at bedtime or when they are sick.

Notice and listen. *"Hi, Kelly! Oh, you look beat."* Pause. If you're quiet and attentive, he'll probably tell you what is on his mind. He wants to share his life, provided that you don't criticize him. He doesn't want your solutions or comments unless he asks for them. He may feel pretty shaky on the inside. He needs your support to help him regain control and self-confidence and to understand the "stuck spots" so that he feels less overwhelmed and depressed. Listening to him proves that you care and are there with him.

Take care of yourself as well as your teen's depression. Has your job lately required extra hours away from home? Have you been preoccupied or drinking or sleeping more than usual to drown out your frustrations? Have you neglected to attend the last few parent nights at your teen's school? Take a look at what's going on with you.

For more information on this topic, read *Coping with Teenage Depression* by Kathleen McCoy (New York: New American

Library, 1982); *Understanding Depression* by Donald F. Klein and Paul Wender (New York: Oxford University Press, 1993); and *Overcoming Depression* by Demitri F. Papolos and Janice Papolos (New York: Harper & Row, 1987).

WHEN TO SEEK HELP

If you're concerned that you have a depressed teen, you probably do. Get her to a therapist for a consultation. Several sessions may be required to determine whether treatment is recommended.

You may need to get help for yourself in order to deal with your worries about your teen. Recognizing the seriousness of the situation and getting a professional evaluation takes determination. It is imperative that you get yourself together so you can help your teen.

When there is crisis, the entire family may need to make some adjustments. Family therapy can be helpful. If it wasn't a family problem before, it is now. Everyone needs to rally and pull together.

Any sign of eating disorders or talk of suicide needs to be taken seriously, even when it seems manipulative. Find a professional immediately.

Research both sides of the family for information about relatives who were depressed.

Learn as much as you can about depression, which is a medical illness just as asthma is. Support your teen if professionals recommend medication. Antidepressants are nonaddictive and usually quite safe. Learn more so you can help your teen and yourself through this difficult, though not hopeless, illness.

See also: Alcohol and Other Drugs; Anger; Bullied; Bullying; Counseling; Eating Disorders; Hanging Out; Learning Problems; Losses and Grief; Mood Swings; Stress; Suicide; Worry

DIVORCE

*"I have enough of my own problems. Can't she be a little
more sensitive to my needs? I can't wait for the
weekend so her dad can deal with her."*

*"I don't know where I belong. My clothes are all over the
place. My friends never know where to find me. Don't
they ever think about me?"*

UNDERSTANDING THE SITUATION

Divorce happens, and it happens a lot! Every divorce is a loss of
a relationship and long-held goals for every member of the
family. When children are involved, avoiding the pitfalls and
long-term negative impact is a major concern for both parents.
Children are pushed into a position that they have little experience with and no control over. *"Where do I fit in? I can't count
on what was before. What can I count on now?"*

Patterns change. People change where they live and sleep
and sometimes where they go to school. Seeing their parents
emotionally upset, unsure of themselves, and preoccupied with
divorce details, teens are reluctant to add to the burden. They
are apt to avoid expressing their feelings.

Divorce is neither good nor bad, it is just very difficult.
Many books have been written on this critical topic. Studies
following children of divorce for a decade and more show that
divorce has lifelong effects, not just on the immediate family
but on the entire extended family. An adolescent needs a strong,
solid environment to push against, rules and dependable parents
to hold him accountable. He needs calm and patient parents to

withstand his occasional bad moods and sometimes his rejection. He needs a consistent adult to listen with sincerity. This is a big order for any parent, let alone a parent going through a divorce.

Every divorce is a loss, even if it is a loss of habitual fighting. It is a critical transition for children, sometimes changing where they live, sleep, and go to school. The process of grieving is painful and requires a lot of time to express what is happening and eventually to construct a new life. Though divorce is often a necessity, sadness, confusion, fear, and anger tend to overwhelm children. Their feelings are very important and need to be handled sensitively so that they can recover and grow in a healthy way.

Remember, parents are not divorcing a relationship with their children, and in most cases the kids need both parents. Both parents need to accept some responsibility for the divorce in a mature way, and teens need honest explanations. The loss is great, even when it is for a good reason.

Teens need to be able to express their feelings about the divorce, safely. This takes a strong parent, or, better, two. Parents who can restrain themselves from showing criticism or judgment about how their child feels are the best listeners. The expression of angry feelings is very complicated. A teen may fear hurting an already stressed parent's feelings and so may not reveal his strong feelings of blame. *"I hate you, Dad!"* is tough to take, but Dad needs to be able to accept this fury and to continue to listen and to love. Angry feelings are normal. The more open and direct teens can be about their feelings, the less likely they are to act out negatively.

Teens separate from families at their own pace. Divorce may speed this up. If it happens too fast, too soon, feelings of abandonment surface. This may trigger anger and disappointment and eventual acting out in a variety of unhealthy ways: poor school performance, use and abuse of illegal substances, and sexual promiscuity, to name a few. When feelings are repressed, then unpredictable, counterproductive, and sometimes self-destructive behavior may emerge at some future time.

Many of the challenges society faces are due to families in transition. Grandparents, aunts and uncles, cousins, and so forth are scattered across the country and around the world. This creates tremendous pressure on the nuclear family. Today, single parents depend on the community for support through after-school programs, community center activities, and ongoing groups organized for children of divorce. It is every adult's duty to help all children feel that they belong, to be interdependent, and to be held accountable. We must face the effects of divorce with new attitudes, ideas, and solutions, and continue exploring better ways to cope. Concentrate on the many positives that come from ending bad situations. It is an opportunity to build strength and flexibility through hardship. Remember the adage, "Adversity builds character."

New life patterns can emerge after a divorce. Fathers who used to escape the home environment for the golf course now invite their teens to join them. New skills, interests, and opportunities develop. All can benefit. A mother who no longer worries about her husband's disapproval may begin to spend time with a long-forgotten hobby or find self-satisfaction with employment. Divorce can open the door to all sorts of new relationships and opportunities, after the grief and loss period has passed. Ideally, the separation process is done carefully and sensitively. A professional family counselor can be of great assistance in creating a happy, healthy future for all concerned.

Therapy can also address some very difficult issues that emerge from divorce: What does a teen learn about commitment and long-term relationships? What does she learn when Dad's income remains the same as or better than when he was married, and Mom's drops below her normal standard of living? What is the message that a dating parent sends to his teen about sex before marriage? What is the outcome for an adolescent living with parents who place their needs first as they struggle to put their lives in order? What does a young teenager learn about reliability and trust when her mother doesn't show up for scheduled visits?

Good family discussions can decrease these concerns. It is

imperative to sort out what your teen observes as the family makes important adjustments and readjustments, though it is often a painful and challenging process. One girl stated positively, *"I'm having so much fun learning that my parents are two separate people! I never thought it would be like this."* Teens benefit from getting to know a parent as an individual. The process of divorce is always difficult, but adjusting to it does get easier with time.

WHAT TO SAY AND DO

Most teens who have lived through divorce agree on one most important piece of advice for parents: *"Do not verbalize negative things about the other parent."* One twenty-two-year-old said, *"I knew things that my mom hated about my dad, but it was really destructive hearing it verbalized. It made me feel self-conscious when I visited my father to know that my mother had just berated him for late payments, which to me meant just one thing: He didn't like me enough to put food on my table. I was worthless in his eyes. This has plagued me for life!"*

Commonly, one spouse tries to hurt the other through the children. This is unfair and hurts the children.

When a parent doesn't show up on time, children feel discounted. It sends irresponsible messages: *"You don't matter,"* and *"Don't trust what others say they will do,"* and *"You don't have to be accountable."*

Avoid "his house/her house" problems by meeting as a family and establishing rules and routines together. This can be done with a counselor if the family needs an unbiased person. Maintaining good communication and setting a consistent structure with similar rules helps avoid teen manipulation. Establish a parenting plan, and review it periodically with your kids. They want to know, *"Where do I fit in? Where do I stay when? Who will be there to pick me up? Who buys my lunches, my clothes, my school supplies? Who gives me my allowance? Who can I depend on when?"*

Anger and depression stem from feeling, *"I have no say. I have no control. I don't matter. Everything is in an uproar."* Matt has no control over the divorce; it's his parents' business. But it's important that he express his angry feelings, openly and directly, to the people with whom he is most upset—his parents. Be alert for anger and blame: *"Mom, it is your fault that I never get to see Dad."* With sincerity, answer, *"Matt, I know you're angry that I am divorcing your father—that's understandable. But I am not divorcing you. It's not about you. I love you and will continue to be your mother, always. I hope we can work out a better schedule for you to see your dad."* A defensive remark on your part will not encourage him to tell you his feelings. Your understanding will be reassuring. Latent fears that he might lose you, too, are usually lurking.

During divorce, big decisions are being made without teen participation. Provide opportunities for your teen to make important, meaningful choices in his life, such as which school he will attend, and accept his input on where to live. He should be consulted about the details of his time with Mom and with Dad.

Listen. Make time to be available; bedtime, when the lights are off, is generally a safe sharing environment for the self-conscious teen. Even if you are so tired that you can barely hold your head up, take the time. Whether you say prayers together or sort through the day with her, you are sending the message that you care and that she's the most important person in your world at that moment.

Stay rooted when possible. Divorce is an enormous change, and to leave a community as well is very tough. When you are late coming home from work, it is comforting to know a familiar neighbor will be there for your teen. Remember, when both the familiar community and a parent are removed, the teen has little security. Having to adapt to a new environment makes the transition more difficult. Be sensitive.

When you are unhappy, upset, angry, or worried, tell your teen. This is good modeling. Say, *"I am feeling _____ about _____ because _____, and this isn't about you, you are not at fault or responsible."* Clear up all confusion your teen may have about your actions. It is easy for him to misinterpret, thinking, *"I'm a bad person. This must be because of me."*

Don't use your teen as your counselor. You are the parent and she is the child. She should not have to take care of your emotional needs, nor is she responsible for your feelings. She has her own emotional issues to deal with. You do need support, but find it with trusted friends, relatives, your church community, or a support group.

PREVENTIVE TIPS

Take care of yourself—this means a good support system, a healthy diet, required sleep, daily exercise, and time alone. It may sound like a tall order, but that's what it takes to raise a teen in any situation.

Most children hold hopes for their parents' reconciliation. Even after remarriage, some fantasize, *"Well, she could divorce him and get back with my dad."* Periodic discussions are very helpful for a reality check. Be sensitive to your teen's fantasies and acknowledge her feelings: *"Heidi, I bet you wish you and your dad and I could all be living together."* Include her in both short- and long-term family plans: *"Craig and I will take you kids on a backpack trip for summer vacation."*

Rebellious behavior is common at this time. The unspoken fantasy is, *"If I'm bad enough, maybe they will stay together."* Explain, *"No matter what your behavior, it will not change the divorce. It will not change our minds. We will continue to work with you so that you don't feel so angry."* Counseling may be necessary at this point.

Talk with your teenager's school counselor and teachers about the current family situation. They care about your teen's education and well-being. They can watch for significant changes in his personality, friendships, or schoolwork and help him as well as notify you.

Your support systems are vital. Many churches, community centers, hospitals, mental health clinics, and so forth have support groups that can help both you and your teen.

Your teen as well as your younger children may be afraid they caused the divorce. They need reassurance that this is not so.

Learn new communications skills to replace arguing and fighting. Your children will grow up using these new skills, which will increase their chances for healthy relationships.

Do not give up on a troubled teen. Kids are very resilient. Trust that he will survive this and be stronger for it. Your son may rebel. His schoolwork may suffer and his circle of friends may change. He may experiment and act out. With a strong support system, your guidance, and a lot of faith, you will all survive.

Parents must be fully aware of and alert to signs that their teens are struggling with concerns. Teens need time and space to grieve over the changes in their family so that they can then go on with their lives.

For more information on this topic, read *Second Chances* by Judith Wallerstein and Sandra Blackslee (New York: Ticknor and Fields, 1989); *Surviving the Breakup: How Children and Parents Cope with Divorce* by Judith Wallerstein and Joan Berlin Kelly (New York: Basic Books, 1980); and *The Stepfamily: Living, Loving and Learning* by Elizabeth Einstein (Ithaca, NY: E.A. Einstein, 1994).

WHEN TO SEEK HELP

When approaching divorce, it is wise to see a family counselor. The effects of divorce are long-lasting, and you may see ramifications several years later. Anytime a teen shows signs of depression—sleeplessness, eating disorders, high-risk activities, use of alcohol and other drugs, poor grades, or indications of learning problems—things are not going well. During the divorce proceedings it is not uncommon for teens to act out in these ways. Their behavior serves to divert their parents' attention away from the divorce. Seek counseling.

See also: Dating, Parents; Depression; Losses and Grief

DOCTORS

"I don't understand her. She's never given me such a hard time over going to the doctor before. Do I have to hog-tie her?"

"She wants me to go to my baby doctor, and I feel weird. I don't want to talk about myself or have him see me. What's he going to do to me?"

UNDERSTANDING THE SITUATION

Preventive health care is part of a healthy lifestyle. If your teen has developed a good relationship with a physician in early adolescence, he is likely to continue trusting this same physician as he begins to grow older and more independent. Other options are available to teens today. Planned Parenthood and health clinics are all alternatives to the family doctor, and often allow the teen to feel more independent and anonymous. Your teen needs encouragement to continue regular exams and to seek a physician's counsel when necessary—eventually, independent from you.

Your teen is dealing with a changing body and surging emotions, along with self-consciousness about new sexual feelings, so it's easy to understand why she may resist a visit. This can be a matter of extreme concern. You both are full of questions: *"Which doctor should she see? Does she need a woman doctor now? Should he be seen by a woman doctor? Is he too old for a pediatrician? What will they ask? Does a mom go in the room? How confidential is the visit?"* These are tough questions. A discussion with the doctor or nurse before the visit may help.

Health issues alarm us as we read or hear the news reports about cancer, AIDS, deadly viruses, and bacteria. Teens are very sensitive, often wondering and sometimes jumping to fearful conclusions: *"Is this supposed to happen; am I normal?"* *"Why am I tired all the time?"* *"I have headaches—maybe I have a brain tumor."* Parents wonder, *"Is my child overweight? She's suddenly gained ten pounds."* *"He's so small for his age—the other boys are so much bigger—could he need hormones?"* *"Do we need dietary counseling?"* *"She has a lump on one breast and it's very tender—could this be a tumor?"* *"He complains of pains in his joints—should I be concerned?"* *"She has had mononucleosis—is this normally followed by depression?"* *"Her ankles and knees are hurting—should she stop playing sports?"*

Your physician commonly hears these concerns and should be more than happy to ease your mind. He can also help with healthy communication between you and your teen. Doctors report that some parents are too distant (one mother hadn't a clue that her daughter was menstruating), and others are much too intrusive. Your doctor may serve as a good mediator. Some teens prefer to have an authority figure or other third person talk with their parents about private, personal matters. It is always comforting to talk with someone informed, someone who can stop the worry.

As teens grow, some health issues change coincident with behavioral changes. Now the body is sexually developed, and birth control issues, pregnancy, and HIV and other sexually transmitted diseases are all considered. Alcohol and other drugs, smoking, and driving are all issues physicians discuss with teens.

You can help an older teen by encouraging him to make his own appointments and get himself to the doctor, with or without you. This comes in handy if he needs to see a doctor and you're not around. You'll feel more comfortable knowing that he is able to go to the doctor by himself. An unprepared teen commented that she couldn't make herself go to the college infirmary because her mother had always accompanied her to the doctor; her roommates finally had to take her.

WHAT TO SAY AND DO

Give choices if possible. Select physicians who are covered by your insurance or within your payment plan. Then, let your teen choose which doctor has the best bedside manner, sense of humor, and listening skills. He needs to trust his physician and feel as comfortable as possible.

Teens want to know what to expect. The nurse will be happy to brief you in advance. Most doctors begin with casual questions: *"How are you liking school? How's the team this year—are you still a quarterback? Are you in the school play again? Have you any concerns?"* More direct questions often bother parents more than their kids. Even younger teens seem to understand why he might ask, *"Do you smoke? Have you started menstruating? Are your periods regular? Any cramps? Are you sexually active?"*

Your teen will be seen alone (unless he requests otherwise). You know, from his closed bedroom door and whispered phone conversations, that privacy is important to him. In most states, doctors are bound to keep visits confidential. However, if she senses life-threatening problems—abuse, depression, personal safety, suicidal tendencies, or eating disorders—she is likely to explain to the teen that by law, parents need to be made aware. If you are very worried, it is okay to ask the doctor or nurse for a summary of the examination.

Teens worry, *"What will he do to me?"* Again, question the nurse before the appointment. Reassure your teen that a third person will be in the room with her and the doctor. Most girls will not be given pelvic exams unless periods are irregular or birth control is recommended. Boys' exams are generally the same as they were at age eight, but now the boy is more aware and self-conscious.

PREVENTIVE TIPS

Many teens are sexually active by age sixteen but will not tell a parent or their family doctor. There are good clinics that counsel teens in pregnancy prevention, sex education, and alternatives to sex. Give your teen a choice: to take care of these private matters responsibly, either at a clinic or with the family doctor.

If you have a very specific concern that may be embarrassing to your teen, it will be helpful to the doctor to make it known prior to your teen's visit. This needs to be done with your child's knowledge but not necessarily her approval.

WHEN TO SEEK HELP

Health issues are a matter of safety. If your teen is not being responsible, you need to firmly and kindly confront him with your observations and say, *"I've made an appointment for you. I care too much to see you hurting yourself."*

See also: Acne; Alcohol and Other Drugs; Eating Disorders; Hygiene; Overweight; Sex, Talking About; Smoking

DRIVING

"My son and his friends are nearing driving age. Help!"
"Mom doesn't have any faith in me. All I hear is how scary it will be to see me drive."

UNDERSTANDING THE SITUATION

You may feel relief that you won't be on call to taxi your busy adolescent and his friends, and it may mean help in the errand-running department. Nevertheless, there is often considerable anxiety in knowing that your teen is now able to drive a car alone. At first, your nerves are on edge each time your teen drives away, feeling so independent. Yet, you know he has his own anxieties and needs your encouragement.

Seek information and support on driving issues. Most states provide and require driver's training. Have your teen practice with you in the passenger's seat; this will help ease your anxiety. Rather than your fear, convey your trust, enthusiasm, and confidence, and he's likely to behave responsibly. Celebrate this great event. This is an important rite of passage into American adulthood.

There are likely to be hassles in the next several years. The first time your daughter scrapes a fender, gets a ticket for speeding or rolling through a stop sign, leaves the gas tank empty, keeps the car out an hour too late, puts an extra eighty miles on it in one evening, or damages the engine because she ignored the low-oil warning light, you will be sorely pressed to hold on to your sense of reason and your temper. You are not alone. We all made some of these mistakes as teens, and we have learned from them. Keep reasonable expectations, stay patient, and help him to learn from the consequences of his actions.

WHAT TO SAY AND DO

Be very clear from the beginning about the level of maturity you expect. Run scenarios past him: *"Scott, the car is a lethal weapon. I'll feel better about allowing you to drive if I see you behaving maturely. What will you do if someone tries to distract you either inside or outside the car?"* Role playing is a good training tool and can be done with humor.

Practice, practice, practice! Take every opportunity to drive with him. Let him drive in as many different situations as possible: the country, the city, with others in the car and without, and so on. Be careful not to criticize and direct constantly, or he will tune you out. Ask questions: *"What do they say about how close you should follow another car?"* Or, *"I'm very uncomfortable about how fast you approach stoplights. What does your teacher say?"*

Be honest about how you feel: *"Becky, this is tough for me."*

However, she will perform better knowing that you feel she can handle the situation, so give her positive affirmations, too: *"I am very excited for you—you're becoming so independent! You make good decisions and will be a terrific driver!"*

Set a good example. Your teen learns a lot from watching you drive. A policeman asked a girl, as she was taking the driving portion of the state driving test, why she was going five miles over the speed limit. *"Oh, that's okay, you can do that,"* she said confidently. She was quite surprised when the examiner said, *"Pull over. You can try again another day."* Her mother always drove five miles over the limit and said it was fine, so that's what the girl had learned.

Reinforce the concept that driving is an enormous privilege and responsibility, and together set limits and consequences ahead of time. Occasionally, ask your teen to recite the rules. Show humor: *"Brett, I know you know the four rules about driving. But pamper me—tell me again what they are."*

1. We must know where you are at all times.
2. Absolutely no alcohol or drugs in the car, or even "in" anyone who is a passenger in the car.
3. Wear your seat belt at all times. Everyone must have his own seat belt.
4. Leave the car with at least a half tank of gas and free of trash.

Post these rules and any others you might have along with the consequences of not following them. Keep rules few but important. Written contracts are very helpful.

Set your rules regarding riding with other teens and add them to your teen's driving rules. For example: no riding with your friends unless they have had their licenses for six months with a clear driving record.

PREVENTIVE TIPS

To avoid the common, *"But, Mom, I told you where I was going,"* or the your-word-against-his issue, use a written contract.

Alex's Itinerary
I'm with _____.
I'll be at _____, phone number _____
I'll return by _____.

Months before she takes her driving test, take advantage of the driver's training manuals. Ask to see the material and become familiar with what she is learning. Invite her help on updating you on current driving instruction: *"Elsa, tell me what they teach about parallel parking. I'd like to know."*

See also: Alcohol and Other Drugs; Money; Safety; Trust; Worry

EATING DISORDERS

"I don't know what to think. Tania looks great, so thin, but she's lost weight very fast."
"Every time I look in the mirror I look so fat. I hate my body, especially my hips. I hate it!"

UNDERSTANDING THE SITUATION

Even though eating disorders are discussed openly in some schools and various media reports claim that one out of five teens experience them, when it is your teen who is anorexic or bulimic, you may well not recognize it. Even if you are told face-to-face, *"Your daughter has an eating disorder,"* it may be a surprise and you may still deny it. Eating disorders are generally hidden from the parent and not recognized as a problem by the teen for many months. The nature of eating disorders is secretive, and they are often experienced as something unique to the teen. *"Shelly has always been a picky eater"* indicates that this is "just her style." One worried mother, realizing that her fifteen-year-old daughter, Susan, was dieting and losing weight too quickly, made an appointment with a nutritionist to counsel her on healthy eating. A few months later, after seeing signs of vomit in Susan's bathroom, her mother took her to counseling. After two visits, Susan refused to go again, convincing her mother that she was fine and that the counselor wasn't helping. Two years later, Susan was hospitalized for six weeks for bulimia. Susan had gone from anorexia to bulimia, and faced a life-threatening situation. Susan's mother reflects, *"It was all so secretive. I never knew how bad she was hurting. She felt fat and ugly. I never knew how badly she was feeling or doing, though I suspected something. I never dreamed it could come to this."*

The term "anorexia" actually means an absence of hunger, though a true loss of appetite is rare. People with anorexia nervosa deny the physical sensation of being hungry because their desire to lose weight has become so important. Anorexia nervosa involves a true fear of fatness or of gaining weight. Individuals have an unrealistic and distorted view of their body image. As self-starvation advances, the preoccupation with food (obsessive thoughts) grows. Anorexics often experience their lives as being out of control, and by contrast they exert extreme control over food and their bodies.

Most people with bulimia tend to be of "normal" weight but are just as preoccupied with food, body shape, and weight as are anorexics. Bulimia is characterized by binge eating (eating large amounts of food in a short time period) followed by a process of getting rid of that food through self-induced vomiting, use of laxatives, or drinking purging teas. Binges can be followed by several days of not eating or by excessive exercise to prevent any weight gain. Some anorexics display signs of bulimia, too.

As with anorexia and compulsive overeating, bulimic behaviors are secretive. Parents are often the last to notice, or to admit to themselves what they may suspect. And a parent's intuition is usually a "red flag" that should be taken seriously. Their concern may require more than what can be done at home without professional intervention.

Eating disorders can be curtailed early with proper guidance. An informed parent is critical. The cause of an eating disorder often is a separation or loss of some kind: a death, divorce, breakup of a significant relationship, or a move, for example. The eating disorder behaviors are not necessarily done consciously. Feelings related to thoughts like, *"I have no say about what happens to me"*; *"I want to be accepted, and boys like thin girls"*; *"I'm not smart in school, I need to be noticed,"* are contributing factors. Discouragement and depression generally accompany eating disorders.

Self-esteem is always an issue. When eating problems begin, an informed parent will listen for underlying feelings, and respond with good thinking rather than irrational emotion. For example, one mother seemed to be continuously nagging her son about his eating. *"She stood over me like the police. I got so that I left banana peels in the sink and ditched the banana so she'd think I ate it. We were at war, we fought about what I ate or didn't eat constantly."* This mother eventually learned with good counseling to stop policing his eating. With help, the family learned better listening skills and ways to build good communication, which resulted in building her son's self-esteem.

One asks the question, Why is this kind of preoccupation with weight happening so frequently these days? One answer may be that years ago when families stayed in one town, generation after generation, a child was known for his family, and recognized for his abilities. Today's teens are living in a fast-paced, mobile society and, under these conditions, rely on their appearance to be recognized and noticed. Advertising and the media play a large role in this unrealistic image ideal, too.

Eating disorders affect both boys and girls, though girls to a greater extent. Boys may more frequently use body-building techniques in much the same manner that girls use starvation, in order to reach their ideal image—to be a jock. Many boys overdo it with weights at a young age and hurt their backs for life. Other boys are at risk for eating disorders because they are in sports where their bodies are important—swimming, diving, gymnastics—or they want to lose weight so they can make their weight category in wrestling. Still others just do not want to be fat. "Buff" is in. Their reasons are not different from those of girls.

Junior high marks a time when girls typically fall into a traditional *"I can't do it as well as you"* made in comparison to boys. Reduced confidence and lowered self-esteem puts girls at great risk for believing appearance is more important than other kinds of success, such as academics. At a time in life when belonging is so desperately needed with peers, girls are caught in a terrible bind. Their bodies are changing rapidly and naturally gaining body fat. These changes are counter to society's "ideal Barbie woman," a slender, emaciated model look. Any healthy teen going through normal changes is threatened. In today's culture, fat kids are shunned. The stress they experience is far from easy.

In junior and senior high school, girls do "gamble" with diets, green hair, and weird dress. How they deal with food can be odd and is usually as short-lived as the green hair. It becomes an eating disorder when it becomes secretive and obsessive. They are no longer talking about being a vegetarian. Instead they are not discussing their preoccupation with food, yet food and body image monopolize their thoughts. An anorexic will diet but generally won't discuss dieting. One girl confessed that she was so obsessed with the eating disorder, she couldn't follow the plot to a movie she went to with friends. She was thinking about her next binge and purge. Each time she purged she promised herself that would be the last, but it never was. She felt so guilty and ashamed for doing this, she began withdrawing from her friends.

Some indications of anorexia nervosa are:

- Loving cooking for others, and especially cookies and cakes, yet not joining in the eating
- Avoiding meals with excuses such as going to the library, already ate at a friend's, will eat in my room while studying, etc.

- Thin and often complaining about feeling cold
- Hair loss
- Missing periods
- Wearing layered and baggy clothing
- Isolation and withdrawn behavior from family and friends
- Mood swings more excessive than normal, irritability, and high tension
- Poor concentration or other impaired thinking
- Grades dropping or other changes in school performance (though, due to perfectionism, some are straight-A students)
- Excessive exercise or hyperactivity

Indications of bulimia:

- Use of diet pills, diuretics, or laxatives
- Swollen glands or puffy face
- Signs of vomit in bathroom
- Leaving table abruptly after a meal
- Enamel wearing off teeth or increased cavities
- Mood swings more excessive than normal, irritability, and high tension
- Isolation and withdrawn behavior from family and friends
- Stealing or other compulsive behaviors
- Grades dropping or other changes in school performance (though, due to perfectionism, some are straight-A students)

Your teen may display only some of these characteristics. That is why this disorder is so very difficult for a parent to detect. You wonder, What is normal? Questions usually produce strong denial. If you question, your best bet is to seek good professional counsel. Eating disorders are not usually successfully treated without professional help and the sooner the intervention, the greater the chance for successful recovery. The urge to binge on foods is not unlike the alcoholic's urge to drink. The repulsion for eating food and the need to resist intake is just as strong an urge. When not treated, an eating disorder can be extremely harmful and even fatal. When it's caught in time, recovery can occur. Treatment is slow, and progress is marked in tiny increments. Becoming aware of what is going on at the feeling level of a person with an eating disorder is slow going. It demands learning how to control the urge to eat. There is not a switch to turn on and off. Instead there is a pattern of behavior that needs "rewiring." What makes it really hard is that the "mechanic" is also the victim. The eating disorder has taken over the controls. The owner/victim needs to be reinstated and drive her own body again.

Depression and obsession are frequently linked to eating disorders, and antidepressant drugs are known to be extremely helpful in conjunction with therapy. Again, the earlier you seek help with experts, the better the chance your teen will have for a healthy future. This may be the hardest issue you have ever faced. As terrified as you feel, understand that you are not alone. Many other parents have felt terribly inadequate and guilty. *"How could we be in such a plight? What did I do wrong? Why didn't I spot it earlier?"* Divorced parents may blame themselves or the ex-spouses, but none of this thinking is helpful. No parent would ever wish an eating disorder on his or her child. The positive parent says, *"We have a problem. What is the solution?"* Remedies include parent and teen counseling, and optimism. Effective treatment utilizes a team approach—including the doctor, a nutritionist, and a counselor—that offers a variety of individual, family, and group therapy. It may take some time and some hard work, but the more effort you put in, the better the outcome.

WHAT TO SAY AND DO

Act on your suspicion by talking with a doctor knowledgeable about eating disorders who will advise you on how to approach your teen. A good first step is for your teen to meet with this doctor. If the advice is that she needs an evaluation, tell her directly. Respect her privacy. *"Jamie, you need a physical evaluation. Some things are happening I don't understand. You have an appointment with Dr. J. at 4:00. I'll drive you, and if you want to see him privately, I will wait in the waiting room." "I am not making the decisions, but your doctor is. We need to follow her advice."* You are doing this out of love, rather than hurt, anger, or fear. The doctor may recommend to you a professional eating-disorder clinic or specialist.

Do not nag your teen about what she eats, how much she weighs, or her obsession with food. Talk to her at a good talk time. Your questions will probably force her to lie; falsifying dietary issues is part of the illness. She wants your acceptance. She may feel scared and she doesn't feel good about what she is doing. Be direct: *"Shelly, I found vomit on the toilet. I know you are dieting and occasionally throwing up. I love you and I want to help."*

Keep your own eating issues separate from your teen's. If you feel fat, quietly deal with it yourself.

Do not comment on her weight gain or loss. She is trying to please. Notice other specifics about her, such as her intellect, her great sense of humor, her sportsmanship, her strong character. A counselor may ask you to help monitor her eating and give you other instructions. Otherwise, do not comment on what or when she eats. At mealtime, avoid noticing what she eats; rather, carry on an interested conversation about her school and other aspects of her world. Don't feed a power struggle.

Have healthful foods and fewer junk foods available. Be aware of what you buy and how fast it disappears.

Give specific compliments to your teen. You may feel, *"I wish she were more outgoing." "I wish she were more like her sister, got better grades, cared more about helping around the house."* She will grow and improve with, *"Thank you for . . . I appreciate that . . ."* Notice specifically what she does right. Mistakes must be okay. When a teen feels she cannot live up to parental expectations, thinness may become the way to gain acceptance and control.

PREVENTIVE TIPS

Educate yourself. Go to parent meetings, volunteer to help at school, work on committees. Learn about the pressures your teen experiences day in and day out. You will be better able to listen and discuss relevant issues, such as how the boys heckle over-weight girls. Your teen needs to be reminded about what is really important in life despite what society and media images say.

If you know that the sport teams are encouraging weight loss, or if body fat is being measured in P.E. classes, talk with the school counselor and principal. This is often handled very inappropriately and publicly.

Your teen needs special time with you and other favorite, positive, and mature adults. An older, well-balanced teen is a wonderful influence. An evening out on a regular basis, a ski weekend, and, better yet, an extended visit with a caring family member away from her peer group, may help.

Healing requires that she feel capable, needed, and useful. Explore activities that build her confidence. She may enjoy volunteering for the elderly or for a children's center, joining a 4H club, or participating in an alternative summer school experience. One teen spent a summer working on her grandmother's ranch. She moved large sprinklers, cut and baled hay, worked in the vegetable garden, and cared for animals. She left feeling quite accomplished. Some teens respond very positively to attending a summer wilderness program. One psychiatrist said *"A two- or three-week good wilderness program is equal to six months of therapy!"*

If you think your daughter is depressed, act on this notion. Depression is very painful and can lead to eating disorders.

For more information on this topic, read *Reviving Ophelia: Saving the Selves of Adolescent Girls* by Mary Pipher (New York: Ballantine Books, 1994); and *How to Get Your Kid to Eat, But Not Too Much* by Ellyn Satter (Palo Alto: Bull Publishing, 1987).

WHEN TO SEEK HELP

If your teen displays persistent signs of an eating disorder, talk to your doctor. Get a referral to a medical person who is familiar with eating disorders. Many hospitals are associated with eating-disorders clinics. The sooner you act, the better the chances that you will help curtail your teen's obsession before it becomes a lifelong struggle. An eating disorder is life-threatening.

See also: Chapter 1, What Happens During the Teen Years; Counseling; Depression; Mealtimes; Overweight; Shyness; Sports

FRIENDS, CHOOSING

"Margaret wants to bring a friend everywhere she goes."
"Can't I bring a friend? I can't stand it alone with you that long."

UNDERSTANDING THE SITUATION

Many parents notice the "frenzy of friendships" as soon as their adolescents enter junior high. Your family meals are interrupted with boys and girls calling, notes are passed back and forth in class, and groups of kids gather in the hallways at school and at lunch, their favorite time. Kids you've never met show up in your kitchen. Family activities and trips are no longer easy to plan unless a friend is invited along.

Welcome to the stage where friendships become more important than family. Making friends, and keeping them, is a major issue for your teen. What's happening? Your teen is defining himself by whom he chooses to be around. No one else can understand so closely what your teen is feeling about daily "stuff." Friends give him consensual and tangible validation that *"I am a cool person."*

Teen groups are all about belonging and guarantee that there will be company around. Groups, or cliques, are perhaps an antidote to being just a number in a large school. A clique can be as informal as a group of friends who always meet at lunchtime. It usually reflects status, interests, and local or ethnic differences. Often it reflects values, grades, sports teams, and family income level. These groups provide grounding and identity for their members. Styles in hair and clothing, as well as pierced ears or other body art, identify teens as a part of their group.

Belonging to an identified peer group helps a teen. Lacking the confidence to "go it on his own," in his group he feels accepted and important. Belonging is part of growing up, and is desirable unless the group begins to stand for things your teen may not like or want to be associated with. Getting out can be devastatingly hard. He may need support while extricating himself.

Some teens are able to flit around the edges of several groups, being friends with many of the members but not fully joining in. These kids are not strongly dependent on what any particular clique may represent or think of them. While the risk of standing alone at times does not bother them, these teens are apt to feel secure enough to befriend peers who are different from themselves, perhaps even those who are troubled or are acting out. This type of relationship may give your teen a chance to care for, counsel, and help another. It may help him to get in touch with his nurturing, unselfish side.

The importance that friends assume sometimes threatens parents. Do not feel rejected or replaced. Your role is to continue to give unconditional love, to be there for her, to set boundaries, and to discuss morals and values, which are very different from what friends provide. Both friends and parents are necessary.

The turmoil of choosing friends and keeping them may seem to preoccupy her world. Teens today are exposed to a much wider variety of kids than was the case when you were young. The friends you find at your kitchen table may not be the types you would choose. Be patient with her, listen, and guide. Eventually she will learn good judgment. For now, she needs to learn to avoid peer pressure and to think for herself. She will come to realize that there are many friends to meet in a lifetime, and only a handful of truly best friends.

WHAT TO SAY AND DO

Your teen will undoubtedly have friends whom you neither like nor trust. Do not mistake these for lifelong friendships. If you badger him over his choices, he'll feel that you don't trust his judgment and will defend his friends all the harder. Have faith, give him space, and let him discover for himself that some of the friends he picked are creeps.

Invite his friends into your home and try to get to know them. Good icebreakers: Set up a volleyball net, use the driveway as a makeshift basketball court, let them cook over a barbecue, invite those who play to bring their instruments. Remember to be respectful. Don't criticize.

The rules in your home should apply to your teen's friends. You are not attacking your daughter when you are specific about a friend's inappropriate behavior. Buffer your comments with something positive: *"Cindy, I know you like Laura."* (Use, *"I feel _____ about _____ because _____, therefore _____."*) *"I don't like the swearwords Laura uses, we don't talk like that in our family. Please tell her not to swear in our home; if I hear it, I will remind her as well."*

If you truly object to your teen's friend because of safety or moral issues, say so. Your son may need you to set the limits: *"Steve, I don't want you hanging out with Brian anymore. His attitude leads people in the wrong direction. I don't want you going to jail because the police thought you were an accomplice."*

Teens are fiercely loyal to their friends. Your teen needs to talk with her friends in private and know that you won't pry or snoop. Intrusiveness invites rebellion.

PREVENTIVE TIPS

Discuss the concept of protecting friends. A true friend knows the difference between tattling on a friend and helping save her life. When a friend flirts with danger, for instance with alcohol or other drugs, or sex, a true friend seeks help. *"Anne, you can always talk to the school counselor or a trusted teacher or you could write an anonymous note about your concerns to them if you don't want to tell her parents. That would be being a good friend."*

At a good talk time, ask with sincerity about his friends. Dream up questions that will make him think about the characteristics of a good friend: *"Is every friend a best friend?"* *"What's the difference between a best friend and a group of friends?"* *"What kind of friend do you want to be?"* *"What do you do when a friend wants you to do something that you don't think is right?"*

Your teen may be involved in a relationship that is possessive or bullying. This is common among inexperienced or unassertive teens. If she thinks you disapprove or are prying, she may try to protect her friend by being silent. If she feels you're sincerely interested and trusts you to keep it private, she may reveal concerns or problems she is having. Then you can help with problem solving.

Much as he may complain, your teen needs time alone with you and his siblings; family time. She may act as if doing something alone with Mom or Dad is a drag, but when you don't grill her and you show genuine interest, she will probably look forward to being with you. One father who had been turned down said wisely, *"Well, if you're too busy to have dinner with me tonight, I'll meet you at school tomorrow for lunch."* That quickly changed her mind about making time to go to dinner with him.

Encourage journal writing. Give her a lockable diary and suggest she write about her friendships. She'll learn more about herself and observe her growth and changes.

See also: Bullied; Bullying; Friends, Left Out; Moving; Suicide

FRIENDS, LEFT OUT

*"I don't know how to help Missy. She came home from
school crying because she was not included. She's being
left out of 'the group.' "*

*"I don't know why they don't like me. They sit in their groups
at lunch and never talk to me. What's wrong with me?"*

UNDERSTANDING THE SITUATION

When your teen is struggling with friendships, everyone in the
family is likely to feel it. When kids are hurting, it often shows
as withdrawal, irritability, impatience, or sudden temper tan-
trums. If she feels rejected by a group, she may not discuss it
readily. Though her behavior may be volatile and exasperat-
ing, with patience you can help her understand her hurt feelings and support her through the situation. Feeling left out
is extremely painful and common. Most kids are even more
sensitive to acceptance or rejection when they start a new
school year, especially at a new school.

Friendships are extremely important. At this age, self-esteem
is shaky; when a teen is rejected, his sense of self can plummet,
just as it skyrockets when he is accepted into a coveted group.
Being on the outside, wishing to be accepted, can be very
painful. Members of a clique can be self-centered and mean,
with cutting or snide comments to those who are vulnerable.
The person being shut out may not even like what the "in"
group stands for, but the rejection is still very hurtful.

Do not pass this off lightly, as in, *"Oh, you'll find another
friend."* Your biggest job is to listen. You cannot fix hurt feelings, but you can certainly sympathize or empathize, which

will help her to apply good thinking and good judgment. She is capable of deciding what is best for her in the situation. Encourage her!

WHAT TO SAY AND DO

From the outside, a tight group of friends is like a tight knot. Help him to understand that keeping a particular individual out of a group is a way for the "in" to feel special; it feeds their wish for superiority or popularity in a competitive arena.

Help him to understand that many other kids feel just as he does. Nothing is wrong with him. This is a very common situation.

Her rejection may trigger old wounds from your past. Do not confuse your experiences with hers. When she comes home feeling rejected and angry, wanting never to talk to Danielle, Marie, and Kathleen again, use reflective listening: *"Nancy, you are really hurt by what they said to you. I don't blame you. I'd be hurt, too."* Do not join her in calling them names and saying how horrible they are. The next day they may all be best friends again, and you might regret what you said.

One boy went to a drinking party to be with the guys on the lacrosse team. It wasn't fun, and he came home early. Even though it was his choice to leave, he felt sad and lonely. Questions helped: *"Rob, what do you like about these friends? What makes them important to you? Is it possible to enjoy some things they do, such as play lacrosse, but not attend the parties? Are there any others who don't like the parties?"*

You cannot take responsibility for your teen's poor decisions. It is not your failure or your success. Buying him new clothes or the baseball mitt he's wanted so badly will not make up for his pain, so don't try. Do listen and make time for him. He may just need to feel bad for a while. He's trying to figure it all out and needs to do some of this on his own.

A kind comment or wink to let him know you're glad to see him emerge from his room is all that's needed. Do not dwell on the problem. He's probably embarrassed to let you know that he's been rejected. Respect his privacy and feelings.

At a good talk time, discuss the concept that friendships take time and patience. Teens are so wrapped up in the immediate happening, situations are black and white, and there's a sense of both urgency and finality: *"I got invited—I'm popular!"* Or, *"No one invited me to sit with them at lunch. No one likes me."*

Find a good time to discuss how to make friends. *"Rachel, you need to approach the group. Choose a friend who looks approachable. It takes courage. Ask something about her. What does she like? What classes does she have? Don't wait for them to come to you, and do not give up. You may have to try and try again. You are worth it . . . no one is better than you. Have patience and be persistent."*

PREVENTIVE TIPS

At a good talk time, help your teen cement values that you feel are important. Can you be popular and a thoughtful, kind person? Someone with a weight problem doesn't deserve hurtful remarks. Intolerance is learned, and you can be very influential. Being aware of how your comments affect others is a first step. Your attitude will shape hers. Say, *"Nora, Martha's clothes are rumpled and unfashionable, and she gets teased about it. What she is wearing is not wrong. It is right for her. It's just different from what 'the group' wears."* You may get, *"Oh,* Mom!" but more sinks in than she'll ever let you know.

Introduce the concept of "dare to be yourself." Independent thinking is an important skill.

Outside friendships can be established during summer vacations or long weekends. Make time to visit relatives and friends outside the school community. Community volunteer work offers the opportunity for your teen to make new acquaintances and see herself in a different environment.

Arrange activities and excursions with other families. Bonding with other mothers and fathers is very healthy for your teen, who may feel easier talking with them than with you.

Coaches, teachers, church leaders, and responsible older siblings are also excellent mentors.

Volunteer in the school community. This will give you an opportunity to observe your teen's peers and other groups. When you get to know other parents, your child's name becomes familiar to them. This is important networking.

See also: Bullied; Bullying; Friends, Choosing

GANGS

"I am afraid when George leaves the house in his red shirt, baggy jeans—he might get shot."
"It's cool to wear my pants low. It's in."

UNDERSTANDING THE SITUATION

Parents have every reason to feel frightened about gang activity in their communities. Media reports of gang violence and insensible cruelty are terrifying. It is sad that children cannot wander the community in safety. Warning them of the dangers has become a commonplace part of responsible parenting.

If your teen has joined a gang, it means he has actively and aggressively made the decision to do so, has been accepted by the group, which has an established hierarchy and protocol, and has actively rejected his family. This is no small decision. It comes with a dress code, tattoos, and antisocial behavior including theft, gun "play," drug-culture activity, and worse. It sounds scary, and it is.

Gangs are no longer just for inner-city, disenfranchised kids. Suburban teens who suffer from a lack of belonging are increasingly drawn to gangs. Years of latchkey living (emotionally or physically absent parents) combined with poor school performance can produce anger at having been abandoned, along with a need to fill an inner emptiness. Gangs offer "love," a brotherhood, structure, and acceptance. Violence and other risky behaviors become enticing. To kids who feel helpless and hopeless, gangs offer a way to be somebody. To know that a fellow gang member, a homeboy, will die for you is a high. This is no exaggeration. In many communities, the most common cause of death among teens is shooting.

Initiation into gangs is extremely dangerous. To join, prospective members have to prove themselves by being beaten up by the gang members, shooting someone, raping or being raped, and/or other dangerous acts. Girls and boys are unaware of the traps until it is too late. Blackmail is a common way to initiate new members. For example, a teen will agree to date a gang member; this gang member will reveal gang secrets; the teen will then be threatened with various initiation rites or death for knowing the secrets.

How can you distinguish a gang member from a regular kid wearing a baseball cap backward? The biggest difference is attitude. Parents and other authorities are not respected, and there is little willingness to cooperate. Schoolwork is ignored; skipping school is commonplace. When a teen joins a gang, only his homeboys matter; he lets the rest of his world go. He may still live at the family home, but he does not participate. However, he may be protective of his younger siblings, warning or threatening them never to get involved in a gang. This is about as much family loyalty as you're likely to see. One eleven-year-old brother of a gang member got the message. In response to being asked what it means to be in a gang, he said, *"It means you're a jerk."*

Dress codes are coming back. Some schools prohibit the wearing of gang colors and baggy pants and will send kids home if they dress against the code. Other schools are requiring students to wear uniforms to solve the problem. Learn what colors and styles mean in your community. When teens mimic gang dress, they may become innocent targets for real gang members.

Do not hesitate to question your teen about his friends. Are they gang types who make you worry? Is your teen ignoring curfew or constantly challenging other family rules? Is he skipping school and avoiding thoughts about his future? Is his behavior out of control? If so, you have cause for concern and will need support to resolve this. Adding more police and making more laws is not sufficient to stop gang activity.

WHAT TO SAY AND DO

If your teen leaves home looking like a gang member, you have reason for serious concern and must tackle the issue head-on. Learn as much as you can about gangs in your area. Talk to the police, community youth workers, counselors at school, youth centers, and parents who have been through it. Learn whether your teen is associated with gang members or is actually a member. These are very different! Do not accuse your teen of being a gang member unless you are certain that he is. Otherwise, you may lose him. You must maintain your credibility. When Alan discovered that his fourteen-year-old daughter was enthralled with the excitement of gang life, he introduced her to an ex–gang member. She told her, in terrible, graphic detail, what happens to girls in gangs. During this conversation, Alan was at home, stripping her room of all gang posters, baggy clothes, and other gang-related items. This girl thinks her family saved her life by arranging that meeting. She soon started family counseling and bought new, appropriate clothes.

Consider moving your teen to a new school. This may seem to be an overreaction, but it has worked for some. Look at private schools. You want her surrounded by peers who want to go to school. A new school offers new opportunities and the chance to begin again without a bad reputation. There is a possibility for change.

Do not criticize the gang friends, though you can object to their behavior. No one likes to hear criticism of friends, and your teen is no different. He will probably be defensive and even more uncooperative.

State your firm disapproval of her activities as well as your concerns for her safety. This is proof that you care.

If your teen begins to find excuses to stay at home, to avoid being out with the gang, it is a sign that he needs your help. He may be terribly frightened; something he has experienced has had a sobering effect. To get your teen out of a gang is not easy. It usually takes the police, the threat of jail time, or threats of death to himself or other gang members whom he has come to love.

Listen carefully to him. Don't push him out. You might try making a deal: *"Stay in school, clean of gang activity, and keep your part-time job, and we'll pay your car insurance."* This proves that you believe in him, that you are willing to help him as long as he shows responsibility. You are offering another opportunity. It is never too late.

Find resources to help. Some counselors are quite savvy about teen and gang issues. Do not try to handle this without support.

PREVENTIVE TIPS

Your teen needs to know how important his safety is to you. Communicate regularly that you love him and care about his safety. Be aware of risky situations and communicate your specific concerns sincerely and firmly. Clothing styles and colors are traditional gang symbols. An ignorant young teen wearing a Raiders jacket or a blue shirt at the wrong time and place could get shot.

Balance your interest in his well-being with being informed but not intrusive. Intrusiveness pushes teens toward secretiveness. Use questions: *"What do you know about . . . ?" "How do you think . . . ?" "Where do you suppose . . . ?"*

Be there for your teen. Listen without feeling you need to give your advice.

Know where she is and with whom she hangs out.

Deal with your problems and concerns with her at a set meeting time. Ask for her input in problem solving and setting limits. Try to spend all other time focusing on what she does right. This will show your faith in her, and will help her to see that home is an okay place. This is very hard with disruptive teens. However, with support you can do it!

If your teen is troubled with schoolwork, take heed. Have him tested for learning problems and build his confidence with an education counselor or a tutor. Find a teacher, coach, or other adult at his school he might attach to. Teens who manage their schoolwork and feel they belong at school have stronger self-esteem and rarely join gangs.

Being cool is important to teens, and to some, gangs seem cool. Find less destructive activities that are considered cool, such as country western line dancing or good rap. Line dancing takes a good deal of practice, coordination, and concentration.

Encourage your community to establish more teen centers and activities that offer healthy choices.

For more information on this topic, read *Always Running: La Vida Loca: Gang Days in L.A.* by Luis J. Rodriguez (Willimantic, CT: Curbstone Press, 1992).

WHEN TO SEEK HELP

Gangs are dangerous. Once a teen has joined a gang it is very hard to convince him to leave. Therefore, if you suspect your teen is hanging out with gangs, get help immediately. Locate gang intervention specialists through your local police and begin family counseling.

See also: Alcohol and Other Drugs; Body Art; Bullying; Hanging Out; Rebelliousness; Safety

GOING STEADY

"I wish he weren't going steady yet. I worry where it may lead."
"My parents don't understand. I love him."

UNDERSTANDING THE SITUATION

Despite knowing intellectually that your teen will grow up and choose a life partner, you may truly worry when she begins dating one person exclusively. You hear the reports of promiscuous sex and pregnant teens; unfortunately, you seldom hear about the majority of teens who are balancing their lives and making fine choices.

Teens today are more mature and sexually aware than in your day. However, this doesn't mean they have developed good judgment yet. When you sincerely convey that you will always love and have faith in her, she will be far more likely to use caution. She will also tend to talk and share more, knowing that she will be accepted no matter what. This is the heart of unconditional love.

Watching your teen begin to choose people to love and care for can be wonderfully rewarding. Does her boyfriend share her interests? Does he fit in to our family, or are we too boisterous for him? What are his friends like? What is important to the two of them? These questions may help you enjoy the process from a distance.

Your reflective feedback is important. These same questions, asked at a good discussion time, will help your teen know himself better and realize what he wants in a partner. Going steady presents life lessons, such as the fact that first impressions are seldom reliable, that falling "in love" too fast can lead to errors in judgment, and that moderation comes with experience. Relax and trust your teen to learn these lessons on his own. Couples today enjoy many more activities, as girls have become more assertive. It is not uncommon to see teen "steadies" playing tennis, skiing, and sharing other interests.

The most devastating difference between today and when you went steady is that sex can be a life-or-death choice. The good news is that better sex education is widely available. Teens are taught about healthy choices, abstinence, and safe sex. Although we are still battling the old, rigid role expectations—girls are passive and boys are in control; girls are possessions and boys with steady girlfriends are macho; a girl's identity depends on her having a steady boyfriend; boys are not responsible ("boys will be boys")—a better balance between the sexes is evolving.

It is comforting to remember that today's teens are more comfortable with the opposite sex, and many close friendships are not of a romantic nature. Boys and girls can go steady and break up and still be friends. Could you have done that at their age? One practical teen said, *"Pat and I were such good friends. Getting serious messed it all up. We decided to stop going steady and just be good friends."* At any age, your teen needs to know that you have faith in her, that you listen to and take her seriously, and that she is becoming a responsible person who can make good decisions.

WHAT TO SAY AND DO

Be a good observer and listen for clues. Without being a peeping Tom, try to assess how serious the relationship is. It is safe to assume that after six months of going steady, the two teens have had at least a "brush" with sex. Encourage a dialogue about sex. *"Diane, when a girl has gone steady with a boy as long as you have with Eric, the question of whether or not to have sex must be faced."* Issues such as abstinence, teen counseling, and birth control should be openly discussed. If you see signs of an unhealthy relationship, such as dominance, you need to discuss that, too, with your teen. Don't lecture. Do not criticize the steady, for that is likely to push them tighter together. One mother and father were very concerned about their daughter's steady relationship. He was controlling, and she deferred to his opinions and decisions exclusively. She had lost her spark. Any criticism infuriated the girl. Dad said, *"Angie, you have somehow changed. You've lost your sparkle. You don't seem to be having much fun lately."* About a week later, she broke up with the boy. *"I didn't feel like me anymore,"* she said.

PREVENTIVE TIPS

Much of the music and other entertainment we enjoy paints a false picture of life. Point out the humor when you see a movie or TV show or hear a song that portrays an unrealistic view of relationships: *"I need him to survive"; "I couldn't help it, I promise to be true from now on"; "I'm crying in my beer over you."*

Encourage your older teen to pursue interesting activities with his steady, such as spending a day in the city visiting museums, galleries, the aquarium, or the zoo. Invite them to join you on occasion—take them to a play. Offer them cultural experiences that promote growth. This also will give them more opportunities to determine their likes and dislikes.

Encourage her to have her friends over for a barbecue, dancing, and so forth. When your home is welcoming, kids will come. It is especially important for young teen couples not to be isolated.

Encourage a strong sense of self. She needs to believe that she's capable without him. She needs to set goals for herself. Both girls and boys need to think about the qualities that will take them into the future as individuals, not as half of a couple. Dependencies often develop with long-term high-school relationships. (*"I can't live without him."*) Teenagers need to feel strong enough to make decisions on their own. Will she choose a college based on her interests or because her boyfriend goes there? Will he choose to work instead of go to college so that he can be near her? Will she give up Grandmother's graduation trip to Europe because she would miss him?

Support activities outside her peer group at school. She needs to meet other teens. Youth groups, summer camp, vacations with the family, visits to relatives, and the like should be encouraged.

Honesty is vital. If you can say it sincerely, tell your teen that you're glad she has chosen such an interesting person to be with. Tell her the positive things you have noticed: *"He seems to listen attentively to your ideas."* It's easy to be critical, but we don't always remember to voice our approval. However, this needs to be shared matter-of-factly. You do not want to give the impression that it will displease you if they break up. You have given a stamp of approval; you have not begun to write wedding invitations.

Breaking up is tough, and rarely is it entirely mutual. It's not easy for the "dumped" or the "dumper." Your compassion is especially important now. Be there to soothe the feelings of rejection or to ease the guilt, and to reinforce your teen's strengths and many other attributes.

WHEN TO SEEK HELP

If factors such as dominance, drinking, partying, and sex are of concern, seek professional help.

See also: Body Image; Counseling; Dating, Teens; Mood Swings; Sex, Talking About

GRADES AND HOMEWORK

Younger Teens

*"Barbara's grades have fallen. I know she can do better!"
Or, "Joy worries herself sick over the idea of not getting
an A."*

*"I try so hard and I can't get good grades. I must be
stupid." Or, "Why does any of this matter? I don't
care about the dumb homework."*

UNDERSTANDING THE SITUATION

Panic is the best term for what you feel when your child's
grades fall to an unsatisfactory level in junior high. He finished
elementary school with average grades or better, but now he's
getting poor marks. No parent wants to hear her child say, *"I
must be dumb,"* or, *"I don't care."* Equally distressing is the
young teen who feels that nothing will do but an A; self-worth
is based on being perfect.

This is typically a time when homework hassles begin. You want
your young teen to be doing homework and learning good study
habits, skills that are important for a successful high-school career.
If grades seem to fall, parents worry and typically apply pressure.
Parent expectations can and often do clash with a young teen's priorities. Academically, the junior-high years are for stimulating a curiosity for learning, teaching how to gather information, and learning
organizational and study skills. You are needed to guide your
young student through this developmental process, focusing on
long-range goals rather than pressuring for immediate results.

Your junior-high adolescent is beginning the greatest overall physical, intellectual, social, and emotional growth since he was age two. Thirteen-year-olds are not noted for having their wits about them. The transition from elementary school to junior high is very stressful. For the first time, your child will be with six or seven different teachers who see him only forty minutes a day. The additional reading, note taking, math comprehension, organization, and focusing may be very difficult. Many young teens still need a close teacher-student relationship. Some learning problems don't show up until this age. An observant junior-high teacher may be able to catch a problem early and address it or guide you or your teen to someone who can.

You may feel that her grades are top priority, but your self-absorbed daughter may put her social activities far ahead of her schoolwork. Establishing new friends and competing among so many kids can be overwhelming. This is the age of, *"Why should I have to do this?"* *"It's too hard, I can't."* The *"I can't"* may mean *"I won't,"* for various reasons. The fear of failing after trying very, very hard is common. Many junior-high adolescents resist the discipline academics require. Sports are more fun; TV and video games are intriguing; hanging out at the mall, or doing most anything with friends, is better than staying at home to study. Your ideas about what is and isn't important may definitely clash with hers.

This is also the time when sexual identity becomes a paramount issue. Any junior-high teacher will tell you that hormones seem to run the classroom. Boys often feel an urge to compete in the classroom, while many girls yield or defer. It has long been considered uncool to be smarter than a boy if you want to impress. Today such values are gradually giving way to healthier ones, though it is necessary for parents to encourage and reinforce intellectual capabilities.

A wise principal believed in these three goals for his students, in order of importance:

1. To develop a strong, positive attitude toward learning
2. To learn the skills necessary to gather information
3. To acquire knowledge

Your job now is to nurture a love for learning and to make it—rather than the finished product, the "grade"—the goal. Approach struggles over grades and homework with care. When you apply too much pressure, nag, and interfere with schoolwork, she may rebel by getting poor grades. Teens can't cooperate when they're in a state of rebellion, and you do not want to create a battle. Kids usually want to do well in school, though some get discouraged early on, and when parental pressure is too great, they may resort to lying or cheating. Your job is to set up a good learning environment, establish a regular study routine, teach good study habits, and win cooperation with encouragement; work with her rather than trying to fight her. Parents who read, rather than fill all their free time with TV, set an example for the love of learning.

Healthy self-esteem comes from the process of applying effort, practice, and concentration to any challenge, whether it is playing a sport, learning French, or playing Chopin. Your goal is to expose your young teen to many exciting challenges, set goals together, and make sure that the necessary skills are taught. It will pay off.

WHAT TO SAY AND DO

Together, design a study space that he can call his own. *"Jason, you are older now. Schoolwork requires more time and concentration, both at school and at home. Let's design an office space for you to study in."* His own space, with a good desk, comfortable chair, and proper lighting, will encourage him to work harder at home.

Together design rules regarding homework. When she starts junior high, set clear boundaries for her, with the understanding that, depending on effort and responsibility, they may change. Your list may look something like this:

- No TV on school nights, unless negotiated beforehand. Tape what you want to see and watch it on the weekend.
- Quiet time, one hour each evening. No telephone interruptions. Use the time for reading if there is no homework.

• Friends after school only on days when there is no other after-school activity.

Evaluate the rules after each grading period.

Suggest that occasionally she find a buddy to study with. Studying with two or three friends is often better than doing it alone. Be a good observer; kids this age can be productive and have fun at the same time.

Do not rescue him by doing his work for him, but be there to discuss projects and homework. Parents are needed to stimulate interest and to clarify confusion over schoolwork. You should not do the work for him. This sends the not-so-subtle message that he is incapable. If grades fall or you see confusion about schoolwork at home, meet with your child and his teacher to learn how you can help.

Your young teen's grades, good or bad, are not really accurate measures of how much he actually understands. Ask him about what he is learning throughout the semester, and talk to him about how he feels about the work and the classes. When grades come, continue to notice his interest, or lack thereof, in various subjects. Notice the better grades first. *"Bud, you did very well in science this term. Why do you think you did so well? What did you find the most challenging? What was most interesting?"* By focusing on the subject rather than on just the grade, you will help him think about what he is learning.

It is hard to show a parent a poor report card. Often it is presented with denial and lying, rooted in insecurity rather than deceit. Say firmly, *"Riley, report cards have come out. I'd like to see yours."* Then, thank him. Lying and sneakiness may continue if you respond to his report too harshly. He needs to know that you love him regardless.

Focus first on work that reflects her interests and efforts. Comment specifically: *"Awesome comment from your French teacher. This shows a lot of effort." "Wow! It looks as though you really enjoy pottery class. You must be really good with your hands. I always thought that about you!"* Next, bring up the lower math grade. Use, *"I feel _____ about _____ because _____."* For example, *"Alice, I feel most concerned about the lower math grade because I didn't see much effort this term. What do you think would make a difference?"* Then, drop it! Let this brief interaction settle. If only one grade is low, you might consider praising the others and not saying a word about the low one. She is plenty aware of it and may just fix it on her own.

If underachieving continues, meet with the teacher, the school counselor, and your child even if she pleads with you not to. Together, clarify each person's expectations. Leave this conference knowing that you, your daughter, her teacher, and the counselor will be working on this together and will keep one another posted.

Occasionally a real conflict will arise between your young teen and a particular teacher. Teach him to be his own advocate. Show understanding and encourage him to talk with this teacher. Say, *"I'd hate to see you jeopardize your learning because you don't like the teacher or you feel she doesn't like you. This is common—I had to learn to work with different teachers, too. You need to talk with her."* This gives your son the responsibility if it is his problem, and helps him learn to address a teacher, which can be scary at his age. If the problem continues, you may need to schedule a conference with your son and the teacher and possibly the principal or the school counselor. Moving your child to another class may be possible.

"Great job" is not telling your daughter what exactly was great. Be very specific: *"I liked the way you described the dog and the cat in this middle paragraph";* or, *"How about more development about the cat getting lost. How did it feel?"* Teach her to ask what the teacher specifically liked or disliked about the work. She'll work for excellence when she gets more feedback than just a grade or a written *"nice work"* at the top of her page.

If your teen's grades slip, stay away from rewards or bribes, but consider incentives: *"If we see effort and improvement, we'll set up the clothing allowance you've been wanting. I'm sure that when you show responsibility for your schoolwork, you'll be able to handle a budget. There's no better way to learn math than with your own money."*

The grade should not be tied to identity, as in, *"I'm a D student in foreign language."* Labels become self-fulfilling prophecies. She may do better next year, with another teacher who uses a different technique. One girl raised her national math scores by twenty points when she had a math teacher who taught visually and used a hands-on approach. All children gain a better understanding of concepts as abstract thinking develops, and not all children develop at the same rate. Don't compare. Leave the door open for her to change. Say, *"Helen, you're making C's this year in math. Next year it could be different."* Encourage her efforts and help her seek the skills needed for improvement.

You cannot make him do better, but you can work with him, gain his cooperation, and problem solve with him. Listen closely when he wants to communicate. If he acts arrogant, try to understand; he probably is hiding a feeling of discouragement.

Try, with sincerity: *"Matthew, I don't understand this new attitude. You've always liked schoolwork. I'm confused."* Allow your teen the space to figure it out. As he reveals his feelings, he will begin to reflect on what might make a difference.

To say to a young teen, *"You need to try harder,"* can be very discouraging. Instead, propose specific remedies or tactics: *"Greg, can't is one of the worst four-letter words I know. If you run into a roadblock, think of another approach."* Or, *"Ruth, use positive self-talk. Tell yourself, 'I can try another way. It's not like me to give up.'"* If she responds, *"I don't understand her accent. She talks too fast. I can't take notes and listen to her at the same time,"* ask her, *"Ruth, what might make a difference?"* Together, brainstorm solutions: *"I could sit closer to the board. I could ask her to teach me with something I can manipulate, a hands-on approach. I could rewrite my notes every night. I could borrow notes from someone the teacher suggests. We could find a tutor."*

You may have an overachiever who struggles to be perfect in all areas. When he falls short, and it is inevitable that he will, he may be devastated. Ask, *"Sean, could you handle a B in this class?"* Or, *"You work awfully hard to excel. I could handle your getting a lower grade—I wouldn't feel embarrassed or discouraged for you.*

Your curiosity and understanding is what's important, and working for an A is fine, as long as you don't believe that you count only if you get an A."

PREVENTIVE TIPS

Communication between home and school is more difficult than it was when your child was in elementary school, yet it is vital when helping young teens be responsible for their own learning. Many parents of preteens complain that their children won't talk anymore. You may feel cut off, wanting to give privacy, yet stay in touch. Do show interest in your child's homework. One community created a hot line that parents could call to hear their child's teacher outline what they were currently covering in the classroom. This hot line, sponsored by a local city newspaper, has helped teachers communicate with parents, and has kept parents informed, better preparing them to discuss pertinent lessons and assignments with their young teens.

At night when you give your final hugs, ask, *"Betty, what's different this year from last year? What do you like the best? What one thing is the most frustrating?"* This may lead to talks about pressures, friendships, studies, or grades. Do this regularly.

Promote good attitudes. At a good talk time, ask provocative questions: *"What kind of student would you like to be?" "What would you like to get out of this class?" "What would you like others to know about what you think?"* You may get a grunt or a shrug, but the questions will make her think.

Explain to your child that these years are building blocks for the future. At this age, most children live in the here and now and see the future as irrelevant.

One girl attended eighth grade in Germany. She later remarked, *"I had to work very hard there. I learned what 'doing my best' was. I never knew what this was before."* There are ways to learn this much closer to home. Teens learn to "do their best" in sports, music, or dance, where frequent practice is the only way to get the swing or the chord or the step right. The same level of effort and concentration will improve schoolwork.

Be involved at the school. The fact that you are interested and are attending PTA meetings or being a chaperon is very important. She may moan and complain, but your involvement is an intrinsic motivator.

Extra reading choices should be left up to him, but he needs you to show interest in what he's reading and to model an interest in books. Occasionally, read a book your teen is reading, even sci-fi, and discuss it with him.

Offer support systems such as a study buddy or a tutor. Tutors can teach organizational and note-taking skills that sometimes need reinforcing.

WHEN TO SEEK HELP

Sometimes a child is too discouraged to do the work demanded of him. You will need to make an action plan so that success can happen before failure takes place. Today, learning specialists are available. Generally these experts have an educational counseling background. They help define learning styles and identify learning problems. If you feel discouraged, your teen probably does, too. Your school counselor may help you to find a specialist. Failing grades may be an indication of the use of alcohol or other drugs, or that the teen is suffering from depression, or that another serious issue requires your intervention. If you are concerned, seek the help of a professional counselor.

See also: Chapter 1, What Happens During the Teen Years; Grades and Homework, Older Teens; Learning Problems

Older Teens

"A B is only an average grade these days. She has to do better."
"Why do grades have to be so important?"

UNDERSTANDING THE SITUATION

If you panicked over your teen's grades in junior high, you may really feel strung out during high school. In today's very competitive world, grades count. Nevertheless, there are lots of other arenas for success. For every student who gets A's, many others achieve success through music, sports, drama, or art. The important thing is that your teen feel significant in some way and be developing into a responsible, caring, resourceful adult, with your help.

Stress over getting good grades in order to be sure of being accepted into college can be a debilitating and consuming worry for some teens (and parents). Courses on how to pass the SATs abound. Luckily, colleges seem to weigh a balanced background more heavily than straight As. This needs to be communicated to your high schooler. You and the college counselor may also need to explain to him that there are lots of top-rated colleges that are not well known. He need not be discouraged with middle-of-the-road grades. A student who graduates with marginal grades can go to a community college, do very well, and then move on to four-year college despite not taking his high school years seriously. Developmentally speaking, he may simply need more time before he's able to view his future realistically. Keep the faith.

Smart educators view high school as a time to learn attitudes and skills for any number of career choices. One young dentist feels his high-school vocational arts class prepared him for dentistry. He learned welding, the patience involved in planning a project, and the hard work that followed. Whether teens go on to college or technical school or start working right out of high school, the mental outlook must be that learning never stops.

That is essential in our fast-changing society. The A is important only if it represents good thinking, honesty, good communication, emotional control, responsibility, and basic work ethics.

Kids put a lot of pressure and many unrealistic expectations on themselves. They make varsity soccer, run for a class office, keep up their guitar lessons, hold a part-time job, and maintain friendships. Something has to give, and often it's the grades. When grades drop, so does self-esteem, unless other measures of success can be pointed to. One couple devised a creative "living life" report: *"You went up in math and dropped in English, history, and French. You went up in making new friends, volunteering for trash pickup, reading to your little brother, and helping on trips with Gram's retirement home. I'd say you've done very well!"*

You may see her make mistakes, miss assignments, and possibly even flunk tests, all with an *"I don't care"* attitude. But it's likely that she does care. She wants to feel significant. The living-life report helps keep things positive and in perspective. Most important, it restores self-esteem. Listen, help her see her mistakes as learning opportunities, and guide her to organize her priorities.

WHAT TO SAY AND DO

Do not assume your freshman understands what a four-year grade point means and how it is figured. Take time to teach her the realities; then the rest is up to her, and you can get off her back. One girl brought home a 3.2. Her mother asked her what she thought her grade-point average might be at graduation and she answered, *"A 4.0."* Mom gently said, *"Now you have a C and three Bs so you can never have a 4.0. But you still have a chance of doing very well,"* and went on to explain how GPAs are figured, something this freshman had not understood.

Be honest with yourself. What do grades mean to you? Do they measure your success as a parent? Admit it or not, our egos are often very wrapped up in our children's successes and failures.

If her grades drop, your dreams of her going to the college of *your* dreams may be in jeopardy. Keep that fear to yourself; that is your problem.

In some states, certain car-insurance companies offer reduced premiums to teens who maintain good grades. This provides a significant incentive. *"As long as you maintain B's, the insurance will be less and I'll help pay for it."*

Grounding her until she can bring up her grades will do neither of you any good, nor will it help to throw your hands up and say, *"I give up. It's your life. I've done all I can do!"* What your teen needs at this time is your loving support. A parent should never, ever give up.

Bragging, moralizing, or lecturing about your teen years does not motivate. Kids don't like to hear, *"Why, when I was your age I held down two jobs, and played varsity football, took care of the yard for my mom, and still got straight A's."* Likewise, sharing your teenage struggles can be discouraging and can be interpreted as not understanding. Avoid remarks such as, *"Toughen up. School wasn't easy for me, either. I was tutored for four years in every subject."*

This scenario describes a universal problem: *"Some of my friends called me a geek because I did too well on the quiz. If I get good grades, they'll tease me more."* Empathize with her. *"Teasing is hard to take, Jill."* Use questions to make her think. Some boys don't want their girlfriends to do better than they do. Ask, *"Why do you suppose he wants to determine what grades you should have?"* Jill may figure it out. Sometimes kids are envious of others' successes in school and may attempt to cut them down in order to make themselves feel better. Affirm, *"You can be a 'regular' girl and also manage your schoolwork really well. The teasing hurts, but I think that your real friends will secretly admire you."*

PREVENTIVE TIPS

Encourage your teen's visions of what he wants to be. No dream is too big. He will reset his sights without your nay-sayer comments. College planning can be very exciting for a student with a vision. Help him identify his strengths and skills. For example, dexterity may point to a future as a mechanic, an electronics engineer, or a surgeon. Career-planning programs provide a wide range of opportunities for older teens.

Grades improve when a teen is interested in or has had experience with what he is studying in school. Travel, visit museums, and take field trips with your teen. Find ways to enrich what she is learning. One family traveled several hundred miles to attend a Chinese cultural exhibition because their son was studying China. Hosting exchange students is a fun way to bring a foreign language into your home. These experiences give validity and motivation.

Community volunteer work provides opportunities to develop the sense that *"I am capable, useful, and needed,"* which is necessary to healthy self-esteem and the ability to make good career choices. After volunteering in a women's shelter, one sixteen-year-old girl said, *"I wanted to follow my boyfriend, Randy, until I met a woman who had a baby at sixteen. She is struggling to manage school, work, and raising her child. It isn't that romantic. Now I know I've got to set a goal for myself."*

Be available. If you are at home when he feels like opening up, he's likely to talk to you when he needs to. As a rule, teens communicate on their time.

Side trips and other activities as a family are important because your teen will often need a break from his highly pressured environment. A long car ride provides time to talk.

Studies show a positive correlation between teens succeeding in school and parent involvement in the school community. Find ways to make meaningful things happen; help other parents on various committees and seek a parent support group. One high-school parents' group developed a quarterly newsletter addressing parental issues. One mother showed it to her teen and said, *"Chris, it says right here that the majority of parents do not want parties at their homes when parents are not there to supervise."* High-school PTAs are not well attended because many parents lose interest once their children are out of elementary school, and many others simply do not have the time.

For more information on this topic, read *Emotional Intelligence* by Daniel Goleman (New York: Bantam Books, 1995); *Keeping A Head in School* by Melvin Levine (Cambridge, MA: Educator's Publishing Service, Inc., 1990); *School Girls, Young Women, Self-Esteem and the Confidence Gap* by Peggy Orenstein (New York: Doubleday, 1994); and *Educational Care* by Melvin Levine, M.D. (Toronto: Educator's Publishing Service, 1994).

WHEN TO SEEK HELP

If your teen occasionally gets a poor grade, it's nothing to worry about. If grades continue to fail, you may see other disturbing signs: discouragement, changes in friendships, poor sleeping, or apathy. Don't wait. Experts feel most teens who are involved in high-risk behavior have a history of poor grades and learning problems. It is time to talk with the school counselor or a teacher who may be aware of changes in peer groups or other influences at school. It is not unusual for learning problems, which were manageable in elementary school, to crop up in high school. Your teen may benefit from a learning specialist; when coupled with tutoring, grades and self-esteem often improve. There are also many specialized schools to help kids do better in problem areas such as reading or math.

See also: Chapter 1, Tools of the Trade, Parent networking; College; Learning Problems

GRADUATION

"Jess is finally graduating. We're faced with decisions about limousines, restaurants, hotels and all-night parties, unchaperoned trips. I'm having trouble knowing what is reasonable."

"Graduation! I'm done and on my own! This is the biggest day of my life. I'm free of rules! Party on!"

UNDERSTANDING THE SITUATION

Graduation day seems to come amazingly fast. It is indeed one of society's last rites of passage and can be emotionally and mentally overwhelming.

Graduation is a universal mark of growing up and separating from one's parents. As your teen is imagining an orgy of wild graduation parties, you may be gripped with separation anxiety: *"He's not a child, yet he isn't an experienced adult, either. How do I handle this? How much can I still parent?"*

Graduation is a hallmark of teen independence, but your job is not finished. This is not the time to throw your hands into the air and be done with it. You are still very much needed. Parenting is forever. With luck, there will be more graduations, more milestones to celebrate, and more opportunities to raise your glass with pride.

WHAT TO SAY AND DO

Be an active parent: attend graduation planning meetings, join committees. Your teen will probably feel honored, and you will feel informed. Your parent committee should discuss past school-related traditions and feel free to modify or add to them. For example, one parent group discussed last year's student-organized, expensive, unchaperoned senior trips. These parents elected not to support such events for their seniors and instead put more emphasis on the chaperoned senior party after graduation.

Senior year events may include:

Prom
Baccalaureate
Graduation and graduation all-night party
Ditch day (unauthorized day off from school to picnic, etc.)
Class trip (one high school bused eight hours to Disneyland)

Whether you are a mother and father living together, a step-parent family, or a single-parent family, discuss and establish graduation family traditions that will help to establish a pattern for younger siblings to look forward to. Following are some examples.

- One family gives the graduate a family party, inviting close friends and relatives, sometime around graduation. Along with the socializing, the parents squeeze in some videos of the graduate's growing-up years.
- Both boys and girls enjoy personal touches on graduation day. Your teen will know this day means as much to you as it does to her when flowers arrive at the door, a friend or relative calls long distance, a thoughtful poem or a note is left in the bathroom, a singing telegram is a wake-up call, or balloons fill her bedroom.
- A gift of a cherished piece of family jewelry says, *"You have earned something special."*
- Anything that will help your teen stand out in a graduation ceremony is fun. One father ordered a bright helium balloon to tie to his son's robe so that he would see him in the crowd. Girls wear wrist corsages or garlands in their hair, and some boys appreciate leis or boutonnieres.

PREVENTIVE TIPS

Early in the year, discuss options for graduation: responsible, affordable, rewarding experiences. Be creative. Teens really want to have a good time, and it's a milestone worth celebrating. However, a graduation party can easily get out of hand. With careful planning, your teen can enjoy a fun and memorable time, and you can feel as if you have contributed to the special event.

See also: College; Leaving Home; Parties; Safety; Traditions

GRANDPARENTS

"Susan never wants to go to her grandmother's house anymore. She seems to have lost all the respect I've taught her."

"I have nothing in common with Granny. She makes me feel uncomfortable; she's always sick, and besides, I want to be with my friends."

UNDERSTANDING THE SITUATION

It's not uncommon for a teen to announce, *"I don't want to go to Grandma's."* You may be embarrassed by and impatient with such thoughtlessness. Most adolescents do go through a stage of wanting nothing to do with their families. Don't be surprised to hear, *"Mom, don't bring Gram. She talks so loud."* Teens feel that all eyes are on them. When a teen who was close to his grandparents when he was growing up now seems to lose interest, it leaves grandparents feeling hurt and rejected, and this takes a toll on you. Do you find yourself in the middle between two sets of needy loved ones?

Some grandparents live with or are actually helping to raise the family while parents work or for some reason are not present. They are invaluable and fill a surrogate parent role that is of paramount importance.

Some grandparents seem to have an easy time loving their grandchildren for who they are, while others criticize them for what they are not. Some who participate in the daily lives of the family feel they have earned their stripes and the right to tell you and your children everything you're doing wrong. Grandparents who once spoiled their young grandchildren are often amazed at self-centered teen behavior and tend to moralize, lecture, or correct with shame and guilt: *"After all I've done for you, you won't even give me the time of day!"* Still other grandparents feel a strong need to defend their own child: *"Don't you ever talk to your mother that way. You show respect for your elders!"*

Many grandparents have a healthy perspective on life. They don't take everything so seriously and so can act as levelers: *"Oh, he's just young and made a poor decision. He'll get it eventually. Remember when you stole those cupcakes from the church banquet? You didn't turn out to be a thief."* They can cajole and make fun. Grandparents often offer much-needed wisdom and support to both generations.

When a divorce, remarriage, death, or move occurs, the bond between children and grandparents can be disrupted. This is a significant loss, and it takes a great deal of effort to keep this vital relationship alive.

As difficult as it often is, your job is to establish understanding between family members. Try not to overreact to incidents, and see if you can identify the feelings behind the actions. Your teen may need your help in understanding why a grandparent says what she does or acts as she does. You may have to stop a grandparent from intruding on a teen's space. It is a very lucky family today that has active grandparents who want to participate in the overall family picture. It takes hard work to keep communication open so that this valuable relationship works for everyone.

WHAT TO SAY AND DO

Try to bridge the generation gap and develop family pride and identity. Invite your parent to share some history as it relates to your son: *"Dad, Luke and his friends are reconditioning an old car. What did you do at his age for fun?"*

Grandparents can enhance a teen's search for identity. Many teens love to listen to family history and anecdotes about their relatives. Encourage your son to ask his grandfather how he decided to be an engineer or came to own a small business. What steps did he take that got him where he is today? Dinnertime conversations can be exciting. One teen exclaimed, *"Dad, did you know that Grandpa had a butterfly collection, and before he left Wisconsin he gave it to the town museum? It's still on display. I never knew that. One day while he was mowing a field he noticed all these bright butterflies flying around. He started to collect them to see how many different species he could find. He collected twenty-five different kinds!"*

Be alert to your teen's feelings. Before getting angry with her rudeness (*"I don't want to go, I hate being with all those old people!"*), listen for what she's thinking. *"Megan, you don't want to go. What's going on? I'm a little confused. You used to enjoy going to Grandma's."* With reflective listening you may hear, *"I might miss something important with my friends,"* or, *"Carolyn might call and I'll miss it."* An expected telephone call may be enough for her to have an old-fashioned hissy fit over having to join the family picnic or birthday celebration. Once you've recognized the real feelings, firmly state your bottom line. Your values are the priority—family first! Present it with choices once, and don't argue. *"Megan, I understand you might miss a phone call. Leave Grandma's number on the message machine or give it to your friends and have them call you if needed. You need to spend the afternoon with the family."*

Overly critical grandparents can be a problem. Some are disagreeable and downright rude, picking on certain children and playing favorites with others. Be aware when your parent is unfair or disrespectful of your teen's feelings. He needs your support. At a good talk time, explain to your son what may be behind his grandmother's behavior. Address the guilt or shame. *"Tim, it is not because of you that Gram is so rude. You are not the cause. It is not your fault."* Lightly, with humor, add, *"I think she's worried that I'm not doing a good job at parenting and feels she has to help me!"* (You might actually laugh together at the concept.) Be understanding and compassionate. *"That's just how Granny is, so we all have to enjoy the parts of her that we can and let the rest go."* Share a little about her life and why you think she is like this.

Physical and mental deterioration are hard for everyone. One grandfather became a very difficult old man, which made relationships strained. Mark, sixteen, had been taught by his mother to sit quietly and let his grandfather rattle on about his past; Mark's job was to daydream or "veg out" but to be polite and appear to listen, at all costs. He learned to be kind and respectful to elderly people and to be comfortable with them.

Spoiling is what grandparents are famous for. At Grandma's, chores are forgiven, candy is an easily procured commodity, and television time isn't limited. The transition back to home isn't always easy. Be ready for the reentry. *"Tyler, the vacation is over. You are now back and are a contributing member of the family. Life at Gram's is different from home—it's a wonderful break!"*

PREVENTIVE TIPS

Older people have a lot to offer. If grandparents aren't nearby, perhaps a neighborhood grandparent could be "adopted" by your family. Volunteering at a nursing home might be an exceptional experience for your teen.

When grandparents live with the family, it's important to discuss issues that could otherwise be misinterpreted. Rules and routines help bridge the generation gap and take care of the pervasive problem of "who's in charge?"

When you see a positive interaction between your teen and

your parent, compliment them both. *"It's great having this lunch. Imagine, three generations having a good time together!"*

Your parents need time alone with you, just as your children do. This takes energy and planning, but the results are great. If you have a good relationship with your parents, they will better understand how to offer their perspective to you and to their grandchildren in a diplomatic fashion, rather than blurt out their opinions in thoughtless ways.

Research is showing that older people benefit greatly from aerobic exercise. Be sure to consult a physician first. Moderate weight lifting is said to help as well. If your parents are in good health, encourage them to be active: swimming, walking, biking, and the like are good. Cognitive thinking, especially organizational skills and information processing, can improve with a regular walking program. Gram will have more energy and will cope better with your teen.

Grandparents raising teens are faced with complicated issues. Resources that are specifically designed for this special role are available. Classes are offered through community health centers, hospitals, and local agencies. Take advantage of all of them.

WHEN TO SEEK HELP

When a constantly critical grandparent causes tension, rather than make excuses for why your teen is keeping her distance, talk with a counselor or other professional who understands the issues facing the elderly. You don't want your daughter hurt by Gram's thoughtless comments, and you do not want Gram feeling rejected, either.

See also: Arguing; Birthdays; Traditions

HANGING OUT

"Kids today do nothing but hang out with their baggy pants and skateboards. Why don't they go do something! I've called the cops twice."

"We aren't hurting anything. We just want to hang out somewhere."

UNDERSTANDING THE SITUATION

Many teens today aren't interested in the traditional teenage lifestyle of sports, school activities, part-time jobs, and so forth. You may want him to be more interested in good grades and school sports, but you know that he has always been one to do things his own way. Now that he's older, it is a bigger problem for him and for you. He's hanging out with others like himself, not really counterculture or heavy drug users but rather, as some label them, disenfranchised youth. These kids usually are not into gangs or illegal activities, yet from the outside they look like a fringe group. Still, many adults feel threatened by them.

Store owners complain to police that these kids intimidate customers by their very presence. People complain about the baggy pants and loud music blasting on the street corner. Clashes occur, and the teens move on to a different corner. Many of these teens appear chronically depressed, so you worry about drug use even if you have seen no indication of it. Your concerns are valid as you find yourself rather helpless to generate much interest in other activities.

One savvy teen said of her parents, *"When they want me to do something, I'm 'mature,' but when I want to do something my way, they tell me I'm not old enough."* This is a typical teen perception. Teens want to be treated with respect, as mature people, and resent being treated otherwise. People who work well with teens understand that most would rather not hang out on a street corner. They would like a place that is "cool," has food, a few video games, pinball or pool, and an older person who is "with it" to help them get what they need. Some forward-thinking communities offer such places for teens to hang out. The positive message to the entire community is, *"You kids are worth something, we respect you."* One community-center worker observed that barely half the teens in town took advantage of the activities and classes at the center, while the other half hung out on the center's steps. The structured activities offer a legitimate reason for them to be there, even if they don't participate in them. Many of these kids are not secure enough to compete in pinball or pool or computer games, but they know they can be there, no questions asked, no hassles from police.

Your "hanging out" teen is no different from others. He needs your understanding, your faith and trust, and your support. Communities must adopt a more positive attitude about these teens; we all do better when treated with respect. Reflect on the proverb, "It takes an entire village to raise a child." All adults, not just parents, must make a great effort to create an accepting community for all.

WHAT TO SAY AND DO

You are a responsible parent when you ask to know where she will be. Some parents have had success with a written contract. Aimless wandering may not be safe. Agree to a contract and a consequence when agreements are broken. As long as your teen tells you where she'll be, with whom, and when she'll be home, let it be. If she has a problem with this, you need to follow through consistently with the agreed consequences.

Acknowledging your teen's feelings is important. However, avoid judgments and criticisms. Say, *"We know you need a place to hang out, and we realize that it's hard to find one. Your favorite pastimes are talking and listening to music. Where can you and your friends do that?"* Problem solve with him. Even if you can't come up with an immediate solution, taking his situation seriously will help him to mature.

No matter what your teen has done, or is not doing, do not call her names or label her. You may truly be discouraged, feeling that she's lazy, a liar, a punk rocker, and so forth. Kids tend to live up to their labels, so keep them to yourself. Notice what she does well—there's always something. *"Cindy, you're so thoughtful to pick up that junk your father left there. It's been in the way for days. Thank you."* Or, *"Ted, you're the only one who can get the cat to come with only one call. You really have a way with animals."*

Help him discover his strengths. Think back to how he spent time in his childhood. If trucks were important, could he be interested in working with a mechanic? Could you help pave the way for him to work a few hours a week? Has he always loved animals? Is he comfortable with young children? A job may not be so far-fetched: Animal shelters desperately need volunteer help; day camps often welcome teen counselors.

You worry about what your daughter is doing when she's not at home. If you have questions, ask them directly: *"Keri, when you're not home or at the community center, where are you?"* The answer, *"Oh, just hanging out,"* may not satisfy you. *"I know you're just 'hanging out,' but what does that mean? How do teenagers hang out? I know it may sound weird, but I really don't know."* Be interested in her answer. Continue the conversation with her as long as you can. Laugh with her. When she says, *"Oh, Mom, you don't want to know what we do!"* tell her, *"Well, you're an expert after all your hours 'on the job.' And it's high time I learned about it."* This opens up a dialogue with her that will lead to her being more open in general. A conversation like this is different from the highly charged, critical comments she expects, so at first she may feel taken off guard. Initiate such dialogues again and again—you'll be pleasantly surprised. Respect does breed respect!

Teens need structure and may choose the company of an

adult who listens and cares. Nancy, a stay-at-home mother, invited her junior-high-age nieces to her home after school because their mother worked. She greeted the girls with healthful snacks and helped them with their homework. They seemed to enjoy visiting with their seventeen-month-old cousin and never complained about doing their schoolwork with Nancy's supervision. The school contacted their mother, saying that the girls' schoolwork had improved tremendously. What about your teen? If you're a working parent, is there a structured environment she can take advantage of until you come home? Teens need and want adults to be interested in them.

PREVENTIVE TIPS

If your community doesn't have a teen center, you have a challenge. Teenagers want a place to go where they can hang out with their friends and talk and play their music. Teens do not want adults to be present at every moment, yet they do want savvy older people around. Network with others and learn from their experiences. Following are some ideas on how to do this.

Organize a group of interested parents and make some proposals to city officials and the parks department to get a teen center in your community. The results can be amazing when there is commitment behind a project.

Ask teens to be involved in the planning from the start.

Consult members of other communities who have gone through the process: How did they approach their city officials? What role did the school district take? What are the pros and cons of having a chaperoned, open gym offering arts and crafts and other activities? Do they have a teen counselor? What hours work best?

See also: Alcohol and Other Drugs; Friends, Choosing; Home Alone; Learning Problems; Rebelliousness; Shyness

HOME ALONE

Younger Teens

"In June he actually seemed angry that school would be ending. I think he'll miss it because he has nothing to replace it. What activities can I arrange to keep him occupied?"

"I just want to be with my friends and be home alone. Why don't you trust me?"

UNDERSTANDING THE SITUATION

What to do with a teen who is too old for a baby-sitter and too young for a job, when you can't be home, is a valid concern for working parents. An empty house is lonely, even if your son confidently says it is not. He can't hang out at school, and at home he watches all the daytime TV shows and MTV, which are often sexually explicit and violent. So, what are your choices?

Young teens need a place where they can meet their friends and where there are adults whom they like around them. Team sports, music lessons, and other programs designed for adolescents can fill the need and can be very positive influences on your young teen, particularly if you are a single parent. Young teens have many questions about who they are, and if you can't be there, they need other adults to answer their questions and set good examples.

Caring neighbors are a priceless commodity for families in which both parents work. You're a lucky parent to have a neighbor who watches for your teen's arrival from school and cares about her in case of an emergency.

With a combination of an after-school phone call to a parent, chores, homework and after-school activities, an occasional visit from a trusted friend, plus a caring neighbor, a teen can learn how capable he is.

WHAT TO SAY AND DO

If you cannot be at home, provide structure for your teen. Together, plan a routine, set limits, and establish consequences. A chart or list of the after-school routine can be very helpful, showing chores, schedules for practicing music, homework, and so on. Don't forget to add some suggested free-time activities such as watching one favorite television show, playing basketball, or baking cookies or creating a dinner dessert.

Companies should look favorably on employees' daily calls to children after school. Either call yourself or ask your teen to call you at work when he gets home. Try to find a close neighbor who is willing to be on call for emergencies.

Teens complain that when they're home alone, Mom calls only to direct and to give orders: *"She used to call me to tell me where the cookies were. Now I think she wants to keep me occupied. I get, 'Did you see my note telling you to weed the petunias? And don't forget to put out the trash. And, if you have time, write that thank-you letter to your uncle.' "* These kinds of directives should be replaced with agreements at the family meeting and followed up with charts posted on the refrigerator. (However, your young teen still needs to call you daily if he's alone.) Replace the directives with questions: *"What was the best thing that happened today?"* or, *"How did the teacher like your report?"* And always remember the all-important *"I love you!"*

Summers are dreaded by most working parents of young teens. Together, create a plan. Give your daughter a feeling that she has some control over what happens to her by inviting her to brainstorm with you. Supervised clubs such as Scouts, YWCAs or YMCAs, and many after-school activities available through schools and parks departments should be utilized to the fullest, especially when the alternative is "home alone." These activities help to satisfy the need to belong. One young girl who did not like to participate in organized activities every day offered to help a neighbor who had three preschoolers. There may also be jobs such as paper routes, yard maintenance, or baby-sitting that your teen would enjoy. Meaningful jobs or volunteer work help to establish the feeling, *"I am useful and needed,"* and thus contribute to healthy self-esteem.

Give your teen the responsibility of investigating the possibilities. He can call camps and other summer programs for information. In most areas, day camps abound in parks-department programs and churches. He can also have material mailed to your home so that together you can plan his summer. He needs to be a part of this process; it's important that he plan for his future and problem solve with you. This builds his self-confidence and develops his sense of control over his life.

PREVENTIVE TIPS

Affirm your child's good judgment when you can. Compliment him when you catch him making good decisions. The reason for after-school programs isn't lack of trust, though he may assume that.

Your young teen needs to be listened to, supported, and understood as much as when she was a young child. She needs to be appreciated and told she is valuable and lovable.

It is well worth the effort to support sports or other interests such as drama or music when teens are young—when you still have influence over their interests and activities. With hope, their interests will still be with them when they reach high school.

Older Teens

"I worry about Christine being home alone every day. She has friends I don't know well, and I'm uncomfortable with them in the house without an adult."

"Mom, you think I sneak and do bad things. Don't you trust me at all? I don't want anything to go wrong, either."

UNDERSTANDING THE SITUATION

Older teens introduce different concerns about "home alone." You may be truly concerned about new friends and clandestine parties, use of alcohol and other drugs, and opportunities for sexual activity. You may have been informed of your liabilities should someone get drunk or stoned and be hurt, or hurt someone else. These fears are valid, yet parents can go overboard imagining the worst.

Your teen is now very mobile; he can drive places with his friends. The rule that he can't have friends over when he's home alone is now unrealistic. His circle of friends has widened, as it should, and you may not know them. The wise parent will work on establishing a trusting relationship, with open communication, rather than concentrate on adding more limiting rules, which sends a message of mistrust.

WHAT TO SAY AND DO

Read the section above, Younger Teens.

Encourage activities that build her sense of responsibility. Sports give lifelong skills and pleasure. A regular part-time job means she is participating in an adult activity and can save up for a trip, a favorite hobby, or car insurance. A regular volunteer position in a hospital is something to be very proud of.

Your rules must be clear in order for your teen to state her boundaries to others. All teens are at times vulnerable and feel unable to defend themselves from stronger friends who are bent on taking advantage of an unchaperoned situation. If there are girlfriends or boyfriends in the picture, opportunities abound for sexual activity. Peer pressure and the situation may push your teen into activities she doesn't want.

Rules should be agreed upon together. Realistic expectations help to prevent unwanted behavior. It is unrealistic to say, *"No friends when I'm not home."* However, it is logical to limit the number of friends and to say, *"No steady boyfriends alone in the house."* Having someone of the opposite sex in the house does not mean that there will be sex. (When she goes off to college and lands in a coed dorm, she'll be with lots of young men.) It is not necessary to post "no sex in our home" if you've already discussed your expectations.

Don't be too predictable. When your teen is home alone and you always come home from work at six o'clock, opportunities for getting into trouble increase. Vary your schedule when possible. This is being a smart parent, not a suspicious one. Being home alone is counter to your teen's needs at this socially critical time, and asking her to not socialize is like putting her in jail.

Problem solving will be essential for success. No rule will be effective unless your teen and you have thoroughly explored all aspects of the situation and are respectful of each other's position.

PREVENTIVE TIPS

Your trust must come through. Believe that he'll use good judgment when he's alone, and encourage him to make mature decisions. This is the time for him to practice adult skills. He needs to be able to think on his feet, without the benefit of your input. Leaving home without practice in decision making will make the transition more difficult. Take time to teach your teenager what to do if you're not there.

Role-play possible scenarios: *"Mary, what would you say or do in these situations? Soda is being spilled on the carpet. Or, two friends who are dating come over and ask to use your bedroom for an hour. Or, four girls show up drinking beer."*

WHEN TO SEEK HELP

If your teen is not following agreements and is showing poor judgment, seek family counseling. Parents often wonder: *"Is my partner committed to the same expectations?"* *"Is our daughter playing us against each other?"* *"Is her father [or a substitute male adult] a strong enough presence in her life?"* *"Do I worry too much? Is she living out my fears?"* These are important questions and can best be handled with a counselor familiar with adolescents and their families. Many parents face this same problem; you are not alone.

See also: Alcohol and Other Drugs; Dating, Teens; Going Steady; Hanging Out; Jobs; Sex, Talking About; Values

HOMOSEXUALITY

*"My friend's son is seventeen and has never even taken a
girl to a dance. He seems more interested in chess. I
know my friend is worried. Do you think he's gay?"*
*"I like boys, but I'm not interested in dating. I wish people
would get off my back. I've even been asked at school if
I'm a lesbian. I'd be so teased, I'd be dumb to admit it."*

UNDERSTANDING THE SITUATION

You may try to deny it exists, as society sometimes does, but gays and lesbians represent or affect a significant portion of the teen population. You may wish you could protect your teen from this delicate issue, but he may well have classmates who are dealing with this. It is naive to deny that teenage gays and lesbians exist; it is worse to be insensitive to their struggle to come out and reveal themselves.

Questioning one's sexual identity is a normal part of the growing-up process. Same-sex curiosity, too, is a normal part of sexual development and is not to be confused with gay or lesbian identity, yet it often is. Society is hardest on boys. When two thirteen-year-old girls are seen holding hands, scarcely anyone notices. If two thirteen-year-old boys are holding hands, people make comments. The macho lady-killer stereotype is still alive and well in our society. It is very difficult to grow up as a straight teen, who in the normal course of development worries about his prowess: *"Am I attractive to girls?"* *"How do I kiss them?"* *"Will I be able to 'do it'?"* One twenty-six-year-old shared that he hadn't had sex with a girl by the time he was sixteen and wondered if this meant he was gay. This caused him great anxiety. Many boys who are late bloomers and not particularly macho struggle with the "expected norm." These concerns certainly add to their distress as they search for their sexual identity.

By comparison, it can be horrifying to a teen to discover that he may not be straight. He might be gay! When a teen finds himself in any group that society discriminates against, he may very well feel like it's the end of the world. It is no wonder that an incredible number of teen suicides are committed by gays or lesbians.

With the onset of puberty, some boys find that they are aroused by thoughts of other males; girls may not be of any interest to them. Most adolescent boys and girls who discover their same-sex attractions do not tell anyone, at first. In school, "fag" is perhaps the worst possible name that a person could be called, so to admit you are gay invites cruel teasing and chastisement and sometimes the possibility of physical violence. Though physical attacks on lesbians are less likely to occur, the emotional cruelty that accompanies the label "dyke" is much the same. It is no wonder that some teens keep their sexual identity under tight wraps through the high-school years.

The numbers show that homosexuality is far from rare. It is common, though not generally discussed. Many parents' biggest fear is that their child may be homosexual. Feelings of inadequacy as a parent (*"What did I do wrong?"*) become incessant. Biblical passages flood back from childhood about being damned for homosexual acts. In our culture, parents' success and self-esteem are almost always tied up in the success of their children. To admit that your child is gay or lesbian can be devastating unless you've accepted and become comfortable with it.

In the Mandan Indian tribe, mothers would pray that their sons would be gay so that they would be designated to stay in camp, helping the women with their heavy work; this way, sons would not have to go to war and risk being killed. In ancient Greece, the love between two homosexuals was considered the most pure, and the highest form of love. In our culture, it is quite a different story.

It is unfortunate that gay teens have few role models of gay, successful, professional people. Many do not "come out" and are not recognizable by appearance, unless they choose to "dress the part" in order to make a statement. This is the minority.

Sadly, because some parents fear, *"If I raise my son to be considerate and gentle, he may become gay,"* boys can miss out on the type of parenting that teaches them to be sensitive, caring people.

WHAT TO SAY AND DO

Therapy cannot persuade a homosexual to become a heterosexual any more than it can persuade a straight person to become gay. Kicking your gay son or lesbian daughter out of the house will not help either. There is only one choice for responsible parents: Remember your teenager when he or she was a little child and needed love and help; he or she is that child, still. Your understanding and continued love are imperative now to create an accepting environment, though this may be very difficult for you.

Usually, when a teen tells her parents she is lesbian, they are stunned and at a loss for words. *"We love you so much, we don't care,"* might be the most supportive of all comments. *"We will*

not have you in our house—you are no child of ours!", at the opposite end of the spectrum, is more often the response. It is no
wonder that many never "come out" to their parents. One
father, a minister, lamented that he was not able to help his son
as he struggled through the ordeal of hiding his homosexuality:
*"Some of the pain for me is realizing that between the ages of fourteen
and twenty-two, when Mike came out, he was dealing with it alone.
That's what really hurts."*

Your first job as a parent is to be outwardly calm; then, learn
as much as you can from your teen. Remember, she is as terrified as you are to discuss this with you. Your body language,
your facial expression, and your tone of voice will reveal your
true feelings. Stay calm and ask with sincerity, *"How long have
you known? Have you discussed this with and found support from
anyone else?"* Finally: *"How can I help you?"* Next, seek information from libraries, doctors, other parents, and close friends and
relatives. You may be surprised at the number of people who
will tell you about a lesbian sister or a gay uncle. People you
trust may be wonderful supports for you, if you can "come
out" too. You have to decide whom you want to tell and to
practice talking about it. Of course, you have the option of
keeping the secret, but that will only maintain the pain and isolation that your son or daughter is going through. It is far
healthier to share.

Get comfortable using the word *gay*. Say it in connection
with a role model like Greg Louganis, the Olympic diver, or
tennis star Martina Navratilova, or someone you know personally. Discussions with others will usually be healing, once you
have become more informed about what it means to be gay or
lesbian. There are many organizations and groups to help you
along the way.

Talking to your straight children about sex is difficult
enough, but it's even harder when talking to a potentially gay
child about sex with a same-sex partner. Such conversations
generally are avoided, but the concerns cannot be dispelled
unless they are discussed. *"Are you using safe-sex practices? Where
did you learn about them? How do you know that you will be really*

safe? How do I know you will be safe? Your father and I don't want to worry that you might die of AIDS." At first, some conversations are too hard to conduct alone; but the presence of a trusted friend, sibling, or other third person can help everyone get through it. Therapy or support groups can help people deal with the incredible confusion and the adjustments that must be made in people's thinking about one another and about homosexuality in general. Counseling can help families express their feelings, encourage understanding among all, and facilitate honest communication.

PREVENTIVE TIPS

Sensitive parents do not make disparaging remarks about gays or other minorities—ever. They teach respect, acceptance, and tolerance in every sense of those words. If your teen is gay, he needs to know that you are forgiving and accept him. If the opposite has been heard in your teen's upbringing, he will be terrified that he now is among those you scorn and ridicule. This will make it very difficult if not impossible for him to approach you with his discovery.

When you hear your teen or others making fun of gays or lesbians, do not let these comments go by. Say, *"Negative talk is not called for. Some of the most respected people in this community are gay, and you never know if you might be hurting someone's feelings. It is not okay to talk that way."*

Provide information about gay role models: *"I always thought Uncle Ned was gay, but it was never discussed. He was my favorite uncle because he made up wonderful children's stories and seemed to genuinely enjoy life."*

Learn about homosexuality. One expert in the field said, *"What I'd like to suggest is: 'Hey, folks, this isn't just a heterosexual world. Be aware that the natural way of being a human being has a lot of variety in it. Who we are is rich with variety. Be open to that possibility.' "*

Recently, the media have been more open in reporting about the double lives that homosexuals have had to lead. These courageous people have risked much to "come out," stand their ground, and try to teach that gays and lesbians are just like any other people. A teen who had been acquitted of a pickpocketing charge remarked of the judge who heard his case, *"His sexual orientation may be different, but it didn't get in the way of being a fair judge. He really understood."* This judge had recently admitted his homosexuality in a newspaper article.

For more information on this topic, read *Parents Matter: Parents' Relationships with Lesbian Daughters and Gay Sons* by Ann Muller (Tallahassee: Naiad Press, 1987); *Free Your Mind* by Ellen Bass and Kate Kaufman (New York: Harper Perennial, 1996); and *Growing Up Gay/Growing Up Lesbian: A Literary Anthology* edited by Bennett L. Singer (New York: New Press, 1994).

WHEN TO SEEK HELP

If your teen is struggling with sexual identity, it may be helpful for him or her to attend counseling or a drop-in group for gay, lesbian, or bisexual teens. There are many teens trying to answer the same questions, and many groups devoted to helping them.

PFLAG—Parents, Families and Friends of Lesbians and Gays—an organization in the United States, Canada, and Great Britain, is an excellent resource for parents who want help in understanding their children's sexual orientation. They have a series of pamphlets for parents that is invaluable. It is especially helpful during the adjustment process. This group can save the relationship and the communication between you and your gay teen.

Suicide is too often the choice for a depressed homosexual teen. The identity adjustment she must make is mind boggling and frequently leads to serious unhappiness and isolation. If you are concerned, do not hesitate to get professional help. Find a therapist who works with gay and lesbian adolescents.

See also: Chapter 1, What Happens During the Teen Years; Depression; Safety; Sex, Talking About; Suicide

HYGIENE

"I don't know how to make Laurie understand that she needs deodorant and a shower every day now. She's so unaware."

"She won't get off my back. I do shower sometimes."

Six months later:
"Laurie takes the longest showers and sometimes twice a day. Our hot water bills are tremendous."
"My parents are never happy. Now I take too many showers!"

UNDERSTANDING THE SITUATION

Many kids need to begin using deodorant as early as age ten. It can be very embarrassing for both of you to have to say to your teen, *"You need to bathe more."* Most young teens need parental guidance in learning how to take care of themselves as they develop. It is a lucky teen who has an older sibling, other relative, or friend who can share her wisdom. One young girl said, *"Thank gosh for my two older cousins. I learned how to shave my legs one summer staying at Grandma's with them."* Kids get a lot of good information at camps, church retreats, and so forth from older, mature teens.

Unfortunately, we tend to get angry at what seems slovenly behavior. One mother complained that her daughter had left a used feminine napkin on the bathroom floor before stopping to think, *"Have I ever taught her how to take care of them?"* Hygiene needs to be taught, and too often we assume that kids automatically know what we consider so obvious.

WHAT TO SAY AND DO

Be direct and matter-of-fact. It's great that he's growing up. Many parents are uncomfortable bringing up issues such as oily hair and body odor, but you do your teens a disservice by not mentioning hygiene. Buy some deodorant and hand it to him: *"Congratulations, Mark, this is yours to use every day from now on. You are definitely growing up!"* Buying him shampoo for his type of hair, and so forth, will be appreciated.

Use humor: *"Michael, it doesn't matter if you have purple hair and a ring in your nose; as long as you're clean and smell decent, you will have friends."*

You can remove yourself from the driver's seat by assigning some of these tasks to others. For example:

- Ask the family doctor or nurse to discuss hygiene when your teen has an annual exam. A professional explanation is likely to result in greater responsibility.
- The dentist or oral hygienist can discuss cleaning teeth and keeping breath fresh, especially with braces.
- Ask a dermatologist or cosmetics expert to demonstrate proper skin care, which can reduce acne.
- Find a barber or beautician who is good with teens. A perky, young role model can be a good choice to teach your teen proper hair care.

Take time to teach (but avoid old myths such as "chocolate causes zits," etc.). For instance, we often take for granted that they know how to wash their ears, because we told them once when they were eight years old. Don't assume anything. Instead of giving a lecture, ask her to tell you what she knows, then show her, if need be. Remember, there are more ways than one to get a job done, and she may teach you a helpful hint or two. Age thirteen, when most kids begin to care about how they look, is a good time for them to begin doing their own laundry. Wool and some other materials need special care. Hairbrushes and combs need to be washed. She needs to know how often to wash her everyday clothes, her towels, her underwear, and so forth. Just think, your workload is getting lighter!

PREVENTIVE TIPS

At a good talk time, discuss the importance of good hygiene. Everyone wants to belong. *"Laura, the way someone smells or looks leaves an impression on other people. People don't want to be around others who have smelly, greasy hair or bad body odor. At your age you need to wash every day."* One mother reflected, *"When I went to my thirtieth high-school reunion I saw a classmate named Kirk. He's now forty-eight and I'm sure a very nice person, but all I could think of was how bad his greasy hair always smelled. Smell is such a primitive sense, I guess that's why I remember that about him and nothing else."*

WHEN TO SEEK HELP

Teens don't seem to mind peculiar dress or hair coloring and so on, but when they aren't clean, they can be shunned by their peers. Poor hygiene is an indication of how a teen feels about himself—it could mean he is angry, depressed, using drugs, or experiencing a number of other problems. Proper counseling may be of help.

See also: Acne; Doctors

JEALOUSY

"Terry is so jealous. She constantly dwells on what others have and what she doesn't have."

"I hate Pam. She thinks she's so great in all her name-brand clothes. If it wasn't for her, Bill would still like me. What a bitch!"

UNDERSTANDING THE SITUATION

Jealousy is the stuff of soap operas and great novels. Look for it in the workplace (the jealous employer not promoting a promising employee); in families (an older brother giving up basketball because his younger one has taken a keen interest); in the classroom (*"she sucks up to the teacher, she's the teacher's pet"*) and school hallways (*"he's walking with* my *girl"*). Teens' self-esteem hangs largely on their being accepted. If acceptance is threatened, the green-eyed monster may pop up.

Jealousy often becomes a problem between steady couples. "Steady" denotes possession, and both boys and girls are known to fight for what they feel is theirs. A boy may harass another boy who's interested in the same girl. Some boys fight physically, and some are quite violent. Girls usually are a bit more subtle, backbiting and starting ugly rumors about other girls who flirt with "my boy." This leads to grudges and sometimes lifelong estrangement. (Just bring up this subject at a high-school reunion.)

Jealousy is a real feeling but not a productive one. You need to discuss these feelings openly with your teen. She has already had many opportunities to experience jealousy, whether over friends, teachers, or siblings. Because any uncomfortable feeling needs to be identified and understood, it's very important to explore how to handle jealousy.

Help her manage and resolve her feelings first by validating them and then exploring their origin. Often, jealousy is the result of not having something you want, whether it is a boyfriend or a CD player. Help your teen identify where her jealous feelings come from and find ways to reduce them. Reassure her that dealing with jealousy is part of growing up. She can learn to cope and keep her integrity.

WHAT TO SAY AND DO

Jealous feelings often lead to anger. Help him understand the root cause. Use questions: *"Hank, are you angry because Troy got what you consider your position on the football team? Are you a little jealous because you think the coach favors him? I can see why you might think this and why you're furious with Troy, even though he has been your good friend. What would you do if you were in his place? Do you think he might be feeling a bit uncomfortable, too? After all, is he responsible for the change on the team?"* If you have some advice, offer it: *"Would you like an idea from me?"* If he wants help, brainstorm some solutions: *"How about telling the coach that this is very hard for you. Perhaps his way of looking at this would help you. Also, you can talk with Troy. Let him know, too, that this is difficult for you."* Writing is a helpful tool for understanding the feelings in order to talk about them. *"Hank, to organize your thoughts, you might want to write them down first. It might help you come to grips with it all."*

Humor helps, too. *"Wow, now that you and Troy have talked about it and you have 'slain the green-eyed monster,' life is looking up. Good job! Too bad these things have to be so painful, but that's life. These sorts of situations will get easier for you with practice, even if they never feel good at the time."* With disappointments come new perspectives and healthy resilience.

Overindulgence is a common fix for hurt, jealous feelings. Don't attempt to rescue her or soothe her with a shopping spree, a slumber party, or support of a counterattack. This approach won't help her manage her life in a responsible way. It will, however, guarantee repeat performances of "poor me."

Help her understand her jealous feelings. *"Jennifer, I know you're jealous of Cassie's new clothes and you wish you had as much money to spend as she does. There will always be people with more, and many with less, than you have. What could you do to make yourself feel better?"* One high-school girl decided to continue to shop with her wealthy girlfriend and try on all the clothes until she got bored with shopping. She said, *"You know what, Mom? After trying on all those clothes, I recognize the good brands that are at the thrift stores. It'll be fun to start looking for great finds."* This turned out to be a good lesson. A little gentle counsel and perspective, given at the right time and in the right way, was indeed useful.

Take time to teach him the difference between his wants and his needs. He may *need* new jeans but *want* the very expensive brand name. Ask him to pay the difference in cost. When you ask your teen to be responsible, he will have a better sense of self, blame himself less, and handle competition better.

PREVENTIVE TIPS

Be aware of your actions. You may not realize that you express jealousy every day: *"Look at that beautiful Porsche. He's gotta have bucks!"* Your comments and actions may be teaching your teen just what you don't want him to do.

Limit competition among siblings. Try to stop comparing kids. Find family activities that do not call for winners or losers. Hiking and camping stimulate teamwork. Appreciate and celebrate each child for what he or she is.

Teens are less jealous when their world is secure. The better their self-esteem, the less likely they are to be jealous. Limit your criticism, and compliment him on what he does right.

Help your teen to set goals and to stay on track. When he follows his major plan (such as going to college and then medical school), he has something to lean on when an obstacle gets in the way.

When you read or hear news reports of domestic violence disputes, discuss them in the context of personal values. Many tragedies could be prevented if jealous feelings were handled better. Help your teen put these sensational stories into a healthy perspective.

Discuss boundaries with your teen: "Do not let anyone persuade you to do something that you know in your heart isn't right. A jealous person may try to get you to do something against your will. Listen to what you really believe. Stick with your convictions!"

Give her a journal or a diary with a lock. *"Toni, here's your own private book to write in. I promise, no one will read it but you. Write out all your feelings, thoughts, and experiences, bad or good. It will help you feel better and may help you decide what you want to do."*

Remember that your teenager is learning a lesson of life. You can't fix the jealous feelings for him. He will learn that with disappointments come different solutions and new results. Life does go on; he will weather the storm. After he has gotten through the hurt and has managed his jealous feelings, you can discuss the incident to see what he has learned and to offer advice on how he might handle it better next time.

WHEN TO SEEK HELP

Jealousy can lead to impulsive and hurtful behavior. Talk with a school counselor or a therapist if you are seriously worried. One jealous boy pushed his ex-girlfriend out of a moving car. One girl cut herself with a knife when her boyfriend went out with her best friend. Teens often need help in dealing with strong feelings of anger and hurt.

See also: Anger; Bullying; Depression; Siblings; Trust; Values

JOBS

"Danny got a job cleaning and feeding animals at the pet store. Wow, was I surprised!"
"It feels so good to be earning my own money. I love it!"

UNDERSTANDING THE SITUATION

It's a true milestone when you and your young teen consider the possibility of a real job outside the home. You may wonder, *"Am I ready for this?"* What age is appropriate? Which jobs are appropriate? You have no model to follow, so the "baby" may never seem quite old enough. But remember, jobs build healthy self-esteem, offer an opportunity to be responsible, and provide an environment separate from the world of family, school, sports, and peers. Jobs provide opportunities to interact with other adults and to learn how the "real" world works. For some, the first job is a rite of passage.

Applying for a job can be very difficult. It involves being judged and being chosen. It is a very disappointing blow to be turned down for a job. In order to save face, your teen may act as if he doesn't care; or he may feel that one rejection means that he'll never get a job. You need to keep it in perspective. Getting a job is often a matter of sheer luck or of good timing rather than expertise.

Your teen needs to be prepared for her job duties and to know what to expect, even for "odd" jobs. For instance, some hospitals offer classes to certify teens for baby-sitting; these classes teach an understanding of children's needs, which in turn boosts self-confidence. Learning safe practices when working around machinery is another must. For the unprepared or un-supported teen, such a job may end in disaster.

Some teens will try a number of different jobs as they learn more about their personal interests. Not all kids will want to baby-sit; maybe mowing lawns or delivering papers is more appealing. Many fast-food establishments hire teens. Take the time to help your teen explore various options and to follow through. Parental involvement is extremely important; taking time from your busy life to show interest and to support his work experiences will be well worth your effort. There will be days when he would prefer to "veg out" or do something with his friends rather than be on time and dependable. Hang in there with him through the tough spots.

Some teens take on too many work hours. The trick is to balance work with play. Virtually every teen can benefit from the experience of working, but there are other important things in life, too. Young teens have plenty of time to become a part of the nation's workforce. Pushing too much, too early, can cut into necessary, normal social life.

Exposure to the job world can come in many ways, not just by holding a job. Some schools have "career days," and some communities offer opportunities for kids to visit their parents or older friends at their jobs, because they realize that many occupations are a mystery to teens. The road grader's job may be easy to identify with, but what a banker or a publisher does all day is not so clear. Encourage your teen to talk to people about their jobs—why they like them and how they got there. This will help him to begin to think about his future.

WHAT TO SAY AND DO

Give positive feedback. Your teen may think she is unqualified, when in fact she has many skills. Make a list of the chores she does at home and the skills she has learned from each of these tasks. For instance, cleaning the kitchen requires noticing what needs to be done and making decisions about which tools, techniques, and cleansers are appropriate for the stove top, the refrigerator, and the countertops. If she gets the kitchen done in the quickest way possible, she has learned expedience. She also has to do a good job to please her boss (Mom). List her skills and responsibilities: She gets her brother safely to his lesson, being trusted to be a careful and safe driver; she is on time for commitments; she plans ahead and is an excellent organizer; she follows detailed directions when baby-sitting. This can be a real eye-opener for your teen. The language of the employer is very different from the language of household chores, but the skills are much the same. It's all in the packaging. Phrases that encourage: *"Linda, you helped Eddy learn to tie his shoes, and that shows stick-to-itiveness; you encouraged him to learn."* Or, *"You're conscientious about how you do your chores, and you do them on time. You'll do great at a job!"*

If he applies and is turned down, put it in perspective and encourage him. *"They hired someone who has more experience. This doesn't mean there is anything wrong with you. It means the company saved money by not training a new person."*

Older teens have to manage fairly complicated pressures. You may feel it's important for your teen to pay for her car insurance, but when she also has to balance sports, schoolwork, community service, and friendships, you might take a look at how much pressure she's managing. It may not be conducive to good learning or to keeping a realistic, sane schedule. You might do better to help her with car insurance payments during the school year; during the summer, when she has time to work, she can pay you back. It is great for your teen to be responsible, but too much stress often becomes a real health issue.

Listen well when your teen relates stories or situations regarding his new job, such as dealing with bosses, following unclear directions, and getting clear feedback. Sometimes it is not good to stick with a poor work environment. If he decides he wants to quit the job, discuss how to give notice in a responsible, thoughtful way. Many first jobs are menial and can become boring. Talk to him about how to avoid creating hard feelings and about the importance of references: *"Brad, think ahead to when you want another job. You'll have to list past employ-ment and will need good references. It is advisable to give two weeks' notice. What will they say if you just don't show up? Comments like 'unreliable' will hurt you in the future."* Consider alternatives to his job carefully.

Teens often feel that their jobs are their turf and tell parents not to embarrass them by visiting. This may be exactly what you should do if you have concerns about the environment or the responsibilities. Your teen is spending many hours a day in this location with people you don't know. Unfortunately, not all job sites are positive. Ask him to show you around. When you give feedback, be careful not to alienate him: *"Maury, it was good for me to visit; now I can appreciate what you do on the job. But I'm concerned about how rough your boss is. Does he always talk to you like that?"* A flood of tears followed as Maury admitted his hurt feelings and his fears. Dad helped him to quit in a responsible way.

Teens tend to feel they have to do it all, now. Remind them that they have their entire lives to work; perhaps they can get more satisfaction out of volunteering at the Boys and Girls Club than they can out of menial fast-food types of jobs. Volunteering is work, a chance to earn recommendations and possibly a future paying job with the organization. The ini-tial reward is earning a sense of self-satisfaction rather than a paycheck.

PREVENTIVE TIPS

When teens spend all that they earn, they develop an unrealistic attitude: *"I'm rich!"* Explain the difference between "wants" and "needs." She may want to spend her newfound wealth on mani-cures, hairstyling, the tanning booth, or athletic equipment, and forget about saving for special events such as concerts.

Both older and younger teens should learn to save a portion of all earnings. "Save it for a rainy day" is the adage many of us were raised with. It is not old-fashioned. It is prudent and responsible and establishes good habits.

Teach moderation and how to delay gratification; these important values are necessary to a successful life.

If you notice that your teen is working longer hours and suspect that his hard-earned money is being spent on alcohol or other drugs, confront him.

See also: Alcohol and Other Drugs; Clothing Allowance; Money; Stress

LAZINESS

"We cannot get Ralph to do anything. All he does is sit and mope around all day."

"Dad, you don't understand how tired I am. I couldn't mow the lawn if you paid me a million dollars!"

UNDERSTANDING THE SITUATION

Some teens are apt to be lazy, and this can be extremely frustrating. There are jobs to be done and she resists. Her coach tells her to stay in shape and she lies on the couch. You wonder, *"Should I pay her? Should I bargain with her? What have I done wrong? Is something seriously wrong with her?"*

Laziness is not uncommon and is usually temporary. She may seem obsessed with her private concerns. At times, schoolwork may suffer. She may be in a phase of rejecting you and the family. Try to relax and let these moments go; most of the time, they will pass, and interest in schoolwork, a feeling of energy, and a desire to participate in the family will return.

A lazy teen may be misunderstood. What may seem to be laziness to you is often part of dealing with the pressures of adolescence. One of the jobs of the adolescent is learning how to cope. It takes an enormous amount of time and energy to deal with balancing the social scene, experiencing new sexual feelings, stressing over schoolwork, performing in sports, joining the yearbook committee, not to mention dealing with a disgruntled family as she withdraws to the safety of her room rather than interact as she used to.

Occasionally the teen needs to recharge her batteries and will tend to do so by sleeping in over the weekend and being overtly lazy. A new label may help. Rather than lazy, call it "self-healing," or "recharging." This temporary antisocial behavior usually ebbs and flows with the energy needed to face her complicated world.

Some laziness is just a bad habit. He may be stuck at the TV or the computer, where he only has to press a button or roll the mouse. He may neglect everything you feel is important—hygiene, schoolwork, chores. You feel he is missing the experience of working hard and feeling satisfaction with the results. However, this may be his way of escaping the pressures.

Some teens stay up very late, get up early for school, and are genuinely exhausted. They might be called lazy when they are actually sleep deprived.

WHAT TO SAY AND DO

Household activities may need to be adjusted so that teens can get the sleep they need. Watching late-night TV shows, using the Internet, completing homework following late sports practice, or procrastinating all need to be evaluated in the family meeting. Figure out together how lights can be put out at a reasonable hour. It will help everyone, and your teen's laziness may soon be a thing of the past.

If cooperation is lacking, stay calm. Do not overreact. When you worry, she may worry, *"What's wrong with me?"*

Sometimes a lazy kid lacks motivation. Stimulate his thinking. He needs to feel the excitement of challenging himself to try something he never imagined he might do—for example, climbing the wall in the indoor gym, running the Fall Frolic, or entering the spelling contest.

Refusing to cooperate with you may be a way to get your goat! A pattern of subtle, passive-aggressive fighting often emerges. Your teen conveys an unspoken, *"You can't make me. I'll stay in my room forever."* This is similar to power struggles you and she may have had when she was in her "terrific twos." Learning new ways to relate would be most helpful. Do not allow her to suck you into a battle. Do not lose your temper.

She's been lazy lately, and now you need something done. Give her choices with a note. Most kids who are not in a full-blown power struggle will cooperate.

> Dear Jen,
> The laundry needs folding. Please let me know when I can count on your doing it.
>
> Love, Mom
>
> Before dinner _____
> After dinner _____
>
> Signed _____

PREVENTIVE TIPS

Outside activities can provide the successes he needs for renewed energy. Be creative and look beyond the norm. One boy began rowing for a crew team in a nearby city. No other sport at school or in his immediate community had turned him on. He was surprised to find that he was good at it, and he made new friends.

Laziness can be a sign of discouragement. If your teen's grades have slipped, talk to his teacher or school counselor. He may need to be placed in another class level or have a tutor. He may also be having social problems or be under too much stress.

Become familiar with the clubs and activities your teen's school offers. Then, at a good talk time, you can offer some ideas that may spark her interest.

WHEN TO SEEK HELP

There are a host of medical conditions, such as anemia, hypothyroidism, and mononucleosis, to name a few, for which persistent lack of energy is a symptom. What you interpret as laziness could be a medical problem. Take her to the doctor for a full evaluation.

You should seek help when you notice persistent withdrawal, slipping grades, erratic sleeping or eating habits, or when you suspect the use of alcohol and other drugs, or when you see him joining a group of friends whom you don't know, or when you observe his mood as consistently glum. A lazy kid may be depressed beyond his ability to cope. A talk with an understanding counselor may be of help. Clinical depression is a serious condition and may require psychiatric care.

See also: Alcohol and Other Drugs; Chores; Counseling; Depression; Mood Swings; Stress

LEARNING PROBLEMS

"I'm so discouraged. Kevin really hates school and he's nearly failing. He's very bright when he's doing things he likes. He just doesn't do well at school."
"People expect too much—I can't be good at so many things. I have a hard time figuring out what's expected of me."

UNDERSTANDING THE SITUATION

Learning problems may have cropped up as early as elementary school; however, it may be junior high school with its many demands that brings these problems to light. Some kids even make it to high school feeling incapable and discouraged academically without anyone identifying *why*. Often, learning problems surface as the student becomes older and the demands and need for independence increase. You may hear comments like, *"I'm not interested; this stuff is boring"; "The daily work is okay, but I do lousy on tests"; "School takes too much time—life is too short"; "Every teacher thinks her class is the only one"; "I don't think the teacher likes me."* You may be frustrated and may find yourself nagging your teen to try harder. Or you may have resigned yourself to his poor grades because the pattern has been the same since elementary school. Or you may have given up, thinking, *"He's just a poor student. His father and I didn't do well in school either."*

High-school grades appear on permanent records, and the disturbing reality of "Yes, there is a life after high school" sets in. Kids who fail at school are at greater risk for dropping out, drugs, suicide, pregnancy, gang activity, and the like.

Here are some important issues to consider when you wonder why your teen is struggling.

- Does your home environment meet her needs? Is the atmosphere conducive to learning? Is there an encouraging atmosphere, with established routines that meet the needs of everyone? Or is it excessively strict, or chaotic? Learning is difficult for teens when their families are struggling with drug or alcohol abuse, divorce or new stepfamilies, financial problems, and so on.
- Have there been inconsistencies in his learning process? Was he well prepared for junior high and then high school? Differences in skill emphasis and teaching methods between elementary school and junior high may leave students with skill deficiencies that can become problematic. Particularly if you have moved to a new community, your teen may have some gaps in his education, but these can readily be addressed if discovered.
- Are some subjects chronically more difficult than others? An assessment by school officials or other professionals can

identify problems in specific areas such as reading, writing, language, math, study habits, and social skills. If there is a clear pattern, help is needed. Learning problems do not get better on their own.

- There are many individual approaches to learning that affect comprehension, communication, and concentration. When you and her teachers understand her learning style, you can be far more effective in helping her grasp difficult concepts and stay attentive. For example, Crystal listens well to lectures, is able to take notes, and memorizes geometry concepts easily. Francie has learned that to do well, she needs to copy all her notes in different colors and draw the concepts in the margins before she "gets it."

Learning problems are complex and sometimes difficult to define. Most teens are intellectually developed enough to appreciate their needs and adjust their learning styles. An adolescent can find great relief in discovering that he is not "stupid." He may be able to compensate for a reading deficiency by listening to books on tapes. Listening, he now knows, helps him feel more in control and confident.

Once informed about her learning style, Joanne can evaluate how her teacher teaches; is it right for her? Knowing that she doesn't memorize well, when the history teacher announced that everyone had to learn the Gettysburg Address by heart, she panicked at the thought of being humiliated in front of the whole class. She knew she would do poorly. She asked her mother to go with her to talk to the teacher about alternative ways to complete the assignment. The teacher cooperated, and Joanne was able to present an interesting classroom talk on Abraham Lincoln's famous words. This would not have happened if Joanne had not consulted her teacher. Most teachers are flexible and will provide the needed assistance when asked.

By actively seeking to understand why your teen is having difficulty with schoolwork, and then helping him to come up with new approaches, you are being as supportive as when he took his first step as a toddler. You are saying, *"I believe in you, and we can deal with this successfully,"* and, *"You mean so much to me, I love you."* This is very important to a discouraged teen. You can help, and you can make a difference.

Working successfully on a learning problem requires cooperation among parent, student, and teacher. You will probably learn more about the learning style of your family, and this is bound to help everyone communicate better and feel better.

Your teen's self-esteem will be greatly enhanced when he sees himself as a capable student. A learning-style evaluation, though it may take some effort and expense, makes it possible for him to speak up for his needs. When he moves into a new class with a new teacher, he can tell the teacher, *"I learn best when I sit in the front row, with no distractions. I don't take notes well, so I need to read the lessons to understand them. Can you help me with this so I can do well in your class?"* With increasing success, he will become more confident and competent. This will take time and encouragement, perhaps throughout his school career. Keep the faith. The payoff will be his desire to learn and his belief in himself—priceless gifts.

WHAT TO SAY AND DO

Reinforce the fact that each of your children learns differently, but all are learners for life. If your daughter thinks, *"My brother is the smart one. He likes school and does well. I'm not as smart, and teachers don't like me,"* tell her, *"Mallory, you do not learn like Jeffrey—you never have. I have a feeling that if we could find a way to present this math differently, you would find it very exciting. And you'd be surprised at how very smart you are!"* Then, make it happen.

Your positive attitude is essential. Teens who struggle with school suffer greatly. Often they show anger rather than pain. She may have struck out to hurt you as she hurts. She may feel so inadequate that she gives up. Your most important job is to be persistent. Keep encouraging: *"Heidi, we can lick this. I believe in you. There is no problem too big."* Give an example: *"Remember Uncle Paul? He had a private tutor teach him to fly because he couldn't learn in the flight-school classroom. He's a one-on-one, hands-on learner, and an excellent pilot!"*

If you are concerned that your teen has a learning problem, consider having an assessment done. The following guidelines may be helpful:

Have a medical exam done to eliminate any undetected hearing, vision, or other physical problems. Some teens are so used to adapting to their limitations that they have unknowingly hidden them even from their parents; or perhaps these problems have developed more recently. An assessment generally requires filling out paperwork that identifies your child as a "focus of concern." This step requires that the school do at least a preliminary evaluation. Depending on its outcome, the student may or may not be referred for further testing.

Several full assessment options are available. References can be obtained from your family physician or pediatrician, school counselor, local learning-disabilities association, or other parents who have been through the process.

A good evaluation should include a profile of strengths and weaknesses as well as recommendations for intervention and accommodation. You and your teen will be told what is needed. You also need to know what to ask for. Local organizations and laws protect and support kids who have learning problems. For example, you may be able to have your teen take tests such as the SAT and ACT without being timed. You may also be eligible for textbooks on tape, peer note takers, and special considerations in scheduling.

Once you understand his needs, request a conference with the school counselor or learning specialist. If you have had a private consultant, that individual should be included as well. The purpose of the meeting is to develop a plan of action that you, the school, and the student agree is appropriate. Once your teen feels that he has an advocate within the system, he can begin to work toward self-advocacy. This will not happen all at once and will probably require help from his school-designated advocate, at least initially. This person should also be responsible for informing your teen's teachers of his learning style and needs. Many teachers are responsive, but not all of them find it easy; they tend to teach in the way they themselves learn.

Usually, parents are most comfortable seeing their teen study the way they do. For example, Barry's father felt that the only way to learn was at a desk in a quiet room. Barry felt most comfortable at the kitchen table with his siblings milling around and the stereo on. Each child in your family may need a different study environment.

PREVENTIVE TIPS

A supportive environment is a must for emotional stability and good learning.

Conflicts around homework and learning in general can be very complicated. Remember, you are a parent first. If the chemistry is right, you can also be a tutor, but let this go if you find yourself battling. It will do more harm than good, and everyone's self-esteem will suffer. It is not unusual for parents to have difficulty teaching school subjects to their kids.

Do not do your teen's homework. Your teen may be relieved, but, deep down, the unspoken message from you is clear: *"I can do it better. You don't have the skills or the capability."* This is not lost on your teen and is likely to increase his lack of self-confidence in school.

Learning problems are challenges and are seldom outgrown. Encouraging your teen to understand and work with his learning style will offer him some control over the problem.

Discuss the life skills that education offers. *"Harlan, even if you don't plan to go to college, you need to learn math, reading, self-discipline, and time management."*

Go to open houses; chaperon events; keep in touch with teachers and other parents. She may act annoyed and wish that you would stay out of her school, but don't let that deter you. Your sustained interest is important to her success, though she may not realize it or admit it.

Promote a variety of interests beyond schoolwork, such as

dance, choir, sports, or the arts. Most service organizations love teen volunteers, and helping others builds a strong sense of purpose.

Look at vocational training with your teen. One high-school girl went to beauty school her junior year. She still managed to graduate with her class, and though she failed chemistry, she found it fascinating as it related to hair color. She began to feel like a bright and capable young woman with the skills for a fine career.

For more information on this topic, read *Keeping A Head in School* by Melvin Levine (Cambridge, MA: Educator's Publishing Service, Inc., 1990); *The Way They Learn* by Cynthia Tobias (Colorado Springs: Focus on the Family Publishing, 1994); and *Seven Kinds of Smart* by Thomas Armstron (New York: Penguin Group, 1993).

See also: Anger; Depression; Grades and Homework

LEAVING HOME

"I never thought I would be ready for this, but it is definitely time for him to leave home!"

"I can't wait to leave. It's kind of scary, and I'll miss my cat, but I'll finally be on my own. No one to tell me what to do!"

UNDERSTANDING THE SITUATION

When asked about long-range goals for their children, beyond happiness and security, most parents want their kids to maintain a lifelong friendship with them. Yet you may feel as if you do nothing but disagree with your teen, and his leaving has become a welcome event. What about the friendship you'd hoped for?

It is an anxious time. Minor issues become exaggerated. The process of leaving home may be so painful that, subconsciously, the teen creates turmoil in order to make the separation easier. This may be especially true when the move has no clear direction. Some teens are going to college; others are going simply because "it's time to leave!" Parents' doubts and worries can motivate older teens to leave in order to prove that they can do it. This sometimes works out fairly well for all.

When a teen leaves home, it affects the entire family. Before Jerry left for the Coast Guard he refused to do his chores, was nasty to his brother, and couldn't look his father in the eye and say good-bye. Sue, a younger sister said, *"I miss Bob. He was always there for me—at school, at parties, and at home dealing with Mom and Dad."* Beth felt too much attention was going to her departing older sister. Graduation, parties, and shopping for college clothes took attention from her: *"Besides, this is the first summer we haven't gone to the lake. Just because Roberta's leaving for college, she's wrecking everything."* The departure of older siblings can be complicated. The void is felt by everyone in the family. Ken moved out angrily, leaving a mess and refusing to let his mother come to the apartment he'd found with a friend: *"I want to do this on my own! Bug off."*

While intellectually they may be prepared to say good-bye, many parents are surprised by their strong emotions. One mother said, *"I knew what was happening. I was disgusted with how he left his bedroom, but I decided to let it go. I took him to the airport, hugged him, with thoughts that I wouldn't see him until Christmas, and after a few tears I drove home, deciding to thoroughly dust and clean his room. Then, there was the Lego car carefully placed on his shelf, with the engine he so carefully installed eight years ago. Why should I dust it now? Cleaning his room seemed so trivial, so unimportant next to the feelings of emptiness. I stopped, sat on his bed, and had a good cry, and then I left and closed the door behind me. I decided I could clean the room another day."*

When teens leave home, especially when the youngest leaves, it means that parents must face what is left—their relationship. They must redefine it without the daily interactions and buffers their children provided. They spent many years focused on parenting, with all its joys and hassles. Now . . . ? Conversely, teens who are leaving generally have some subtle feelings of abandoning their parents and sometimes worry about causing a divorce.

Many young adults will stay at home for economic or other practical reasons. The relationship between parent and teen needs to change to allow all to move to the next stage of development. Common sense and courtesy should prevail.

WHAT TO SAY AND DO

Begin talking about leaving home before it happens.

Use of the old bedroom. One girl leaving for college said, *"I just want to be respected. If Mom and Dad need my room for an office or for Grandma, I can accept that, if we discuss it and plan on what to do with my things. I don't want people going through my stuff when I'm not home. Ideally, I'd like my room to stay the same and be there for me when I come home."*

Holidays. Sometimes your son or daughter will not be able to come home for important holidays. Discuss this in advance. Care packages go a long way to help, even if they bring tears and waves of homesickness.

Vacations. For some young adults, this will be the first time they must face obligations that keep them from joining the family for vacations or other special occasions. Just because he can't get away, don't assume he isn't interested. He still needs to be included and invited.

Money issues. Most colleges provide guidelines for freshmen. If your teen will be traveling or working, the guidelines may not be so well spelled out. Your teen should be made aware of the costs of auto, health, and dental insurance, room and board, clothing, and other monetary facts of life *before* he leaves home. Charge card and checking account plans need to be agreed upon. A conference with your personal banker may be helpful.

Telephone calls. If you can afford to, give your teen a calling card with the understanding that you will talk once a week. Knowing he can call you when he needs to will make it easier for you both. Make an agreement that he will pay for any long-distance calls.

Younger siblings. Those left at home may feel a big loss. Plan ahead to make the transition easier. One boy always went to Grandmother's for the summer with his two sisters. When they left for college, Grandmother was happy to let him bring a friend, which made for a smoother transition.

PREVENTIVE TIPS

Transitions are harder for some people than for others. Be aware. If you see unusual behavior such as anger, rebelliousness, or withdrawal, provide extra opportunities for listening and discussing feelings. Leaving home may be troubling you both without realizing it. Look forward to the future; often your relationship improves with distance.

The whole family must make adjustments. The family will never be the same, and this is a loss, even if it is for happy reasons. Grieving is a process of letting go and rebuilding and will not happen overnight. The teen is leaving her home, her friends, her school, and her family. This is a lot to lose. Your continued communication with her may be vital to her sense of well-being and her ability to move into this next phase of her life. (Please read the section titled Losses and Grief.)

For more information on this topic, read *All Grown Up and No Place to Go: Teenagers in Crisis* by David Elkind (Reading, MA: Addison-Wesley, 1984).

See also: College; Counseling; Depression; Graduation; Losses and Grief; Money

LOSSES AND GRIEF

"Chuck has been very responsible ever since his father died. It's as though he's trying to take his place. I worry that this may not be good for him."

"When Rita committed suicide, I thought I would, too. I can't believe she did this to all of us! What was she thinking?"

UNDERSTANDING THE SITUATION

Few teens make it through high school without experiencing some important loss: a best friend moving away; a mother returning to work full-time; a sister leaving home; his parents' divorce; the death of a grandparent or of a high-school friend. Even a parent's loss of a job or income is significant. To a teen, loss can cause extreme turmoil.

No one teen will grieve the same way as another, or even in a way that you might expect. When Leonard's dog died, it was clearly a bigger loss to him than his grandfather's death. His father was amazed at how totally unprepared Len was, even though the dog, Charlie, was fourteen years old. Leonard had trouble eating and sleeping and could not stop thinking about him. What Dad did not understand was that Charlie had been there for this teen for as long as he could remember, wagging his tail and loving him unconditionally. Grandfather was attentive but was present only occasionally. Charlie had heard all about Leonard's hard times, licked his tears and wounds, and slept in the same room to fend off bad dreams when he was younger. It is no mystery that Leonard experienced the losses differently and that the intensity of his grief was different for each.

Some teens may feel guilty for not grieving over the loss of a distant relative as intensely as you do. Accept the differences. There is no right way to react. Losses mean different things to different people.

You may not recognize your teen's behavior as grief as he reels from the death of a good friend. He may have great emotional surges, be frightened by their intensity, and not know how to express his overwhelming feelings. He may withdraw and refuse to talk about it—a common reaction that can make it difficult for you to help. But deep down, your teen needs to be comforted, and you need to be sensitive in offering that comfort. Say, *"Would it be helpful to talk to me about what happened? If you decide you want to, I am here for you. I loved him, too. We will miss his visits very much, but I know I will never forget his wonderful jokes."* Expressing your thoughts may help him to start expressing his.

When thirteen-year-old Sid's father died, he began wearing his father's pajamas; he wore them every night for three weeks. This saddened and upset his mother, yet it was an important way for Sid to keep the memories of his father alive, for the moment. Mom's style was more inward and not as demonstrative. Both had to work through their grief in their own way so that they could let go of father and husband, respectively, and eventually move on. This is how the grief process works. It allows people to readjust and form new relationships with new father figures and partners.

Amanda's mother went back to work full-time. Amanda was sad to come home from soccer practice a half hour before her mother arrived, and she missed the aroma of freshly baked bread or cookies and their familiar, comfortable after-school discussions. Though these weren't everyday occurrences, their absence gave Amanda something concrete to be angry about. Instead of saying, *"Mom, I miss you when you're at work. I wish you were home like before,"* she made hateful remarks to her mother.

If divorce or death forces a move, grieving is doubly difficult. The family configuration changes. An oldest son may feel he has to take on the new role of "man of the house," or a daughter becomes "mother" to younger siblings. A stepparent may enter the picture. In such complicated situations, grieving can be compromised unless the changes are handled in a sensitive, proactive way.

Keeping a "stiff upper lip" was once the accepted, even admired, way of dealing with grief. However, it is now known that unresolved grief is not healthy and can lead to physical and emotional problems. During the grief process, the sufferer must work through feelings of loss, abandonment, sadness, and anger. All these feelings are valid, and repressing them can keep a teen locked into depression and other problems.

Teens who have to adjust to a new stepparent often face a loss of the way things were. Their grief may be replaced by feelings of anger, blame, and resentment. Martie lost a wonderful school when her mother married and moved to a new home in a new district. She felt furious with her stepfather for "causing" the family to move. She was filled with anger and blame, which prevented her from expressing her sadness over missing her old friends and school. Sometimes there is so much at stake that professional help is warranted. This kind of rage at a stepparent can easily lead to negative behaviors such as losing interest in school and starting to take drugs to numb the pain.

Teens need to develop coping skills for hard times. How they learn to deal with losses at a young age paves the way for how they will handle the bigger ones that will surely happen later in life. It may be a key maturing event in your teen's life.

It may be helpful for a grieving teen to hear that time does heal wounds and that though it is hard when the loss is new, there are still many things in life to look forward to. The grieving process can be intellectually understood. This helps. But to gloss over the pain is unhealthy. It takes time, and time must be allowed. It may surprise him to look back and realize that he is not sad anymore, though during the grieving process he could not imagine ever being happy again.

Some college freshmen, away from home for the first time,

have a terrible time adjusting to the loss of their family and the support it offered. Their inexperience in dealing with loss becomes a liability. Surviving and coming out the other end as a wiser, whole, and happy person is a vital life skill.

WHAT TO SAY AND DO

Think back on some of your losses and how you coped. Ask, *"What would I rather have had happen?"* Anything you can do to sensitize yourself to the true feelings you experienced, or shut out, when you were a teen will be helpful now.

Don't discount her pain. It hurts you, too. *"You'll get over it in time. You'll see, you'll make new friends quickly,"* is not helpful. At the moment, the feelings need to be identified and empathized with. *"Erin, you hurt so deeply. I know. I felt that way once. I am so very sorry for you."* When a parent can truly empathize, the grieving process is shared and therefore processed more completely.

The first step is to give permission to grieve. Tell your teen it's okay to hurt, to cry, and to sob. It will eventually get better.

Trauma often causes numbness and shock. This is so uncomfortable that you might see your teen act inappropriately, even laugh about the event. Don't get angry. This is not a sign that she is mocking or that she does not care; she simply has no experience in how to react. She may laugh from embarrassment.

Uncontrolled crying may seem hysterical, and some hold back, fearing a loss of control. This is especially true of boys. You can help with: *"John, sometimes it may feel like you'll never be able to stop crying. It is important to let the tears help to wash the sadness out of you. It's the way to feeling better. I promise, you will feel better if you let out the hurt."*

Anger over feeling abandoned after a death or a divorce is often followed by guilt: *"I should not feel angry for his dying!"* As shocking as such thoughts may be, they are normal.

"If I hadn't told him to leave me alone and never come into my room again, he wouldn't be dead." When thoughtless outbursts suddenly take on imagined power, it is very important to seek

counseling. Guilt can live on to create self-esteem problems or worse.

It is also imperative that your teen hear your grief. Talk about it even if it is painful. Your modeling is helpful. Do not forget to find your own supports. That is what your family and friends are for, and clergy and counselors, too.

Family rituals or traditions can be a great help. For example, the loss of a loved one may come welling back at anniversaries, graduations, weddings, or with the birth of a baby, years later. These are important reminders that someone we loved still is missed. One seventy-eight-year-old grandmother has given a check to her three granddaughters each year, for fifteen years, in honor of the memory of their father, her son.

Anniversaries of traumatic events can be tough; sadness or agitation may surface as the mind tends to reenact experiences or feelings from an unconscious level. Pay attention to your feelings and moods at significant anniversary times. They can affect the family but may have more to do with your inner world. Teens appreciate sensitive personal discussions, and they will learn about themselves at the same time. Your teen is not your counselor, but it is important to share your feelings so that your actions are understood. She may otherwise think she has caused your mood.

PREVENTIVE TIPS

Ask the school counselor or principal if there is a program to help teens with losses. It is important for everyone to know which emotions to expect and to understand why people respond as they do, especially in the event of a schoolwide tragedy involving a teacher or student. Bereavement counselors are trained to help everyone to talk about the loss, anticipate and share feelings, and gain support from one another. They give hope that the pain will decrease, and can be instrumental in allowing memories of the lost person to be kept alive.

If your teen had conflict with the person who died or left, she needs reassurance that her anger did not cause the person to leave. It is very important for her to verbalize her fears. Guilt can develop into extreme stress.

It is important to let your teen talk about her perceptions, allowing for sharing and concerns to be expressed and corrected if needed.

Generally, teens have an uncanny sense about whose help they want and who may be unhelpful to them. If your teen refuses your help, try not to take it too personally. Offer your presence and support, and reassure her that you will not abandon her. She needs her privacy, and your hope.

For more information on this topic, read *Fall of Freddie the Leaf* by Leo Buscaglia, Ph.D. (New York: Henry Holt, 1982); *The Tenth Good Thing About Barney* by Judith Viorst (New York: Macmillan, 1971); *Annie and the Old One* by Miska Miles (Boston: Little Brown and Co., 1971); *Explaining Death to Children,* 3rd Edition, by Earl Grollman (Boston: Beacon Press, 1980); *Talking About Death: A Dialogue Between Parent and Child* by Earl Grollman (Boston: Beacon Press, 1967); *Straight Talk About Death for Teenagers* by Earl Grollman (Boston: Beacon Press, 1993); and *On Death and Dying* by Elizabeth Kubler-Ross (New Haven: Yale University Press, 1968).

WHEN TO SEEK HELP

Watch for normal indications that your teen is grieving. He may withdraw from social contacts for a while, and he may have difficulty concentrating at school and attending to homework. He may daydream more than usual. He may seem preoccupied with details about the crisis or describe the feeling of being in a fog. He may experience disrupted sleep and eating problems. Don't ignore these signs. Tell him you notice that he seems to be having difficulty. Offer to listen and comfort, or suggest counseling. He may be most interested in a peer support group. He may know peers who would benefit from group counseling over the same loss.

A delayed grief reaction may set in several months after a loss. Teens can react in extreme ways, such as drinking, drug-

ging, or engaging in other dangerous, even life-threatening behaviors. School becomes problematic for them. You should
confront your teen with any such behaviors and try to point
out a connection between the behavior and the loss. Counseling can be very helpful to both teen and parent at this time.

In the case of suicide or traumatic death, it is especially important to manage the grief process carefully. A sudden death can be
more difficult than that of a person who has been ill for a long
time. Adolescents tend to be dramatic, and when a friend com-
mits suicide they may lament that it would be better that they die,
too. Put things in proper perspective. Teens need to know that
they can make it through something this traumatic.

See also: Alcohol and Other Drugs; College; Depression; Leaving Home; Mood Swings; Pets; Rebelliousness; Suicide

LYING

*"I don't know if she's telling the truth or lying. She is
really on a bad track and I can't trust her anymore."*
*"She always questions my word. She makes me feel like a
liar, like she won't ever trust me."*

UNDERSTANDING THE SITUATION

"I don't believe she told such a lie." The shock, shame, and anger
when you know that your teen has deliberately lied can be overwhelming. Hanna did not go to Kate's house overnight; she went
with a group and spent the night in a vacation cabin. A force field
of mistrust springs up: *"How will I ever believe what she tells me?"*
and guilt: *"What did I do wrong?"* If the lying is routine, the
normal tension of raising a teen increases, and your relationship

can definitely become strained. Teenagers are testing their power now and may have to stretch the truth to do so. If caught, they can become very indignant and furiously deny the accusations. They want to be trusted, desperately. Does this compute?

Technically, it is much easier for a teen to be honest because he is less likely to get into trouble with his parents, school, peers, and ultimately the law. But teens love to "get away" with things and will lie to do so. Why?

To conceal the truth. The truth may get her into trouble, so she may alter details, like whom she was with or where she was, or she may change the entire event.

To impress or shock. A better story draws more attention. This might be called creative lying, or making the fish a little longer. It redresses a feeling of emptiness and insignificance: *"I'm not good enough; I have to embellish the truth."*

To gain advantage over others. He may embellish his score in a game in order to be admired.

To test boundaries. He may tell you that he drove home a friend who was drunk to test the rule that no one who has been drinking is allowed in the car: *"But I did a good deed. I drove him home."*

To protect friends. He may cover for her so that she doesn't get into trouble. He may feel the consequences are unfair.

For selfish gain. He may be so discouraged that he lies to cover up something malicious or hurtful in order to get ahead himself. Alicia resorted to shaving her neighbor's horse's tail, which eliminated her competition in a horse show.

Your reaction to discovering an untruth is extremely important. Your daughter is developing her moral code and trying to find her way in the world. She will make some poor decisions.

If you have lectured, moralized, threatened, and punished for lying in the past, you need to examine your disciplinary style. It is not working. Likewise, avoiding a confrontation in the hope that she won't do it again is not responsible parenting. *"No matter what I do, she still lies, not all the time, but when she's late for first class at school she has these wild excuses. Otherwise she seems truthful."* Perhaps something is going on in this class that needs to be investigated, rather than her behavior.

You cannot cheat or lie and expect her not to. *"Oh gosh! The dog pooped right on the neighbor's front walk. Let's get out of here."* Evading the consequences, or not admitting something for fear of others' opinions, will be keenly observed by your teen. What you model is very important!

View a lie as a mistake in judgment. Most teens will stretch the truth, withhold information, tell half-truths and occasionally outright lie. This is normal. They also need to be trusted. Kids with healthy self-esteem may feel the need to lie less often, but they can get very good at "harmlessly" deceiving you when it is to their advantage.

Your job is to get past the guilt: *"What did I do wrong?"* and anger: *"How can he say this?"* and instead focus on: *"How can I help him feel strong enough to tell the truth?"* He needs your encouragement. The lie needs to be addressed and a consequence applied. If it happens again, as it may, repeat the correction. It does not mean he is a liar. It's like breaking rules; teens will if they can. Getting away with something is a powerful feeling. Manipulating teachers or parents can be a "high," until they begin to feel a little guilty about it. Most teens lie, and most do not end up in jail. Most eventually realize it just isn't worth it.

Avoiding or pulling away from the family may mean she has been lying to you and feels uncomfortable with closeness right now. Guilty feelings are one of the elements that encourage telling the truth. Learning how to manage them, and learning from mistakes in judgment, is part of adolescence.

Repeated, serious lying may be an expression of discouragement. He needs to know that the deed is wrong, that you feel he is not a bad person, and that you still love him unconditionally. He needs to know you have faith in his ability to change. You must be loving, firm, and consistent, and you must hold him accountable.

WHAT TO SAY AND DO

If you know he is trying to impress, say so. Do not embarrass him; treat it lightly and kindly: *"Ted, that's a little exaggerated. Maybe you wished it had happened that way. Tell the truth."* Say this with a smile to ease his embarrassment.

The issue is often twofold. First, he has done something wrong; second, he has lied to better his situation. For example, you find a brand-new soccer ball in the garage with your son's name on it. When questioned, he lies, telling you that a friend gave him the ball. Say, *"Our family rule is that when you do something wrong and tell me the truth about it, you will be held responsible for the mistake, but there will be no other consequences. You are never punished for telling the truth. But when you do something wrong and also lie about it, you will have to take the responsibility and experience the consequences. You lied about how you got the ball. You took the ball from Justin's garage. You need to return the ball. We want you to stay home this weekend to think about this. No friends. We'll talk Sunday night."*

Never ask, *"Are you lying?"* You will probably throw your teen into a bigger, defensive lie. If you know she is lying, address it matter-of-factly: *"Mary Ellen, I know that is untrue."* Never say she is lying unless you have proof. Likewise, never label her a "liar." Name calling may send an internal message, *"I am a liar,"* which then becomes an identity. Instead, address the deed: *"You have told a lie."* Or, *"That is not true. That is a lie."*

Kids who observe their parents avoiding difficult situations with fibs or "white lies" often do the same. Karen asked her mother to tell Andrew she wasn't home to avoid his incessant phone calls. Steve wants Dad to tell Ray he went hiking to get out of a commitment gracefully. These situations happen to all of us. Relax and help out. Later, have a talk about how this might be handled in the future. However, if "cover-ups" are requested too often, you probably are overprotecting your teen from facing situations directly. Rescuing can encourage dishonesty and send the message that you think the other person cannot handle the truth. At a good talk time, not in the heat of the problem, discuss it and problem solve: *"It is not okay for you to put me on the spot so often. How can you get yourself out of this gracefully on your own? What could you do differently to keep from getting into a bind like this next time?"* Help her practice: *"I can't talk on the phone now because . . ."*

Avoid unreasonable threats: *"All right, young lady, you will not leave this house for the rest of the school year!"* Your loss of control distracts from the seriousness of her action, moving the responsibility to you. Tell her you need to cool off and that she is restricted while she, too, reflects. This can be a killer to your teen. For example, on Saturday morning say, *"Angie, I need to think about what you've told me and what really happened. Plan to stay home until we talk about what this means to your future privileges."* Eager to settle the matter, she may come to you begging or bargaining several times over the weekend. You will be most effective if you are not ready to talk until Sunday night. Angie will have had a great deal of time to consider her responsibility, and this is more effective than your anger.

Rather than emphasize, *"You lied,"* focus on finding a solution: *"Jill, the softball obviously went through the window. I don't know who did it or how it happened. How can we repair the window, and how can we prevent that from happening again?"* This approach is not punitive and encourages your teen to tell the truth in the future. Concentrating on "who done it?" is not positive parenting.

PREVENTIVE TIPS

Examine any "threat" he may perceive from you. Check his perception at a good talk time. He may lie to you so that you won't think less of him. He may be feeling that he'll never be able to do enough to please you or that his mistakes are not okay. He may feel shame over what he has failed to accomplish or cannot achieve. Problem solve with him. For example:

Address his feeling with a question. "Ron, are you feeling that you have to do something to stand out so that others will notice you?"

Show understanding. "I think I'm finally understanding how you feel." Keep it light: "Sometimes it takes me a long time!"

Briefly state your concern. "I'm concerned that you're lying so often."

Restitution - Consequences. Ask for his ideas. "What would it take to make lying unnecessary for you?" Or, "What can I do to help you?" Give him time to think. He may need a few days.

Follow up. Discuss the issue again after a week or two. Ask, "Is it better?"

Do not give up. This may take some time and repetition.

Teens routinely observe society's double standards. Advertisements offer half-truths; campaign messages manipulate the truth; cover-ups for illegal toxic-waste dumps are defended in courts of law. The list is long. These are excellent subjects for family discussions regarding ethics and morality. When is a lie a lie?

Make telling the truth a strong family value. Trust is very important with teens in relation to privileges. *"You will be allowed to take the car more and more as you demonstrate that you're responsible and honest."* And, *"We do not punish for telling the truth. We all make mistakes, and we are responsible for them. We can be honest about our mistakes and still feel good about ourselves."*

Your teen is watching you. Be honest. If you fabricate or exaggerate a story for effect, or tell a lie to protect your credibility, your teen is likely to do the same.

Work on building your teen's self-confidence. None of us wants to do wrong, but when self-esteem is strong, it is easier to admit a mistake. A good exercise is to have your teen finish these sentences:

1. I belong when _____.
2. I am appreciated for _____.
3. I am good at _____.

These questions stimulate good discussions. With this exercise, both parents and teens learn something new.

Positive family time is crucial. Use the family meeting to establish limits and consequences. At all other times, concentrate on what he is doing right. Stop nagging about all that is wrong or undone. He may already feel in a one-down position and need desperately to know he is appreciated and valued.

WHEN TO SEEK HELP

If your teen seems unable to recognize the difference between a lie and the truth or appears chronically untruthful, outside help is in order. Chronic lying can be very frustrating, resulting in negative feelings that only add to the problem. See a therapist who is experienced in working with adolescents and their families.

Depression could be at the root of the problem. If so, it needs professional diagnosis and treatment.

Defensiveness can indicate an inability to face the truth. The common result is lying. This may be a sign that your teen is having difficulty with self-esteem and identity issues and is in need of professional help.

See also: Chapter 2, The Positive Parenting Philosophy; Counseling; Depression; Mealtimes; Spoiling; Rebelliousness; Trust; Values

MEALTIMES

"It seems our family is never together. We're all so busy, we never even eat together."
"Oh, great. Another night on my own and a frozen pizza!"

UNDERSTANDING THE SITUATION

Mealtime is one of the best opportunities to visit with your teen, to talk about everyone's day, and to plan for future family events. Unfortunately, today's fast-paced society has all but erased the possibility of eating together. School activities, sports, and jobs take priority. You may need to designate one meal a week to eat together. This positive tradition will increase your teen's self-confidence, cooperation, and sense of responsibility and belonging. It's up to you to make family meals happen. The pressures will be a challenge, but if something has to give, the family meal shouldn't be it.

Expressing ideas, telling stories, and stating opinions are skills practiced at the dinner table. Set the tone by making interesting conversation about your day. Ask for feedback, and be interested in the things your teens bring up. This is a great time for discussions about ethics.

WHAT TO SAY AND DO

Who cooks is often a concern for the harried mother coming home to very hungry adolescents. Eating healthfully is important, and fast food just does not fill the bill; it may also be too costly. Cooking is no longer the exclusive job of mothers and sisters. Take your son food shopping with you. Teach him how to make his favorite foods, and share the food preparation responsibilities. All family members benefit from presenting and sharing a meal.

Express your appreciation for everyone's effort: *"Thanks for making time for us to have this meal together."* Some families say grace. Some families begin with each person saying what he appreciates about another person sitting at the table. Both methods create a unity that says, "We care about one another."

In the "old days," meals were a time for teaching life lessons about generosity and compassion, honesty, fairness and accountability, right and wrong, and ethics. Families sat around the table deep in conversation and debate. *"What if you were riding your bike by a parking lot and you saw your good friend stealing a stereo from a car? Would you talk to him, tell his parents, pretend you never saw, or turn him in to the police? Why?"* The standard one was: *"You found a wallet and it had four hundred dollars in it. What would you do if there was identification in it, and what would you do if there was none?* Could you live with yourself if you then read in the paper that a homeless family had lost all their savings?"

It is also a good time to discuss pertinent adolescent issues. *"What if a friend told you she wanted to run away from home and asked you to hide her at our house?"* *"What if you knew that your football buddy had been drinking a lot even though there was an honor system to not use or you're off the team?"* *"What if you saw your favorite teacher smoking pot with his students?"* Ask, *"Why?"* and, *"What would you do?"* and, *"Is this the only choice?"* Communicate that you do not necessarily know the answer. These are moral issues that need to be answered "from the gut" as well as the mind. Teenagers enjoy opportunities to use their new intellectual and philosophical skills. His ideas may astound you.

There is no better way to drive your teen from meals than to pick on her while you have her "captive" at the table. Do not use mealtimes to arbitrate the hassles of the week. They make very poor seasoning. Hold negotiations at the family meeting, where emotionally loaded issues can be discussed more comfortably.

Occasionally, bring out the "company's coming" dinner-ware just for the family. Ask teens to help set the table and light the candles. Teach them how to set the table from utensils to water glasses. One mother noticed that her teens were setting the table with the fork on the right side (which is the wrong side). She designed a "Queen Elizabeth Is Visiting" meal and taught them how to set a formal table and how to act should they be asked to entertain royalty. (You never know.) Good manners are important when making first impressions and in social and career situations. Adolescents are not too young to learn them. Remind your son that when he is invited to dine with his girlfriend's family, he will need good manners.

Manners can be addressed with a glance or a short comment: *"Ryan, please, your gum."* Generally, when your conversation includes your teen and is of interest to him, he will be polite. Humor always helps: *"Ronald, would you do this if Queen Elizabeth were here?"* or, *"Dawna, I see Oren,"* which was one mother's private signal for *"you have food stuck on your braces."* Oren was their dentist's name.

Turn off the television during meals. It stifles conversation and can make strangers of family members. Occasionally, a special program will be important to share, but that is the exception, not the rule. Limit phone calls during meals. Take a message or leave it to your answering machine. Your teen's friends will soon learn that this is the norm in your home.

PREVENTIVE TIPS

Many teens like to help plan and cook meals. They are old enough to do some of the shopping and learn to buy carefully and wisely. They can be responsible for cooking one or more meals a week.

Establish new mealtime traditions to fit your family's life-style. One single mother who worked three nights a week set Tuesday nights for family dinner, because that's when she was home to cook. Her teens were permitted to invite anyone they wanted. Her children are now grown and live out of town, yet their friends occasionally come for Tuesday dinner. This tradition obviously was meaningful.

See also: Siblings; Traditions; Values

MONEY

"Kelly seems to actually get depressed when we can't afford designer jeans."
"Dad is such a tightwad. I hate him sometimes."

UNDERSTANDING THE SITUATION

Styles of saving and spending vary just as learning styles do. One mother observed that her two teenagers handled money the same way as they handled their Halloween candy when they were small: *"My son stashed his candy away, eating it only when he thought about it, and it was the Fourth of July before we threw the remainder out. He stashes his money the same way. He doesn't have many wants, and when he needs money it seems to be there. Our daughter ate her Halloween candy in a week. She seems to do the same with any money she gets. Her wants and needs are less defined, and she spends carelessly."*

Most parents complain, *"She just doesn't understand the value of the dollar."* Ask yourself which of your personal spending habits you would like to pass on and which you'd rather not. It is not only the younger generation that needs to understand just how much money is overspent. Too many people of all ages think more about what they want than about their responsibilities. Earning money has little to do with managing it. Some young people have jobs but don't hold on to their money because they have no structure for saving and spending. Budgeting money is seldom taught in schools. This is a parent's job.

The teen years are the last opportunity for this kind of teaching before your child leaves home. She will make mistakes. He'll spend all and want more. Are you enabling bad spending habits rather than empowering your teen to make good decisions and to learn the difference between wants and needs? Sound management of money is a life skill that you and your children will be grateful to have learned. There is a strong connection between healthy self-esteem and how money is handled. When parents and children expand on these skills and begin to feel creative about using them, there is no end to the potential for all involved.

WHAT TO SAY AND DO

Use your teen's allowance to teach her money management. Learning how to manage money can happen only if there's some to manage. Different families use different approaches to giving allowances. Amounts will vary according to the child's age, the needs of her situation, and what your family can afford. This allowance should not be linked to chores or to behavior. Discuss with your teen what the allowance is to be used for. Keep in mind that overindulgence is unhealthy. These are the years to teach budgeting and the difference between needs and wants. If you rescue her every time she miscalculates, she won't learn effective money management.

Darcey, age thirteen, receives a weekly allowance. Her parents expect her to budget for entertainment, birthday presents, school supplies, and school lunches, and to save 10 percent for her favorite charity. She has learned to supplement her allowance with baby-sitting and other odd jobs. Her parents will match any deposit she makes to her savings account. This has been an excellent motivator.

Matching funds teaches how money can grow. One mother, sending her young teen off to camp with spending money, said she would match any amount that she came home with. This motivated her daughter not to spend money on candy, as she had the previous year.

Lending money and amassing credit with teens is generally not advisable. The sums add up, and parents often end up forgiving the loan to avoid a hassle. This is not good teaching. One wise father did loan his son, Kirby, money for a musical instrument for a band he was starting. Dad wrote up a contract stating that Kirby's CD player was the collateral on the loan. Kirby began paying off the loan, earned back his CD player, and felt empowered. It takes love, strength, and consistency not to be an overindulgent parent.

Peer pressure is intense at this age. Be aware of your teen's sudden awareness of how much her friends have to spend and what their parents buy for them. Listen carefully. Don't be defensive when she criticizes you: *"Why don't you make the money that Charlotte's mom does? She has everything she wants."* Stay calm. Rather than express anger or resentment, sympathize, and reflect her feelings: *"You'd like it if I made more money. What would you buy that you can't now?"* Or, *"Yes, I agree, I'd like to earn more. I may not choose to spend our money the same way, however. Let's make a wish list."* Or, to stimulate thinking: *"I might make the money Charlotte's mom does if I worked longer hours. But I'd have to pay child care for your sisters, and I'd miss being home with all of you."*

Don't assume he cannot handle the consequence of his choices. We learn from our mistakes. It takes a lot of love to say firmly, *"Honey, I know you want to go to the concert with your friends. I also know that you chose that designer sweatshirt."* Offer sympathy: *"I know it's hard to learn just how far money goes. Maybe you'll have saved enough for the next concert."*

Teach the difference between wants and needs: *"You need a pair of sandals, but you want the expensive name-brand pair. I'll give you enough money for sandals; you'll have to earn the extra for the ones you want."*

Do not be too quick to rule out your teen's ideas just because they don't seem cost-effective. Much of corporate America was founded on dreams. When you say no too fast, you stop her creative thinking. For example, if your teen wants to sell homemade apple pies, ask serious, thought-provoking questions: *"What a great idea! How will you market your pies? How will you take orders so the oven doesn't get overcommitted and interrupt cooking dinner? I'll bet it can be done!"*

Review your money-management style. If you haven't been keeping a budget, start to, and share it with your teen. This is good role modeling and allows her to see the realities of proper money management.

Find opportunities to teach life lessons. Jeff was forgetful about turning off lights; he left them on all day while he was at school. His mother had him write the monthly checks for the electric bills, and each time that the bill was less because he'd been more conscientious about turning lights off, she gave him twice the difference for extra spending.

Avoid saying, *"We can't afford that."* When you follow this by buying yourself some extras, you send a mixed message. Say what you mean and be honest: *"I love you but I'd rather not spend our money on that at this time."*

Don't fall into the "money-love trap." Is your self-worth tied up in how much you earn or what you can provide? Our teens are impressionable, and they tend to believe that they have to have the best in order to be admired and accepted by their peers. If it's not affordable, insecure teens may feel unloved, and, unfortunately, many parents feel guilty. We do what we can and then we begin to be creative. Used-clothing stores can be an alternative so that bills don't pile up. This solution is realistic and healthy. Your teen may find just what she wants for a fraction of the department store's retail price.

PREVENTIVE TIPS

Hold regular business meetings to establish your family budget, and invite your teen to discuss priorities. This approach replaces the guilt-laden *"How could you demand that when we can't afford it?"* One family planned a vacation they could ill afford. Mom researched the cost of the trip and the family voted unanimously to work for it. From May through August, the four girls (with some help from Mom and Dad) shared a paper route, watered yards and plants, washed cars, cared for pets, and baby-sat. Everyone appreciated the value of that vacation!

Watch for signs of depression. When money is scarce, teens often perceive themselves as less valued than others, and self-pity monopolizes their thoughts.

Listen, sympathize, and explore priorities. Teens are stressed, balancing school, sports, social life, and family. In addition, many need to work to pay for the extras their families cannot afford, especially in high school, when comparisons are so important and some kids have so much more than others. A job can become too stressful and have serious consequences on physical and mental health. If your teen can learn what is important, and can structure his spending on sound, responsible principles, he will grow to be an effective money manager, no matter how much he has or doesn't have. The comparisons will still be there, but the realities will not be as painful.

Teens are keenly aware of those with more money and those with less. Your attitude is of prime importance. One teen needed three hundred dollars to go to camp with her soccer team. Her father had lost his job, so he encouraged her to earn the money herself. She earned every dollar baby-sitting, doing odd jobs, and going without new clothes. Her parents cheered her on. She was the only girl on the team whose family couldn't afford the camp, but after earning the money herself, she felt great.

Teach your teen that credit cards should be paid off monthly. The credit card is often seen as a license to spend an unlimited amount. What is not understood is that credit cards are very expensive when not paid off. A pair of designer jeans may cost sixty-five dollars, but with over-limit penalties the cost can rise to more than a hundred dollars. Today, unemployed kids straight out of high school often have the opportunity to obtain credit cards. One girl owed seven thousand dollars on her Visa card before she was out of college: *"The credit card company made it seem like I'd won a contest each time I maxed out. They sent a letter of congratulations and upped my credit line. I didn't know it would add up so high. I can't believe how stupid I was. It'll take years for me to pay it off."*

The example above is why it is so important for you to stay involved with your teen's spending habits, even when it is his own money from his own job. Impulsive buying, purchase of dangerous items or weapons, or purchase of too many videos all need parental supervision and control. He may have earned the money, but you are still the parent and your job is still to guide him into being a responsible person. You may need to hold his money in a savings bank as a way to insist on better judgment and moderation.

See also: Clothing Allowance; Jobs; Spoiling, Overindulgence

MOOD SWINGS

"I'm going nuts! One minute she's up, the next she's falling apart."
"I don't know why I feel so bad sometimes. Why do you keep asking me how I feel, or why I feel that way? I just want to be alone!"

UNDERSTANDING THE SITUATION

When emotional surges hit in early adolescence, both you and your young teen are likely to feel confused. These emotions are unpredictable, likened to a hurricane or to a roller coaster with forceful ups and downs. Suddenly there is a touchiness and lack of patience with common situations that a year ago would not have been a big deal.

The hormonal onslaught is accompanied by rapid emotional changes. One twelve-year-old boy went from being overly pleasant and helpful at times to pouting and refusing to cooperate in anything. Another parent reported more emotionally overt behavior from her daughter—fun and giggling one minute; the next, crying or slamming a door about something so seemingly incidental as someone having used her hairbrush. These kids sleep with their teddy bears and worry about dating all within the same few hours. She may want to cuddle one evening and the next close her door and want total privacy.

If your teen's self-concept, at any age, does not match what he sees in the mirror, he may go into a tailspin, and moodiness is the result. For him, moodiness is part of the preoccupation with how he looks. Boys can worry excessively about their physiques and girls their figures. Remember what it was like to open your mouth and wonder if what came out would be a voice or a squeak? Or to look in the mirror one morning and see a stranger whose clothes were too tight and who had a big zit in the center of her chin? These kids feel that they have no control over what's happening to the most intimate parts of themselves. These changes happen faster than they can adjust to.

Both boys and girls experience mood swings. Some begin as early as age nine, while others show only barely discernible signs, ever. Your teen's temperament will probably influence how she will manage. One mother described her fourteen-year-old as a spirited girl. *"Leslie has always been a more intense, more persistent, perceptive, and extremely sensitive girl. Her mood swings initially were stronger than her older sister's. She is learning to manage them."*

Your young teen's mood swings may seem unbearable to you, but just think how it feels to her. You have perspective; she doesn't. She is under the sway of her hormones. To feel suddenly out of control can be confusing and scary. Often a teen in the middle of a temper tantrum knows all too well that he is acting foolishly, yet he is unable to stop himself. This is embarrassing.

Many teens at age sixteen or seventeen, who are aware of their emotional surges, learn to recognize and understand them and sometimes can calm themselves and feel in better control. Frequently these surges are related to the menstrual cycle. An older teen may be irritable and yell at her parent, and in five minutes apologize for her loss of control.

You must be the solid wall that your teen can lean on, cry on, or bang his head against. His moodiness may appear to be laziness and annoy you terribly. He may complain of boredom. Through it all you must be there for him, both caring and firm. You need to be like an air traffic controller, constant and dependable even in the worst weather conditions to assist with your teen's takeoffs and landings.

WHAT TO SAY AND DO

Stay calm. All adolescents are self-absorbed. *"I hate Mom"* usually means discouragement or confusion: *"I'm only trying to figure out who I am."* As aggravating as he may be, he needs you to understand that underneath his behavior is a feeling he hasn't identified, may even be afraid of, and certainly doesn't have control over at this moment. Do not attempt to soothe him when his emotions are high. Help him identify or acknowledge his feelings: *"Reggie, you're really edgy. I'm a little confused. I made a suggestion and you threw your books. What's going on?"* He may be able to talk or he may need time out. *"Maybe you can get in touch with what's going on. You cannot throw books."*

Respect her need to be alone even if you feel rejected. She needs to have her space and the family needs to allow it. She needs time to consider. Do not label her. Calling her a "grouch" will only worsen the situation. Do not take her comments personally. Detach yourself when she calls you names or criticizes you. When she shouts, *"You don't love me,"* or, *"You're the meanest—"* stay calm. Say, *"Mindy, this isn't about love, this is about getting your laundry out of the dryer."*

Try to keep it light. In other words, do not get sucked into the moodiness or be manipulated by it. Sometimes you can distract her with gentle nudging. Do not take responsibility for her mood. She may try to manipulate you, but rescuing her from a difficult situation will not help her grow up.

Do not let her mood affect how you treat your other family members. It's so easy to take out your frustrations on your spouse or other children even though they don't deserve it. Your teen will probably seek more attention and notice the power of her mood swings if you overreact. Keep your cool.

Stop her from hurting her siblings. Address the action by stating the family rule: *"Liza, those words hurt. That's not okay. You'd better cool off for a while."*

PREVENTIVE TIPS

Self-absorption is a developmental stage. It often may make her unhappy and limit her patience and her understanding of the world. Encourage her to find ways to help others, such as through volunteer work or doing good deeds for a neighbor. She may be fragile and volatile right now, yet she is also strong, good-hearted, and insightful.

Moodiness can be addressed with patience, understanding, and distracting activities. What are his natural talents and skills? What interests him? After-school sports or classes in painting, jazz dance, or karate might provide satisfying outlets.

Ask questions to make her think: *"How do you feel about this?" "What do you think about this?"* She will learn that these are two different processes, both of which should be involved in decision making.

Don't rescue him. He will make some bad choices along the way and may be upset. To live with disappointment and consequences is an important life skill to learn. You cannot fix it for him. *"Alan, I can't undo what happened, but I wish I could make it easier for you. I'm here to talk when you want."*

Whether hurt by a friend, discouraged by a teacher's comment, or coping with bad hair days, she feels everything intensely. Do not offer a chocolate sundae or take her shopping for new clothes. Instead, help her to identify her feelings, sympathize, and problem solve with her.

Give her a journal and encourage her to write her private thoughts and ideas. This will help her to get in touch with her feelings and to decide what she believes is right.

At a good talk time, help her understand what is happening to her, both physically and emotionally. Understanding emotions is the first step to controlling them. Be available: *"Jeanne, so much is happening with you now. Anytime you want to talk to me, I'm here."*

Moodiness can be related to self-esteem. Help her understand that self-worth is not the same as appearance. Instead of focusing on how pretty she is, compliment her grace, her strengths, her efforts, her internal qualities: *"Your smile is so infectious! People gravitate to you because they know you care."* Teach her to look within herself for validation.

Find time to be alone with your teen. Invite him to lunch, or maybe a short drive out of town to allow for some good talk time. Just because your son is older does not mean you should stop your routine nighttime talks. Replace the bedtime story with listening about his day, without judging or criticizing: *"What was your favorite part of the day? What was the hardest part?"* And remember, he will talk more when you stop talking.

Comment often on what he does right, and be specific: *"Andy, I liked the way you offered to help the lady in the parking lot. I bet you made her day."*

Encourage positive peer relationships. Don't tease about boy-girl friendships being more than just that.

You need not take responsibility for his moods. Don't let your guilt get in his way. The sooner he learns to manage his frustrations and gain control for himself, the happier he will be and the sooner the moods will disappear.

Casually leave a copy of the book *What's Happening to Me?* by Pete Mayle (New York: Carol Publishing, 1975) in her room. She may enjoy learning from it and even share it with her friends.

WHEN TO SEEK HELP

If your teen spends an unusual amount of time alone and brooding, if he does not have friends, or if you notice other changes in his behavior that concern you, it could indicate that he is overwhelmed by sad feelings and needs outside help for what could be depression. Ask your family pediatrician or school counselor for referrals.

See also: Body Image; Chapter 1, What Happens During the Teen Years; Counseling; Depression; Privacy; Stress; Suicide

MUSIC

"Dana keeps turning up the volume on her electric guitar, and now she's begun to play the drums in the school jazz band. I hope I can live through this."
"My dad can make me do anything for him if he threatens to take away my boom box. It's not fair!"

UNDERSTANDING THE SITUATION

Much of today's music is violent, has antisocial messages, and encourages drug use and unhealthy sexual contact. Police and parent groups have begun working to prove that these suggestive messages have a negative impact on teens' morals. Some researchers believe that music represents their inner world and their struggles with growing up and helps them to vent their emotions. In any case, it is important for you to listen to your teen's favorite music, and occasionally MTV, enough to be able to talk intelligently about it. It's fun when a parent can lighten up and find something good about her teen's music, while giving a clear message that not all of it is acceptable. He needs to hear your opinion, even if he doesn't agree with it.

Many adolescents sing in the school chorus or play in the orchestra or jazz band. Teens sing in church choirs, too, and take music lessons after school. Some teens form their own rock bands and practice in the garage or the basement. Neighbors may not like the noise, and limited practice hours may need to be set, but this is a healthy, creative process for your teen.

Like team sports, musical groups teach skills of coordination, timing, and concentration. Everyone has an important role and is depended on to do his or her part. This builds true self-esteem and experience in working with others.

In high school, music courses are often considered part of the fine arts curriculum. The skills used when playing an instrument—practice, practice, practice—transfer to other types of learning. Most competitive universities offer performing musical ensembles as accredited courses.

WHAT TO SAY AND DO

Do keep listening to your favorite music. Your teen may dismiss it as old-fashioned, but in time he may develop an appreciation, just as you did. Remember your parents' objections to your music when you were a teen?

Do keep listening to your own choice of music. Your teen may dismiss it as old-fashioned, but in time he will develop an appreciation, just as you did. Surprisingly, one father found that his daughter enjoyed the oldies station on the radio. He taught her some of the dance moves from the sixties, and she in turn taught her friends. This led to a Dad and Daughter Dinner Dance, which became an annual school affair.

Musical taste is a common battleground between parents and teens. To enjoy your teen's music might be an impossibility, and often battles ensue. But lighten up, loosen up, and try. Remember your own parents' objections to your style of music when you were a teen. Listen for the rhythm and fake a few quick steps.

He'll laugh, and you will, too. It's just not worth straining your relationship by fighting over music. Close his bedroom door or have him use earphones. However, as one school bus driver put it, *"My job got so lonely that I have outlawed earphones and Walkmans on my bus. The only time anyone spoke to me was when their battery went dead."* Agree on times to promote conversation.

If your teen is at all musical, encourage her to become involved in music lessons, an organized group such as a school chorus or a choir, or even musical productions, perhaps through school or a theater group. Knowing how to play music and being able to sing can provide lifelong satisfaction. Alida enjoyed singing in a local youth choir when she was thirteen, and ten years later she decided to sing again. This led to a master's degree from a conservatory of music, and then, much to the surprise and pleasure of her family, a job with a local opera company.

Support school music programs. These programs, which generally gain popularity in junior high school, are a healthy diversion for teens who have musical talent. Band teachers love to turn on new students; it is a mark of success for them. Unfortunately, in some public schools, music isn't considered a cool thing to do. When parents organize fund-raisers for performances, travel to competitions, recitals, and so forth, music becomes a more desired elective. One band teacher, with parent fund-raising and chaperon support, traveled twenty-five hundred miles with his high-school jazz band to audition and play at Disneyland. It was cool to belong to that band!

Don't be afraid to let go of your dreams for her and allow her the space to explore new musical interests. Leah had played piano since she was eight. At fourteen she wanted to drop piano for the flute because she felt that the piano was socially isolating. This lament is often heard by piano teachers, as the piano generally is not a part of the popular school band. Encourage her to explore what works for her. Given the freedom to spread her wings, she may well rediscover the piano at a later date: *"Leah, you don't have to be a concert pianist to receive great enjoyment from your talents. You play well and will never forget how. It's something you will always have inside you."*

Encourage outside performing. If your son is talented, help him come up with ways to perform in public and possibly even earn money. With other musical friends, he may volunteer to play at nursing homes during holidays. This could lead to starting a band. Neighbors may want him to give music lessons to their children. Performances and small jobs enhance self-esteem.

Mistakes made in public can be mortifying. Support the effort and downplay the off notes: *"Evan, everyone makes mistakes. This isn't your first and it won't be your last. I'll bet your band teacher has a few stories to tell about his mistakes. In a few days you'll be able to laugh at this, even though you feel embarrassed now. I think everyone did very well tonight."*

PREVENTIVE TIPS

Expose your teen to all types of music. Try a family picnic at a bluegrass or country-western event. Some communities offer summer nights at the symphony. Let her bring a friend and introduce them both to new forms of musical expression.

OVERWEIGHT

"Everyone in our family is overweight. It must be in the genes. Rachel is out of luck; she'll have to live with being fat. But she eats when she's not even hungry. I worry so much because she has no friends."

"I wish she'd get off my back. I don't need my mom coaching me about my fat body."

UNDERSTANDING THE SITUATION

Being overweight can be devastating to a teen and very sad and worrisome for a parent. Teens may hoard and hide foods rather than eat in front of classmates and may lie about being hungry to avoid being labeled "piggy." The pudgy teen may feel less valued, left out, unlovable, and self-conscious around friends who are thinner. A discouraged teen is often depressed, angry, and sometimes very defensive. She greatly needs your love and understanding, and there definitely are ways to support her. It is wise, if not imperative, to begin by finding your own support system and seeking professional advice. Weight problems can be very difficult to deal with alone.

Statistics show that too many adolescents in the United States are overweight, the majority being female. We have become a very sedentary society—many of us seldom walk much farther than from house to car—and much of our population is at risk for obesity. We can talk on the phone from any room in the house; we can follow the world through the Internet; we can change channels without leaving the comfort of the couch. Though our inactive bodies need less fuel, we have more food than ever before at our fingertips. There are restaurants and fast-food stands on practically every block. You don't even need to get out of your car, just drive through.

Adolescents frequently become slightly overweight just before puberty because as hormones turn on, height and weight become out of sync. Parents tend to jump in too fast with concerns. There are lots of factors to consider. Some teens will grow as much as a foot in a couple of years, while others stay relatively short. Once girls establish regular periods, they generally do not grow more than an inch or so.

Compulsive overeating can be a very big part of overweight conditions. Obsession with food is as hard to deal with as any other addictive behavior. Teens with this problem eat for emotional reasons; eating provides comfort. It is not uncommon for these teens to feel bloated and have bowel irregularities. Hoarding or stealing food can also be a symptom of compulsive eating. Genetics are identified as being a contributing factor of many overweight conditions, but knowing this does not ease the embarrassment or address the health-related issues.

You can make a difference. If your teen is pudgy, he probably feels very discouraged. The last to be chosen for team sports, he has been considered slow physically and perhaps academically and has been teased unmercifully. And, whether you are overweight or not, you are uncomfortable with his weight. Do not give up. This is not a hopeless situation, but he does need your help. There is no room for guilt or blame; there is only room for looking ahead to some very positive solutions. When a teen sees her body slimming down, she experiences self-satisfaction.

WHAT TO SAY AND DO

Food issues often involve power and control struggles that may have started in early childhood. Your physician can recommend a good nutritionist or counselor to work with both of you so that you can get out of the middle. Few families can accomplish this alone. Diet centers may not be right for your teen because most of them don't address teen self-esteem issues and do not always promote lifelong healthful eating habits. They typically push crash diets rather than a gradual, sensible weight loss of two pounds a week through healthy eating and proper exercise.

Overweight teens often need counseling to deal with depression, assertiveness, coping and stress management, and various social skills. The following suggestions may work better when coupled with professional support. That may be your first step.

Be very careful not to make critical comments that your teen might interpret as, *"I am a bad person,"* or, *"I am not doing enough."* You may think it is helpful to make comments such as, *"You are what you eat"; "That crust will look better on the birds than on you"; "You're fat—why are you eating that?"* But if you say these things or even point out the eating problem, she will only feel worse and eat more.

Help your teen accept family characteristics. Be positive, and stress the importance of healthy bodies. *"Ellen, the women in our family do have rounder hips. We are destined to carry more weight. This doesn't mean doom and gloom because fat runs in the family. We just have to accept and live with our body type. It may mean we have to work harder than the Twiggy types, but we can lower the amount of fat we eat and we can exercise to firm and tone our muscles and have very healthy bodies."*

Model a good eating and exercise program just as is recommended for your teen. This may mean changing your lifestyle. Don't expect her to do this alone. Families can plan vacations that involve exercise and good eating, such as bicycle trips, walking tours, wilderness hikes, dude ranches, and so forth. Exercise vacations are usually affordable, especially if you plan them yourself or with another family.

Few young teens are put on diets. Generally, because they are still growing, it is recommended that they increase exercise until they stabilize their weight. For older teens, the weight loss recommendation is one to two pounds per week, no more.

Avoid old power struggles by establishing new approaches. Discuss the following techniques with your teen and a nutrition counselor. These suggestions have worked for many, yet they may require individual tailoring.

Stop nagging. Your teen can set a long-range goal for exercise, making a contract with herself to reach that goal in small steps and designing a monthly calendar with regular "appointments" for exercise. For example, Jenny's goal was to walk four miles in one hour, three times a week. She planned to start the first week walking twenty minutes a day and build up to her goal within a month. If she missed an "appointment" marked on her calendar, she agreed to make up the time later that week.

Add incentive. Invite a friend to walk with or offer to walk a neighbor's dog for companionship. Added support helps with the commitment to the goal. Establish a personal reward for reaching this goal. Parents can support a ski trip, ice skating, bowling, a movie, an audiotape, and so on for goals reached.

Encourage keeping a journal. Some teens do well recording their routine exercise and their feelings, and some like to record what they eat.

Make rules about where to eat in your home. Everyone must abide by the rules. For instance, eat only when sitting at the dining table. This eliminates mindless snacking in front of the refrigerator or the TV.

Brainstorm noneating activities, other than television, that do not involve eating: vacuuming, dancing to favorite music, walking to Grandmother's house, and so on.

On the refrigerator, post a "starved or stuffed" scale from 1 to 10, with 1 being starved and 10 being stuffed. The goal is to stay between 3 and 7 on the scale. The idea is not to get to the starving point and not to eat until stuffed.

Think of food as a fuel, not as a pastime. Teach your teen the following awareness technique, in which he must answer the questions:

- Why do I eat? (Is it because of hunger or a feeling such as boredom, hurt, anger, etc.?)
- What do I eat? (Is it sweet, junk, etc.?)
- With whom and where do I eat? (Some eat nervously when out with other people; others are "closet eaters" alone at home.)

Eat "bad" food, too. Savor it. Eat a small portion and decide that will be all for today or for this week. Guilt is counterproductive.

People who have problems controlling their anger are encouraged to learn which emotion triggers their temper. Often it is embarrassment or hurt feelings. Similarly, people who have developed poor eating habits frequently eat when they are bored or frustrated. Food "feeds" the emotions as much as it feeds the body. The chart that follows may help to sort out the emotional triggers for unhealthy eating patterns. If patterns can be identified, then they can be understood and dealt with.

TUFF CHART

"It is TUFF to think about what we are feeling when we go
to food for comfort."

Time?	**U**tter event!	What **F**eeling?	What **F**ood sought?
11:00 A.M.	stayed home	bored	another bowl of cereal
11:20 A.M.	can't find cat	frustrated	chocolate pudding
2:15 P.M.	date canceled	unlovable	chocolate chips
4:30 P.M.	prep for class debate	anxiety	cold pizza
all night	slumber party	"partying"	chips & dip, ice cream, and much much more

PREVENTIVE TIPS

Many experts recommend reducing television time to an hour a day. Watching TV is a sedentary activity that promotes snacking, and commercials whet the appetite.

Take time to listen to your teen. He needs to share his feelings.

You can't fix bad feelings, but you can listen and acknowledge that you care. This may help him be more accountable, and he may decide to make some needed changes.

At a good discussion time, ask him if he would like some ideas for healthy eating. He may rather read a list than hear you tell him.

Parents can do many things to help:

- It is important to break the snacking habit because it typically leads to skipping meals. Invite your teen to eat at mealtimes, no matter what he has been snacking on, so that he will not be hungry before the next meal and snack all over again.
- Make nutritious meals and eat together as a family. Offer everyone the same foods. How much a person eats is as important as what he eats. For some, using smaller plates is a helpful trick.
- Always have fruit available for snacks and do not provide potato chips and other high-fat junk foods.

American children too frequently do not get enough exercise. Become an activist in your community. Push for better physical education programs in the schools, at all age levels, and for more sports in the community.

Most overweight teens feel very self-conscious playing sports, but creative ways to get exercise can be found. She can walk home from school rather than ride the bus, or get an after-school job walking dogs for people who work late.

School lunches and vending machines are often filled with fatty junk foods. Check out your teen's school. Become an advocate for healthful snacks, drinks, and lunches.

Know what approach the coaches at school use when a teen is overweight. Lindsey came home crying when she was dropped from the first-string basketball team because, in front of her entire team, the coach said she was *"slowing down these days because of too many Quarter Pounders."* Such harmful approaches need to be addressed. If this happens to your teen, see the school counselor or the principal.

WHEN TO SEEK HELP

Overweight affects self-esteem, not to mention physical health. Teens are especially vulnerable to hurt feelings, which can lead to depression, isolation, and self-pity, which in turn can lead to more eating. Such cycles are very destructive and difficult to break. If you suspect this is happening to your teen, talk to your doctor or a professional counselor, or perhaps a nutritionist.

Compulsive overeating is a serious condition that can be recognized by obesity and by a general sense that food has become a substitute for dealing with uncomfortable feelings and difficult situations. Depression usually accompanies overweight conditions and is a large component of compulsive eating. As with bulimia and anorexia, antidepressants can make a big difference when used in concert with therapy. Seek professional help.

See also: Counseling; Depression; Eating Disorders; Mealtimes; Stress

PARTIES

"She's going to another party tonight! She flips out when I tell her I need to know if the parents will be home. She says that I don't trust her and that I'm the only parent that checks up on their kid. She can make me feel terrible."

"My parents actually called Joseph's parents to see if they were going to be home. I was so mortified. I have the worst parents!"

UNDERSTANDING THE SITUATION

Every time your teen leaves the house for an evening out, you fear for his safety. Parties are a big part of the adolescent scene, and you're smart to be concerned about what happens, especially at unchaperoned ones. Teens often don't know when to stop, especially when alcohol or other drugs are being used.

Teens naturally want to be with their friends and free of adult supervision. They want to party on their own, away from the family. Since you cannot lock your teen in a box, your challenge is to help her plan safe entertainment and to use good judgment in unsafe situations.

Some parents conveniently leave so that their teen can have more fun at home with her friends, figuring she's safer there. Wrong! Teens have party-finding antennae. Some may arrive with hard liquor and drugs. As a result, there may be unwanted sex, vomit-stained carpets, and sometimes 911 calls. Teens high on alcohol or other drugs will do things they would not otherwise do. Often, party crashers don't even know whose house it is and have no compunction about damaging things or stealing;

they are anonymous. If your teen is the victim, she may be too frightened to call the police, scared for herself and protective of her peers and embarrassed at having lost control. If police come, the teens take off, driving while intoxicated. By law, you are liable. Such situations have the potential to become a tangled web of emotional, legal, and safety issues.

"Stuff" happens at unchaperoned parties. You need to talk with your teen about the realities. You need to express your love for her and your concern for her and her friends' safety and your liability. It is illegal to serve alcohol to minors, ever, even in your own house. Don't demonstrate poor judgment. Your child should not give or attend unchaperoned parties.

When dealing with these kinds of problems, sometimes you think, *"Oh, for this just to hurry and pass!"* Keep the faith. It does pass. Someday your twenty-something-year-old will tell you about all that went on when you were unaware. You'll be glad that you didn't know then—you may still not want to know, even now—and glad that you continued to set limits and parent with firm and loving support.

WHAT TO SAY AND DO

Family rules are designed to protect. One respected high-school principal's advice to parents was, *"Never leave your teens alone in a home over a weekend without mature supervision. 'Stuff' happens in empty houses. Never knowingly let him go to an unchaperoned party. Always call the parents who are hosting the party, and know whom your teen will be with."*

Consequences must be clearly stated and agreed on in advance. He knows the rule: no unchaperoned parties. Have him sign a contract stating where he will be and with whom and that he'll call if plans change. This way, you avoid *"I told you that I'd be . . ."* And there can be no argument about the consequence. *"Margo, it was signed and agreed. Since you chose . . ."*

Parties need ground rules. If there is to be a teen party at your home, with kids whom you don't know, agree to rules before the party.

All guests hand over their car keys when they arrive
No one may return once they have left
No alcohol or other drugs
Upstairs is off-limits
Inform neighbors about party
Agree to the volume of music
Everyone leaves by midnight
Parents will be called to pick up out-of-control teens

Talk about party dangers with your teen so that she is comfortable calling you to come get her if she finds herself in an uncomfortable situation. Agree not to punish her if she shows responsibility for her safety. It will be a learning experience.

Encourage teens to plan active parties. You might include ball games or other sports or competitive dance teams, ending with prizes and a "barbecue banquet." Put them in charge, even of the cooking.

Peer pressure may be the reason your teen wants a large party. If so, he will probably be relieved when you say, *"I'm not comfortable hosting a huge party. If you want a dozen or so friends over to have a barbecue, I'm all for it."*

Establish limits with your teen regarding overnight parties. Coed overnight parties are common in high school, held at hotels, in parks, and at other places where parents are not present. It is a way to be with friends, use alcohol and other drugs, and feel totally independent from authority. You may feel, *"It's okay. We did it when we were kids."* Rethink that attitude. The potential for violence and legal ramifications are greater today. In many states, hotels are required by law to have a parent, or a person of legal age, sign for responsibility. You and the hotel will be held liable for any illegal action if the room is given to minors. These are laws that are intended to keep teens safe. Here is a good opportunity to be a responsible parent, rather than an overindulgent one.

PREVENTIVE TIPS

Parents need to network. Organize as a community and meet at the high school. Create common ground rules for your teens. The parents who allow unchaperoned parties may not choose to attend your meetings, but you will influence the community at large and empower your teens to find healthy entertainment. Warning: Do not allow parent meetings to include stories about any specific teen. If you say something about your son, it will get back to him, and he will be rightfully upset that you have violated his privacy.

Community centers and Boys and Girls Clubs are great places for casino nights, dances, and pool or basketball games. Teens need safe places where they can hang out together.

Educate both the parent and the teen populations. One very effective parent group sponsored a panel that was presented first to the teens at assembly at school, then was repeated for parents in the evening. The panel consisted of a lawyer, a doctor, a chief of police, a psychologist, and a parent. Each had very interesting information and presented it in a matter-of-fact manner. The lawyer talked about the legal ramifications of unchaperoned parties, the doctor explained the adolescent body's reaction to alcohol, the psychologist discussed developmental ramifications for teens who drink and use drugs, and the parent told of the lawsuit filed against him because of an unchaperoned party at his home, which had cost him his home and the money that would have paid for his teen's college education.

Allow teens to take as much responsibility as possible in planning their parties. This way, they feel more in control and can take pride in their efforts.

Post house and party rules where they can be seen.

Keep family alcohol out of sight. Know which inhalants are in vogue, such as the innocent-looking aerosol whipped cream and various breath sprays.

Be ready to step in if things begin to get out of hand. Call 911. Police are great reinforcement. Remove car keys if drinking or drugging is involved.

Never leave a party of teenagers alone in your house. If you are on vacation and leave your teen at home alone, tell the neighbors how long you will be away and who is expected at the house. Your teen needs to know where to get help in an emergency, and your neighbors need to be available to help out.

Offer alternative types of parties. Be creative, and invite her to plan with you. Offer her tickets to a play and treat a couple of good friends to pizza before the play. If you can afford it, your money is well spent. Take a few friends camping and offer a cake at the top of a mountain. Sign a group up for a ropes course, or encourage them to go to a local sports store or gym where they can learn to rock climb on a wall. Some parents rent space at a bowling alley, an ice-skating rink, or an indoor-soccer building.

Girls just entering high school will be under pressure to date older teens. This is not wise, especially when parties are involved. At their young age, they generally are not ready to withstand the peer pressures to use alcohol and other drugs or to have sex. Freshman and sophomore girls are more vulnerable because they want to go along with the crowd in order to be accepted.

WHEN TO SEEK HELP

When you feel you have lost control, you know she doesn't listen to you, and she is obviously attending many unsupervised parties, start with her school. Talk to the principal and the school counselor. They may direct you to parent support groups formed for just this purpose—to put a stop to unchaperoned parties.

If you suspect your teen is attending unchaperoned parties where alcohol and other drugs are being used, take her for an alcohol and drug assessment. This is a good time for parent networking. Let other parents know what you have learned and what you are doing. This is proactive parenting.

See also: Alcohol and Other Drugs; Chapter 3, Tools of the Trade, Parent networking; Graduation; Rebelliousness; Safety; Sex, Talking About; Sneaking Out

PETS

*"It seems that Argus is the only one Robin will talk to.
I'm so glad we have him."*
*"I can't believe she gave him away. He was my best friend.
I'll never forgive her!"*

UNDERSTANDING THE SITUATION

People are social beings. We seek others for company, comfort, and security. There's a sense of completion to know someone is with you. As teens grow into adulthood, their peers become exceedingly important, providing proof of acceptance and belonging. For many kids, pets have much the same role. A dog can be a true companion for a teen needing a solitary walk, when walking alone may feel awkward. Animals of all kinds allow teens to be alone without being lonely.

For some teens, pets help to bridge the gap between youthful dependency and a more adult, independent lifestyle. They can be a stabilizing and moderating presence during difficult times. They can listen to a crying teen and offer back their silent, total acceptance—just what the upset teen needs most. Ask a teenager what his pet means to him. Jane said, *"My cat is like an extra friend. He calms me down when I'm upset and is always there. He's the definition of companionship."* Another teen said, *"I don't have many friends to do things with, but my dog and I go everywhere. I couldn't be anything without my dog."*

Pets fill a gap especially for teenage boys who feel they must play a macho role in order to be accepted by their peers. *"My teenage son is 'in love' with his kitten. He even cleans the litter pan without my telling him. It's such a surprise to see him so happy with something so small."* One never truly knows how important an animal can become for a teen, or for anyone else. A kitten or puppy allows expression of soft fuzzy feelings without fear of ridicule—it is okay to cuddle and talk baby talk. When the pet grows up, the two are pals. Pets can be a comfort when things go wrong, never talking back or saying the wrong thing at the wrong time. A cat's purr is calming. Friends may come and go, but Buster is constant. Even the fish silently swimming in the tank send a message: *"It'll be okay. When things get tough, just keep swimming and it will work out."*

Pets offer opportunities for learning how to interact with other living things. Animals need their privacy and use body language to communicate it. A turned head and refusal to make eye contact means, *"I'm not in the mood. Leave me alone."* Family members need to respect these subtle signals. The drop of a ball at your feet is an obvious signal: *"I want to play!"* As Tammy retrieves the Frisbee, the family argues over whom she loves the most. Cats are more independent than dogs, and it's fun to watch them as kittens and to hold them when they grow up.

Teens who have allergies to fur need not be deprived of pets. Geckos, fish, snakes, and salamanders can fill the bill. They may not greet you at the door with wagging tails, but they offer a sense of peacefulness and opportunities to learn about responsibility and the characteristics and behaviors of another species. A pet snake can be of comfort sitting on your teen's warm shoulder while he does his homework. This can actually be helpful for schoolwork. There are many other positives, despite the need for frequent cage cleaning.

One father described how important his daughter's horse had become. Through taking lessons and training her horse to jump, she gained confidence in herself and her ability to control a large animal. She said, *"I would never use drugs because my judgment might be affected and it could cause my horse to get hurt while jumping. It's up to me to help him do it, and the timing is everything."* Her attitude toward the use of alcohol and other drugs changed drastically, and her grades went up. Her father felt very good about supporting the expense of the horse.

A teen's first experience with death may be the death of her pet. Accidents, old age, and euthanasia are of great concern. The issue of quality of life versus length of life must be confronted. A good veterinarian will offer a professional opinion and helpful solace. Allow for ceremonies. Grieving must be encouraged. A lifelong pet is very important to a teenager, and her sadness demands respect. If her loss is made light of, it may influence how she processes future losses, including human ones. (Please read the section titled Losses and Grief for more discussion on teens' sensitivity to deaths of pets.)

WHAT TO SAY AND DO

Before bringing a pet home, make agreements about pet responsibilities. A dog is unimaginably comforting to the teen coming home to an empty house after school. However, the teen must be responsible for some of the care of the pet. Dogs are high maintenance. They live with us, bond to us, and depend on us daily for food, exercise, and love.

Hold a family meeting. There is an age-old scenario: *"It is your dog. You wanted it, and now I'm the only one feeding and exercising it. We have a problem!"* Perhaps the role of the pet needs to be examined periodically. Whom is it helping? Has it become a family pet, important to everyone? Who pays for the license? Who pays for the annual immunizations? Should this be a family responsibility, with everyone giving up a few allowance dollars for the dog's needs? Is it important for one member of the family to maintain ownership?

Dogs, especially, need a lot of training, and it should be started as soon as the animal is brought home. This takes time and commitment from everyone. Someone needs to take responsibility for the puppy's training in the house and, if possible, in obedience classes where he will learn how to behave outside the home. He needs to be socialized, thoughtfully, and often before he gets beyond the impressionable puppy age. The whole family must learn the same commands so that he doesn't get confused during his training.

PREVENTIVE TIPS

Planning to adopt a pet? At the family meeting, write down your needs and restrictions regarding a pet. It can be disappointing, even disastrous, to make a wrong choice.

Not all dogs and cats have the right temperament for all households. Kirsten's cat was always hiding, never venturing out in their very active, loud household of three teenagers. After several accidents under Kirsten's bed, a decision was made to find a new home for this very skittish cat. Adopted by a single older woman who lived a solitary, peaceful life, the cat adjusted almost immediately, playing with cat toys in every room and jumping happily onto her new owner's lap for petting. The cat was dearly loved, and Kirsten's tears turned to delight for her cat's newfound comfort.

Before giving up a pet, be sure to discuss it as a family and listen carefully to everyone's comments. Although you may not understand the terrific attachment your teen has to his pet, it can be a significant loss and needs to be handled with sensitivity and care.

WHEN TO SEEK HELP

A teen who is cruel to an animal needs professional attention. Teens who have serious problems with the law, abuse others physically or sexually, or light fires, often show signs of cruelty toward helpless animals in their earlier years. Seek help immediately.

A teen who fears dogs or other animals may benefit by consulting a dog trainer who can interpret animal behaviors. Understanding may be all that is required. She doesn't have to own a pet, but since animals are everywhere, she should feel that she can handle being near them. If your teen has a phobia in one part of her life, there are likely to be others as time goes by. Seek professional treatment before it becomes a bigger problem.

See also: Chores; Friends, Left Out; Losses and Grief

PRIVACY

*"Caitlin wants total privacy. She's never been so withdrawn.
She doesn't want me in her room, she doesn't want me
around her friends, and she won't let us help her with
homework. I can't even comfort her like I used to."*
"I just need space, and my parents are always in my face."

UNDERSTANDING THE SITUATION

One of the first signs of adolescence is the need for privacy.
Parents report, *"Her door is always closed. I feel like a total
stranger."* While you may feel rejected, privacy is important as
she learns to cope with the many changes affecting her. Few
young teens tolerate company in the bathroom as they used to.
As her body changes, she needs privacy to adjust, and hours in
front of the mirror behind closed doors.

As the hormones kick in, privacy can help to calm an emotional teen. Some kids do this naturally very well, while others
need directing. Privacy offers space and time to "just be" with
new feelings and to learn to cope. There is no substitute for an
understanding parent's listening ear; however, it needs to be
combined with alone time. Offer to listen if he wants to share,
but be aware that alone time is also of great help.

Privacy is needed for good thinking. Your teen is now doing
more abstract thinking, and thinking for himself. His thoughts
are not so readily shared with parents. Besides, he wants to "do
it" on his own. Respect his need for privacy. Not to do so is an
invasion of his privacy.

And last but not least, privacy is needed for social adjustment. Peer groups are demanding. The telephone becomes the

tool for working on important matters, privately. Many teens don't want you even to ask who the caller is.

Although your teen needs space—for you to get "out of her face"—she also needs you to be near when she comes for comfort. The junior-high and high-school years are not the time to get out of her life, as she might indicate by insisting on her privacy. You need to stay in the perimeter, active in the surroundings. Be a fly on the wall.

WHAT TO SAY AND DO

The family meeting is a good time to discuss rules and boundaries regarding privacy. Younger siblings are probably not aware of the teen's need and may easily feel rejected as the older sibling demands more time alone.

You may need to direct an angry, tired, or frustrated teen: *"Ben, you've been irritable and pushy with your brothers. Perhaps you need some space. Try relaxing with your stereo in the privacy of your own room."* Kids should know that privacy is needed to relieve tension.

Teens sometimes do not want to be near their parents in public, where their friends may see them. They want to be older, and separate from their parents, who make them feel babyish. Toby walked on the other side of the street with a, *"You don't understand. I don't want to be near you."* Let her do this. It is a normal part of the separation process. She wants a more independent life separate from her old one. You may feel rejected, but she needs space.

Asking him how his day went may get you a shrug and an "okay," with few if any details. He needs to keep his day to himself. Probably he is so inundated with feelings about what happened that it would be impossible for him to give you much of an answer. He needs time to digest it so he can figure it out for himself before he can explain it to you. Later, you might spontaneously learn more, but not if you badger him. Remain open and interested. Offer him something about your day. This is good modeling.

PREVENTIVE TIPS

Teach your teen that being alone can be a chance to refuel. This is different from being lonely or neglected. Teens need to learn to think about what is going on in their busy lives, time to set goals for themselves. This can be done while walking the dog, saying a prayer, writing in a journal or diary, or just "vegging out" to music as he lies on his bed.

WHEN TO SEEK HELP

Too much privacy may mean too little communication. When a teen is discouraged, or is involved with alcohol and other drugs or other high-risk situations, he may withdraw. If you suspect this is the case, you need to intervene. Watch for evidence and confront your teen. Use a support system. A close friend, an understanding relative, a clergy member, or a school counselor can help you decide what direction to take.

The need for privacy comes in short spurts. If your teen has withdrawn for a period of time and is not socializing with friends or involved with the family, he may be depressed. Seek help from a mental health professional familiar with adolescent depression.

See also: Depression; Friends, Left Out; Home Alone; Mood Swings; Pets

PUNCTUALITY AND WAKE-UP HASSLES

"Justin will not get up in time to get ready for school. I'm exhausted by the time the bus comes!"

"My mom thinks I have to get up hours before the bus comes. I only need fifteen minutes to get ready. What's her problem?"

UNDERSTANDING THE SITUATION

"Getting ready" hassles are universal. Teens are expert at staying in bed too long to catch the school bus, hovering by the closet trying on the fifth outfit of the morning, or just standing in front of the mirror, as you nag and threaten in the hallway. It's especially embarrassing when he holds up his friends' parents when they come to pick him up for some event. You may even try putting his clothes out for him, just as you did when he was seven. Nothing seems to help. Such hassles often start at night, as he stays up too late and you know he'll be impossible to rouse in the morning. No wonder your blood pressure rises.

No two teens are the same, and the causes of time-related problems vary. Temperament plays a big role. Some kids just can't be rushed. One mother said, *"I nagged her all her life. Now she's happily married, and she's still slow to start, but her husband doesn't mind. They seem to be a very productive young couple."*

If your teen is having difficulty getting up, she may be having problems with school. Generally, this occurs around transitions such as starting at a new school. Suddenly there are many changes and new expectations from new peer groups. When it seems overwhelming, your teen may just stay in bed.

In fact, teens need more sleep than they did during the elementary-school years. Notice what time your teen goes to bed. Attending parties on school nights, watching TV late at night, and using the computer are all great temptations but result in problems the next morning. Many experts feel we are a sleep-deprived nation, and bad habits can get well entrenched during adolescence.

Getting sucked into battle is a common pitfall. Ask, *"Why am I so caught up in this routine of getting him up?"* and, *"Whose responsibility is it to get up and go to school?"* Your teen must take on the adult responsibilities that are rightfully his. This may fit with other areas in which you are too involved: reminding him to write thank-you letters to grandparents, ironing his clothes because he hasn't time, or giving advances on his allowance.

If you've always awakened your child, nagged her out of bed, and seen that she's fed and makes the bus, she may rebel at assuming the responsibility: *"You don't even care!"* If she sees it as rejection or withdrawal, tell her, *"I care that you learn to take responsibility for yourself."* The transition from childhood to adulthood can be painful at times.

Giving your teen the responsibility for her punctuality will be easier for you if you also let go of *"What will they think when she's late all the time?"* When keeping others waiting and being late to appointments becomes a pattern, it can be attributed to rudeness and lack of respect for others. It is also selfish behavior. However, teens do not always see it that way. Help your teen become more aware of his actions and their impact on others.

Your teen will learn personal responsibility with your patient understanding. If you begin giving more responsibility to your younger teen, it will pay off in high school. And handling responsibility in high school will help her operate more successfully at college and in life.

WHAT TO SAY AND DO

Agree on a bedtime with your teen. By age thirteen, she should have a sense of how much sleep her body needs; however, guidelines are still needed. Agree to a bedtime. She may experiment with this freedom, but probably she will soon learn to go to bed at a reasonable time. If you don't nag over bedtime issues, you will avoid power struggles and she will learn to get her needed sleep.

Do not attempt to solve wake-up hassles in the morning when the bus is coming. When all is calm, hold a family meeting.

Let her know you understand how she feels: *"It must be terrible for you to have me badgering you for an hour every morning. You must be angry until lunchtime."* Then let her know, briefly, how you feel: *"Actually, I don't like myself very much when I do this. I hate beginning the day with anger."* Act bewildered: *"I guess I'm a little confused. Whose responsibility is school? Whose responsibility is it to remember to take last night's homework off the table? Whose responsibility is it to get up early enough to take a shower, dry the wet hair, iron a different shirt, and make lunch before leaving the house?"* Next, invite her to brainstorm solutions. Choose one that might work, agree to try it for a week, and set a time to meet for evaluation. You may have to do this several times during her teen years, as these problems seem to repeat themselves.

Kids who by nature are slow to get going in the morning may need to start earlier. Buy him an alarm with a snooze button, and tell him to set the alarm earlier to give himself more time. These kids need time to drift in and out of sleep as they wake up, more time to contemplate what to wear and what to eat for breakfast, more time to face the day in general. Suggest that he get organized the night before.

It is never too late to teach organizational skills. One fourteen-year-old girl hung a chart on her wall. After forgetting her clarinet several times, she relied on her morning list. Making lists helps teens as much as adults.

	Wake up	Dress	Breakfast	Activity	Chore	Remember
Monday	6:00 A.M.	xxx	xxx	Band	Dog	P.E. clothes, clarinet
Tuesday	7:00 A.M.	xxx	xxx	xxxx	Dog	English paper
Wednesday	6:00 A.M.	xxx	Meeting		Dog	Math assignment
Thursday	6:00 A.M.	xxx	xxx	Band	Dog	History test; research cards
Friday	7:00 A.M.	Drill uniform		Drill team	Dog	Team drills

Your teen should design this chart; do not do it for her. Merely introduce the idea: *"Ellie, would you like an idea to help you be on time and be better organized?"* She may reject it at first and decide to try it later. She may use it for a while, stop, and then pick it up again. This will work best if you do not force the issue. It is merely a suggestion.

Know your bottom line and be consistent. Fighting is no solution. If she tests you, say, *"Ellie, we made an agreement. As hard as it is for me, I would be doing you a great disservice to pamper you as I used to, and I'd be late for work as well."* She may have to be late to class a few times and suffer the consequences. Responsible adult life requires punctuality.

Compliment her when she does it right: *"Ellie, I love you, and it's so nice not to yell in the mornings."*

You may need to get up earlier, too. Be pleasant. If possible, take time to listen to what is on her mind. Compliment her on her choice of colors. Say, *"Thanks!"* when she puts her dish in the dishwasher, and, *"Good luck on your test."* She needs your positive attention more than you can imagine. Your goal is to turn past nagging into pleasant interactions.

PREVENTIVE TIPS

A positive family atmosphere is extremely helpful when motivating a slow-to-start teen. Is your morning a bleary-eyed, coffee-dependent struggle? If so, how can you make your morning brighter? Is something dragging you down? Are too many late nights making it hard to get up in time for his breakfast? What gets in the way of your being ready to face the day? Consider what personal and household changes you could make.

Watch your attitude toward being on time. How many times do you say to yourself, *"Oh well. I'll just be a few minutes late"*? Casualness can develop into callousness.

WHEN TO SEEK HELP

There may be a deeper issue. Does he have friends? Are others teasing him? Is he unhappy about going to school, trying to avoid tests or unpleasant teachers? Does this behavior belie the goals he has for himself? If he is suffering socially, he may be putting a lot of pressure on you. He needs your help. Talk to the school counselor or with teachers who are approachable and honest. If needed, seek professional help for you and your teen. To be isolated at this age can be unimaginably painful.

See also: Bullied; Bullying; Depression; Friends, Choosing; Grades and Homework; Losses and Grief; Privacy

REBELLIOUSNESS

"Each day I wake up with the hope that maybe she'll want to cooperate like she used to. She's demanding and pushing the limits. The battle ensues. She's so disrespectful. I'm scared. Sometimes I feel that I don't even like her anymore."

"My parents don't understand. They just want to control me. They treat me like I'm a little kid, and I'm not."

UNDERSTANDING THE SITUATION

Rebellion is a natural part of adolescence. It hits as suddenly as the terrible twos, those memorable years of saying *"No!"* to virtually everything. Both of these ages represent a time of separating; at two, he is saying, *"I want to do it by myself!"*; at thirteen, he is saying, *"I want to be me, my way."* It's hard for parents. He is challenging the status quo by acting out, and your feelings are hurt by his rude and disrespectful comments. You can't imagine why he dresses in those outlandish clothes, dyes his hair purple, and wants a tattoo. Chores are a battle. You become stressed trying to think of new ways to win his cooperation before you lose your temper. He won't play by the old rules, and he certainly doesn't hesitate to express ideas of his own.

Fortunately, not every teen goes through this stage in an obnoxious, offensive way. Some do their rebelling quietly, such as by attending a new church where their friends go. Some just subtly refuse to do as they're asked; for example, they let the muddy dogs in to leave footprints on the carpet. Others push the limits just as far as they can without causing too much disruption: *"He gave up his tennis, which meant so much to his father, and now he's trying out for football, which makes us both cringe. I think he's doing it just to express his independence from his father."*

Junior high school presents new opportunities for expression. One high-school senior recalled, *"I was really wild in junior high. I snuck out to date older guys and I started experimenting with smoking cigarettes and drinking. By the time I hit high school, I was sick of the parties and that boring life. I decided to work on my grades instead."* This girl feels that she was lucky—some of her friends have never stopped rebelling.

This is an age and a stage when you need to pick your battles carefully. It is easy to fall into the trap of becoming a critical parent, but it is much more prudent to let the small stuff go with a shrug, a laugh, or a joke. Instead of being critical, identify and enjoy, or at least tolerate, the curious ways of your changing teen. Concentrate on the important issues. Maybe he is cutting his hair in strange ways, but is he still pulling decent grades? If you try to control him, you may inadvertently push him closer to what you most fear.

Keep the faith. Your teen needs to hear everything you notice that is good about him, on a regular basis. Be specific and sincere.

WHAT TO SAY AND DO

Rebellious teens are hard to live with. Focus on what he does right. Even the most rebellious teen wants to please at some level. Comment on all that you see that is positive. There is always something! Find a way to send him off to school on a positive note, even if it means biting your tongue because he's wearing those baggy pants again or has left his room like a pigsty. *"Have a great day!"* Save your complaints and concerns for a specific meeting time when you both have had a chance to calm down and the playing field is level.

Rather than continue to nag, use the family meeting to discuss guidelines and to negotiate. Respect his need for privacy; a rebellious teen may prefer to have these discussions without siblings present.

Teens are very sensitive to comments and especially "vibrations" from others concerning their looks, actions, and opinions. Do not jump to conclusions too fast. His wearing his baseball cap in the restaurant infuriates you; it seems disrespectful and ill-mannered. You are sure that he wants to irritate you, but in fact he may feel that his hair looks disgusting and he would be mortified for anyone to see it. A teen's actions may not tell the entire story.

Keep calm through this acting-out phase. Look for the feelings and beliefs behind your teen's actions. She threw her backpack out the window, after her boyfriend took her best friend home from school, alone. Her purple hair doesn't mean she's using drugs; it's because she feels she's boring. When you stop nagging and start acting bewildered (*"Whoa, I don't understand . . ."*), you may help her begin to communicate the real issues. This leads to self-control.

Listen to your teen. Two of the most commonly heard complaints from teens are *"You never listen"* and *"You don't treat me with respect."* Stop what you are doing, establish eye contact, and give him your full attention. Reflect on what he may feel. *"You feel I don't treat you with respect."* Giving advice, judging, and criticizing are not listening.

Let the less important stuff go. Ask yourself a few questions: *"Is what's going on disrespectful or hurtful to others? Is it a moral issue? Is it a life-or-death issue?"* A strange haircut may be embarrassing to you, but it is not harmful. Don't worry about what others may think. Your positive relationship with your son is more important.

If mutually agreed-upon family rules are broken, bring out your written contracts. She will assume more responsibility for her actions. *"Crystal, you signed the contract, indicating you agreed to be home by eleven o'clock. It seems you've chosen to stay home next Saturday night."*

Do not make assumptions. The fact that she disobeyed the rule once does not mean she'll do it again. She needs to be held responsible for her actions, but you need to offer second chances.

When you grow frustrated with her behavior, do not start

your sentences with the accusatory, *"You always . . ."* Your anger "in her face" encourages a defensive reaction on her part. Sometimes, a knowing glance or a word or two are most effective: *"Marcie, the contract."* Your point has been made!

You can better tolerate rebelliousness when you keep your sense of humor. One father came home late one night and noticed that the lawn hadn't been mowed as promised. In exasperation, he told his son that before morning the lawn had to be mowed, and went grumbling off to bed. The next morning, when Dad looked out the bathroom window, he saw OK DAD mowed into the lawn, with the letters facing the window. He laughed all the way to work and bragged about his creative son's antics to anyone who would listen. Enjoy these moments. Harmless acts of rebellion are good medicine for all.

PREVENTIVE TIPS

Spending time with your rebellious teen may be the last thing you feel like doing. But do it anyway. Your goal is to find something you both enjoy and do it together. Don't assume that because you love golf, he will, too. Suggest going out to lunch. Initially, you may not even talk much, but if he likes the meal, he may agree to accompany you again. In time—it won't happen overnight—you'll find you have more and more in common and the silences will be less uncomfortable.

When you're feeling down about this strange kid who suddenly seems so distant, remember the good times you had together when she was younger. These times will return, eventually. Keep the faith! Always believe in her, and tell her so: *"Amelia, it's been tough for all of us lately. You belong to this family and we're here for you. We believe in you."* She may truly feel bad about herself and her behavior as a reflection of having low self-image. She needs your faith in her because her faith in herself is very low.

Decide together on rules and discuss consequences. For example, Janie has been leaving her curling iron on all day. Mom involved Janie in finding a solution. They agreed in writing: If Janie didn't remember to unplug it, it would be put away for a week. No nagging, no arguing.

Your teen may enjoy picnics, hikes, and camping trips with other families and their teen children. One mother claimed that the family overnights, weekend getaways, and week-long vacations, though complained about bitterly, helped to center her rebelling daughter: *"I'm glad we never gave up insisting she join us. She complained bitterly, yet each time she came with us, we all had a good time. It helped all of us by changing environments and being with different family friends and relatives."*

Structure family outings—to movies or plays, swimming, ice-skating, roller-skating, bowling, shopping, museums, and so forth—as well as staying at home with a good book, video, or game at least two nights a month. It is easy to capitulate and leave out your rebelling teen in order to avoid the complaining, but don't. Inviting one of her friends may make this time a little more tolerable for all.

Many teens seek thrills. Sports can offer these and also provide a balance; there are rules to be followed, and coaches demand conformity in ways that teens can follow, even when they are rebelling at home.

A few sessions with a family therapist to sort out teenage "stuff" can help to avoid desperate situations between you and your teen.

For more information on this topic, read *Parenting Without Pressure: A Whole Family Approach* by Teresa Langston (Colorado Springs: Naupress, 1994).

WHEN TO SEEK HELP

You need help when your teen's actions indicate disregard and disrespect for all family values, needs, and agreements. When serious discussions and consequences are not effective, you tend to feel helpless and to fear that you are "losing it." One mother said, *"I don't understand it. I've taken away all privileges. She can't drive, can't use the phone, can't go out on weekdays, and can't stay all night with anyone. She still defies our rules. I feel like giving up."*

This sad and alarming saga can be prevented. Before things get this far astray, see a professional family counselor or therapist who will work with your family to make necessary changes. If the situation is already out of control, it needn't stay that way. Positives can still happen. Though it may take incredibly hard work, this is not the time to give up!

Some teens rebel in the extreme. One mother complained, *"She's rebelling across the board. She's dressing like a whore, she's dyed her hair, her friends are new and wild, and she stays with them to avoid curfew; we know she's drinking, and she refuses to join the family for meals or activities. She's let her chores go and even let her fish die."* Teens who defy their parents on all levels and exhibit seriously destructive behaviors require professional help. If she does not get the necessary help, her future relationships in life are likely to be problematic, not unlike what is happening now in the home.

See also: Anger; Body Image; Mood Swings; Safety; Traditions

RUDENESS

"Gary just doesn't listen to me. It's like I don't exist; he shows no respect for me."
"She won't leave me alone. She bugs me, and she nags me with constant questions."

UNDERSTANDING THE SITUATION

If your teen's aloof and condescending attitude aggravates you, you are not alone. Many teens are noncommunicative; most are preoccupied. They tend to be rudest at home, less so with teachers, and rarely with friends. Sometimes it's silence in response to a question, or maybe a shrug of the shoulders. She may avoid family meals and instead take a piece of toast to the bathroom to eat while doing her eye makeup. You feel like you are forever cleaning up after her and meeting her many little needs, and when you get little or no response, you feel like a doormat—a nonperson.

Stop. Consider what is happening. Intellectually, you understand that teens often appear extremely uncooperative. You know that as he is in the process of developing his opinions about things, he wants to feel he can do it his way and doesn't have to go along with the status quo. But just as you dealt with his behavior respectfully at age two—when he stomped his foot and screamed, *"No!"*—you must deal with it now. He is struggling to shed his dependencies. To avoid the power struggles, you do have to give him some slack. You can decide what to do when he is disrespectful, but you cannot force him to show you respect. This phase will pass—someday! Too often these irritating situations are allowed to escalate into big fights. Do not enter the arena.

WHAT TO SAY AND DO

Be direct. Tell her what she is doing wrong, but do not attack her character. Use an "I" message. If she is sarcastic, do not mirror her attitude. You are the more mature, so don't stoop to rude behavior. Use, *"When _____, I feel _____ because _____, therefore _____."* For example: *"Alison, your behavior is rude. When you throw your dirty laundry in my face and tell me to wash it before morning, I feel angry enough to throw it back in your face. Ask nicely and I might surprise you and do you the favor."*

Stay calm. Vent your anger elsewhere. Then, at a good discussion time, try a problem-solving approach.

Begin by identifying his feelings: *"Pete, I understand that you feel the need for your space. Sometimes it must feel like we're always on top of you."* Briefly, let him know how you feel: *"We don't feel that you acknowledge us. We'd like to connect more. This is a give-and-take family. No man is an island."* Next, pose a question: *"What can we do to create an atmosphere of respect for all?"* This will help to begin a brainstorming process that may result in some new tactics for both sides.

Finally, let him know what you will do the next time his behavior is disrespectful or hurtful beyond tolerance: *"Drew, I will try to have reasonable expectations. However, when this becomes a problem, I will let you know, and I will stop cooperating with you. For instance, if I'm driving you to school, I will stop the car and ask you to get out."*

If others are disgusted by the way your teen is acting, ignore their comments. Grandparents' criticism can be the worst, because they don't want to see you being hurt or treated disrespectfully. If you hear, *"She's always getting her way. I don't understand why you tolerate it when she's so rude to you. You must be working too many hours,"* respond kindly: *"Thank you, Mom. I understand your concern, and I appreciate your noticing. I'm aware of what's happening and I'm working on it my way. Please, trust me. I love you for caring."*

PREVENTIVE TIPS

Rudeness can be a result of stress. Today's teens feel tremendous pressures and have high expectations for themselves, and some experience anxiety because of this. Some kids don't sleep well when anxious about something as simple as a vocabulary test. Acting out against the people they love most is safer than against their friends or teachers.

Share these tips on stress management with your teen:

- Take a ten-minute break, close your eyes, and listen to your favorite music.
- Take a warm, soothing bath or shower.
- Get physical. Throw some hoops, go for a run, or take a walk.
- Play with the dog.
- Throw rocks in the lake.
- Share your feelings with a trusted friend or family member.

- Ask someone for a back rub.
- Ask for space when you feel that you are being pushed.

Help him to recognize and respect his own boundaries. Few teens are aware of their limits. He may not know he is over-tired or too pressured until he loses control.

WHEN TO SEEK HELP

If typical bouts of rudeness become chronic and intense, you need support. Talk with another mature parent, a school coun-selor, or a therapist. Your teen may be feeling overwhelmed and need someone to talk with, too.

See also: Arguing; Bedrooms; Learning Problems; Mood Swings; Privacy; Rebelliousness; Stress

---

RUNNING AWAY

"Angela has never been an easy kid to live with; now she's run away! What are we going to do?"
"I can't stand my parents and their unreasonable rules. I've had it! Anyplace would be better than here!"

UNDERSTANDING THE SITUATION

Most parents have experienced a child's threat to run away. Indeed, many of us can remember packing our bags at age five and getting as far as the front porch. However, when a teen stops participating in family life, begins threatening to run away, or actually leaves home, things have gone too far. Your feelings of guilt, hurt, fear, and failure can be crushing.

Some reasons why teens leave home:

- He feels that the rules are too strict and allow no room for negotiation.
- She is distressed by a parent's negative or unhealthy behavior, such as an alcohol problem.
- He feels that he is the cause of family problems, such as his parents' arguing or pending divorce: *"If I weren't here, my parents wouldn't fight so much."*
- She thinks she'll do better away from a home environment that is unpleasant or abusive.
- He thinks "the grass is greener" in someone else's family: *"I'll have more freedom at Frank's house."*

Running away is usually an attempt to solve an extreme problem. Your teen may be rebelling over seemingly every issue and be terribly hard to live with, yet when he decides to leave home, you are thrown off balance. You may feel a momentary relief because the arguing has stopped, but mostly you feel terribly guilty and confused. You may relive the last few arguments and realize that you were not really listening to what she was saying or feeling.

Fortunately, most runaway teens run to a friend's house and return quickly. Most call to report that they are not only safe but going to school, keeping up on homework, and working part-time jobs. What a relief! All is not lost. Perhaps the break is okay; perhaps you can work this out.

If you are honest, once you hear your teen is safe, you probably admit to yourself that in the past you have thought, *"I wish she'd just leave,"* or, *"Can I kick her out?"* Do not let embarrassment or guilt outweigh your courage to face the problem now. If you have felt frustrated, so has your teen. She is trying to solve the problems by running away, especially if there are long-standing conflicts. You need support in order not to fall into the same old patterns again. Family and friends are imperative. All teens need adults other than their parents on whom to try out their ideas and from whom to receive feedback. These

adults can add perspective for all of you in healthful and helpful ways.

WHAT TO SAY AND DO

Tension between parent and adolescent is normal. If the atmosphere seems perpetually strained and the good times are rare, it
is important to ask yourself if you are minimizing how bad the
communication has become. Is your fear of admitting failure
outweighing the importance of the problem? Perhaps you and
your teen need a cooling-off period to regroup and to reconsider the problems. Look to your family and friends to be part
of the solution. They can invite your teen to come stay at their
homes for a while. They can offer some perspective. Give yourself space to think of alternatives.

If your teen threatens to run away, it is not helpful to say
sarcastically, *"Go ahead, I'll help you pack,"* though that is what
you may feel. Instead, use "we": *"I know we can work through
this. We have just taken a few too many steps in the wrong direction
lately. Let's admit we need a break from each other. Can't we stay in
the same house but not talk? We need someone to help us communicate
positively without fighting."* Keep the faith. Don't give up now.
Your child needs your strength.

If your teen does run, it feels like a catastrophe. You feel
rejected, and you are worried, angry, and unsure of what to do
next. Chasing after her to physically bring her home usually is
not helpful. Finding out where she is, so that you know she is
safe, is imperative. Some initial suggestions:

- Know your local laws. Think about where she might be and
  either call or go there. It is a crime in most states to harbor a
  child. It is not illegal to let a child stay at your house, but it is
  illegal to deny he is there when asked by a parent or police.
- Look in his school, parks, and teen centers.
- File a runaway report so that if your teen is picked up by
  the police, they will contact you. Police may provide an
  intervention, or you may insist on counseling as a condition

for her return. In some states you can refuse to have her returned home if you think you will have no control. The police will then have to place her in a receiving home until counseling is started.

- Have your teen stay temporarily with friends or relatives. Some communities have runaway-teen shelters associated with counseling agencies. This helps when emotions are high and tempers are heated.
- If you have had little success working out issues through family and friends, make an appointment with a counselor who works with teens. You may need a few sessions for yourself at this point.
- Meet at a neutral public location, such as a restaurant. This will help both of you to be polite and to listen to each other without losing tempers.
- Tell her that you love her even though you are having a hard time together. Your teen needs to know that you want her to come home and you love her despite all that is going on. However, a healthy break may be needed first.

Before your teen comes home, prepare for success. You both need time to heal and rebuild your relationship. It will not help to blame or accuse. To teach a puppy to come, you do not hit it for running away. *"Rory, I understand your feelings of hurt and anger. This is painful for me, too. I want us to learn to live together. We need to sort our stuff out with a counselor. Let's not go through this again."*

When a runaway teen, perhaps a friend of your daughter, comes asking to stay at your house, you may want to help but feel awkward. Be helpful. Allow her to stay the night as long as she agrees to call home first. Help her with what to say: *"I'm safe and am staying with the Johnsons. I don't want you to come get me. I need time to think."* Or, *"I don't want to tell you where I am, but I am safe."* Or, *"Joan's mom says I can stay here if we get counseling."* If the teen won't call, do it for her.

Teens who are angry and depressed and into alcohol or other drugs may run to the "streets." By this time communication has completely broken down and is hard to reestablish. Parents and teens may both feel like giving up. A word to the wise: Never give up. There may well come a time when your misguided and misunderstood teen wants to contact you. It may be during an emergency. Take advantage of this moment, and insist on drug rehabilitation or counseling, and welcome him home with clear expectations.

PREVENTIVE TIPS

Even if your child has never run away, chances are good that he has heard of or knows someone who has. Talk about what he thinks happened with that teen. Talk about what you would do in your family if things got bad between you. This is a good time to tell him that you will always love him very much—that even if the tension were awful between you and he felt he had to leave home, you would want him to let you know where he was and that he was safe.

At a good talk time, practice talking things out by finding a touchy subject between you and discuss your differences. Polish your listening skills. You may be driving your teen away with your directing, lecturing, criticizing, judging, or unwanted advising. Some teens like to shock their parents. Bite your tongue. Use reflective listening. Sometimes just a word or two will get him to start talking: *"Oh"; "Mmmmmm"; "I see, and then what?"* You are helping him to work out things on his own by allowing and encouraging him to think about his answers. Listen first. If you're dying to throw in your two cents, ask: *"Holly, would you like to know what I think?"* Be willing to accept *"No,"* and respectfully stay quiet.

Comment on whatever she is doing that is right. You can always find something. Save the other issues for problem solving at the family meeting. Try leaving notes when she isn't expecting it, such as in her lunch, in her bathroom drawer, on her pillow, and so on. Poems and other messages do make a difference. They don't have to be overdone. Just a line or two: *"I care about you"; "You are clever, and I enjoy your sense of humor"; "I believe you can do it. Go for it!"* If you know she is having a hard time, try: *"Hang in there!"*

WHEN TO SEEK HELP

Running away is an extremely difficult issue, and solving it when horns are locked is not easy. Your teen decided to work things out by leaving. Clearly, communication needs to improve. The longer your teen is away, the more difficult it may be to sort out problems. Seek help now from trusted friends, family, and professionals. The streets are a dangerous alternative.

See also: Alcohol and Other Drugs; Counseling; Lying; Mealtimes; Parties; Rebelliousness; Safety; Sneaking Out

---

SAFETY

"Margie is an accident waiting to happen. She has no concept of how dangerous that last escapade was!"

"My parents are so freaked out lately. They warn me about every detail of my life. I'm sixteen now and they still don't trust me!"

UNDERSTANDING THE SITUATION

"Drive-by Shooting Kills Innocent Teen." "Three Teen Athletes Killed in Car Crash." "Teen Paralyzed from Skiing in Marked Danger Zones." "Teen Party Ends in Tragedy." "Teen Raped in Parking Lot." Small wonder that the nightly news causes parents to panic. These are kids from good families. You know that bad things can happen to good people, and you worry about your teen's safety. Why is she so blasé?

One of the most challenging aspects of raising teens is dealing with their feelings of omnipotence, their attraction to fun and excitement, and their certainty that *"it won't happen to me."* When you worry, you may be ignored, mocked, or told just to bug off. Teens in fact do fear for their personal safety. Many have been exposed to a shooting at their school or in their neighborhood; they may have a peer who committed suicide; they may have seen a friend almost kill himself on a dare; and they too are confronted daily with the media reports of tragedy. In school, teens study safe sex, date rape, gun control, and so forth. However, awareness doesn't necessarily breed caution. Most teens will be the first to admit that in a crowd of peers, good thinking may not prevail.

You may be on the verge of panic over your teen's seemingly thoughtless, impulsive, dangerous behaviors. Teens typically feel invincible until something significant happens fairly close to home. *"Just this once, I can have unprotected sex. I know he would never give me something bad. I won't get pregnant—that happens to other people"*; *"I can drive fast without getting caught"*; *"I won't get caught shoplifting just this once,"* and so on. Teens do challenge authority and often "live for the moment." They do not always think rationally or consider the consequences of their actions. Almost every parent has heard, *"I never thought this could happen to me,"* after the fact.

Peer pressure often encourages risky behavior. For instance, a small group of seniors sneaked into the new science lab at school to have a drinking party during graduation week. This ended in the trashing of the lab, causing many thousands of dollars' worth of damage. In a group, a teen may do damage that he would never do alone. Being caught up in the moment and not wanting to be left out can dangerously replace moderation and good judgment.

This can be a truly scary time for a parent. The big mistakes hit the papers and make all teenagers guilty by association. Yet, do you read about the majority of teens who are making good decisions? Do you hear on the news about the twenty non-smoking teens who filled the smoking section in the restaurant so that no one who smoked could come in? Do you hear about the thousands of teens throughout the country who are earning community service credit, volunteering in Head Start programs, hospitals, elementary schools, and so forth?

Teens do engage in risky behavior, and most of the time the experience becomes an important memory and an important life lesson. Many parents will experience a dreaded phone call: *"Mom, I'm, er, I'm in jail."* Or, *"I'm Rosa's mother, and I have your son at my house. He's been drinking and shouldn't drive."* Or, *"Dad, I just had a little accident. I rolled the car."* We can all remember at least one risky encounter that taught us a life lesson. Maybe that's why we're so scared. We would rather our teens never have experiences such as ours, even though we are all the stronger for it. Your fear of "what would happen if . . ." should never keep you from believing in your teen. Your faith and trust in her are all-important.

WHAT TO SAY AND DO

Teens will grow from mistakes and poor judgment when asked to be responsible for their actions. Your teen needs you to support his being accountable, to help him find solutions to his problems, and to apply logical, appropriate consequences. Be strong, loving, and consistent. The police took Don's license from him for speeding with his friends in the family car. Mom and Dad decided that, in addition, Don was forbidden to drive with any of his friends until the revoked license was returned. Dad would drive him and his date to the dance. It takes strength to say, *"No, you can't drive with Ed. If you want to go, we'll drive you."* He needs firm guidance in order to learn from potentially life-threatening situations.

When your teen makes a mistake, do not lecture: *"If only you had listened,"* or, *"This is the last time . . ."* Above all, do not try to rescue or explain away her mistakes. Matter-of-factly say, *"Yup, you skipped class and got caught. What will you do about it?"*

or, *"The neighbor's car door was scraped with your skateboard. How do you think you should handle it? It will cost money to repair."* Let her struggle a bit and find the solutions. She will learn from the consequences. Overindulgence is not healthy. We often do this mistakenly in the name of love.

Watch for opportunities to use *"What would happen if . . ."* Imagining a dangerous situation and how to come out of it safely will give her self-confidence. It is hard to overcome peer pressure, which often sabotages common sense. The embarrassment of being different from the others is too painful for some teens. But when a friend has had too much to drink and is about to take the wheel, it is important to have the guts to say, *"I won't drive with you. I'll call my parents."* If you and your teen have discussed scenarios such as this, she's more likely to rise to the occasion to use her good judgment when needed.

Role-play something that has happened or could happen: *"Joan, pretend you're walking home from the bus and you are followed by three boys who are heckling you. What would you do?"*

Teens are apt to have fears. You need to use phrases such as, *"You can handle this,"* and, *"I know you can do it. I've seen you think through other difficult situations."*

Feel free to call the authorities, including 911. One thirteen-year-old girl and a friend were followed from the neighborhood store by three older male teens. The girls didn't look back, but one boy got in front of the girls and heckled, *"We're going to kill you. Are you scared?"* They ran to Julie's house. The heckling teens yelled, *"Good! Now we know where you live. We'll be back."* Julie's mother, after hearing the girls' story, called 911. The police came, took the report, and gave the girls a case number. The police assured them that they would trace the teens, starting with the store clerk who had seen the boys in the store. This was scary but ended up being a very educational and empowering experience.

If your teen has gotten into some trouble, a very effective first response is to show your love and concern. Anger is a typical reaction, but to display it is ineffective. Whether you have been worried or sick with fear, or are shocked by his actions, the bottom line is that you love him deeply. Stay calm. Ask him to take time to consider the situation and what the consequences might be, while you cool off and gather proper perspective. For example, Brock arrived home at six o'clock in the morning. Mom knew that he had not stayed with Scott all night, as he claimed. She remained calm and said, *"Brock, when I learned that you weren't with Scott last night and I didn't know where you were, I was really worried. I love you, and when I don't know that you are safe, I panic. You need to stay home the rest of the weekend so we can discuss what this means for future privileges. When I feel ready, we'll talk."* Brock waited impatiently and stewed over his actions as he missed a Saturday-night date. Mom calmed herself and got rid of her anger. This resulted in a productive discussion that covered setting limits regarding future driving privileges.

Take time to teach your teen, and try not to assume he will automatically know what to do. One father who skied a lot with his son, James, was amazed when the teen went through an avalanche warning sign with friends. All had to be rescued. Dad admitted that he had never pointed out the signs, nor had he told James any of the stories he knew about others who had gotten into trouble doing just what James had done. Everyday topics such as sex, alcohol and other drugs, violence, weapons, and so forth demand discussion and training, too.

Direct less and question more. Rather than, *"Barry, be sure to take your coat, hat, and gloves when you go,"* try to be light and use a little humor. Ask, *"Barry, it's freezing today. Humor me—what will you take with you today?"* Or, *"Tom, what do you know about the driving conditions tonight? Appease your old mom and tell me what you will do to be safe."* Listen for his response, so that you know what he's thinking.

PREVENTIVE TIPS

Discuss strong values and good judgment at appropriate times. Society gives teens the right to drive at the magical age of sixteen, to vote at eighteen, and to drink at twenty-one. Teens can also have sex, get pregnant, and even marry. There is no protocol on how to manage all these life events. Your family's value system is your unsteady teen's dependable anchor while he is developing his inner controls.

Watch for good judgment and compliment her very specifically on what you see. There is always something, even if it is only that she fed the cat inside because it was raining: *"Good thinking, Sandra. You probably saved Kitty from catching cold."* With practice you will begin to see more opportunities to compliment her.

When something interesting is reported in the paper or on TV, discuss it, don't lecture. Be open to his ideas and value them without judgment.

Self-esteem is related to good judgment. Reward good decision making by expanding the corral, allowing a wider range of privileges. When your teen has made good decisions, tell him so. Trust him to continue to make them. Do not focus on the poorer ones.

"You don't trust me" is a familiar line when a limit is set. For example: You have set a limit—no unchaperoned parties. Explain that it is not a matter of trust but of safety. Explore the consequences of putting herself in a risky situation. These discussions will help her learn to be cautious in the future.

The martial arts teach self-defense and are a popular sport to build confidence and good concentration and judgment skills.

Do not let your past cloud your attitude toward your teen. Just because you flirted with danger when driving with friends doesn't mean your teen will. Likewise, how you were parented will affect your parenting decisions. For example, if you were left to fend for yourself at age thirteen, with no one to support you through your mistakes, you may unconsciously withdraw from your thirteen-year-old when she experiments. If you had an excessively strict parent, you may tend to come down too hard on your teen for her mistakes, or you might tend to be overprotective, wanting to be sure your daughter does not do the things you did.

Notice her (many, many, many) responsible actions. Be specific. Most of your teen's day is handled very responsibly. Do you concentrate mostly on the much smaller part (the part that you want done better)? Emphasize the things she does well and what you most like about her.

Celebrate milestones with your teen. She will act more responsibly when she believes that she is growing older and wiser. Jump on the "first times" and the "big deals." Hurray for the firsts: the baby-sitting job, entrance into junior high and then high school, securing his first paid job, passing driver's education, and of course sports and scholastic achievements. Don't forget the physical changes as well, though a little more discreetly: her first period, first bra, his first shave, and so forth.

Mentors are needed outside the family. Older teens, youth leaders, and coaches who help point out talents and successes are helpful.

Do not blame yourself for your teen's problems. As hard as it is, you must make the distinction between his problems and yours. He is a separate individual, influenced by his friends, teachers, life experiences, and perceptions of the world. He is responsible for his behavior!

WHEN TO SEEK HELP

If you are concerned that your teen tests fate in dangerous ways, listen up. Very dangerous and daring behavior, such as dashing in front of cars or walking on a balcony rail thirteen floors above the ground, is a call for help. He may feel that showing off is the only way to win the attention and approval of his peers. This may also be a sign of depression. If extremely dangerous behavior is occurring regularly, you need to consider what is happening in other areas of his life. Consultation with a professional is prudent and may even save his life.

See also: Alcohol and Other Drugs; Dating, Teens; Depression; Driving; Mealtimes; Sex, Talking About; Spoiling, Overindulgence; Stress; Trust

SCHOOL CONFERENCES

"I would really like to talk with Jackie's teacher about her math. Five minutes on back-to-school night is hardly enough time."

"My mom wants to come talk to my teacher just like I was in second grade. She's so embarrassing!"

UNDERSTANDING THE SITUATION

You may feel uncomfortable asking for a school conference to discuss your teen's progress. Typically, parents ask for conferences less often as their teens enter high school, as if their jobs are done. True, teens do need to feel capable of handling their own lives, and parents do need to let go for this to happen. However, there are times when you may need to be your teen's advocate and a school conference is necessary. Your teen may cringe, and you may feel embarrassed, but you are right to discuss your concerns rather than avoid or discount them.

There are many reasons to arrange a school conference. Do not feel stupid for your concerns. Your teen may be complaining over and over about a class, *"It's too easy. I learned this last year. I should be a level higher,"* or, *"Our teacher goes too fast. I can't follow her lecture well enough to take notes."* You may have concerns about his welfare in other areas—he isn't making friends, he is being bullied, or he is having stomachaches and not sleeping well. You may worry because he complains that his knees hurt after football practice.

There are many departments at the junior-high and high-school levels. You may have access to a principal, one or more vice principals, an athletic director, academic counselors, and college and career counselors. Your teen may have six or seven teachers as well as coaches and other activity advisers. Figuring out which person to see about your particular concern may seem overwhelming. Most schools have a knowledgeable office staff who will direct you to the proper person.

The staff members at your teen's school are there because they like kids and like working with them. They sometimes get tired and cranky just as you do in your field of work. Sometimes they even get discouraged and may seem abrupt. Have patience. When you approach a tired teacher or administrator with understanding, you both will have a greater chance of success.

WHAT TO SAY AND DO

Talk with your teen first. Rarely would you need to have a conference without your teen knowing you were doing so. This is about her, and it is her life. When you include your teen in your concern, she may say she will handle it herself. Encourage her to do so. When kids are raised attending teacher conferences, they often have the courage to speak for themselves to the teachers, advisers, administrators, and counselors. Tell her that you trust her to handle the problem and help her decide on a plan. Set a time to review the situation and, if needed, together decide on the next approach.

Be a facilitator, not a rescuer. If your teen cannot resolve the problem, you may need to help, and a reasonable first step is to call the school for an appointment. If your student has talked with a teacher, coach, or other staff member and not met with success, make an appointment. Often, a phone discussion between you and the teacher or counselor will help enough for your teen to finish resolving the problem.

Start the conference off with your best communication skills. Many times parents go to a teacher with strong feelings and the teacher immediately becomes defensive. Following are four steps to win cooperation from any person. (Your first talk may be over the phone; this strategy works either way.)

1. Begin by identifying feelings and showing empathy. Humor helps: *"I'm aware that you teach a hundred twenty teens a day. Wow! That's a lot of homework to correct and kids to follow."*

2. State your concern and feelings as an advocate for your teen. State something positive before mentioning your concern: *"John loves your humanities class. He likes your dramatic approach. He has talked to you regarding his papers. He would like more input on his written work. He feels frustrated by the letter grade with no specific feedback. He doesn't know how to improve."*

3. State what you need with a question: *"How can you help him improve his papers?"*

4. After hearing a solution, say thank you and decide on a time in the future to follow up. For example, your teen could consult with the teacher in three weeks, and if he's not satisfied you may follow up as well.

There is a hierarchy in every school. Start at the teacher or coach level and move up through the ranks as needed.

PREVENTIVE TIPS

Attend the general meetings at the beginning of the school year and at the onset of a new season of sports or other extra-curricular activities. Understand what your teen will be learning and doing. He will appreciate your interest.

When you volunteer at school, such as to work on a homecoming committee, freshman orientation, or senior prom, or to help in the office or nurse's room, your name and face become familiar. Teachers, counselors, and administrators will welcome your concerns and take you seriously because they know and trust you to be a helpful resource for the school.

See also: Chapter 3, Tools of the Trade, Listening, Problem solving; Grades and Homework; Learning Problems

SEX, TALKING ABOUT

"I feel I should be talking to her about sex. It's every-
where—on TV, in magazines, in rap and other music. I
don't know how to begin, and she clearly doesn't want to
talk to me about it. Is sex education at school enough?"
"My dad is such a prude, I would never talk to him about
sex! I know far more than he does. He just doesn't
understand the world today."

UNDERSTANDING THE SITUATION

Today's teenagers are probably more comfortable talking about
sex than you were at that age. Some are ready to talk about it at
eleven and others not until sixteen, but at any age, parent–child
talks about sex tend to be extremely awkward. However, at
whatever age it happens, "the talk" is enormously serious and
hard for most of us to do well, and it is a huge responsibility. It
is ideal if it can become a topic that is frequently addressed in
normal everyday conversation.

One mother, finding it difficult to talk to her thirteen-year-
old son about sex, urged her husband to tackle the conversation. She handed Dad a book, and soon heard gales of laughter
coming from her son's room. The next thing she knew, the
two were throwing hoops outside. What could that five-minute
conversation have accomplished? she wondered. Probably not
much from an instructional point of view. But it did loads to
promote a relaxed atmosphere, which set the stage for more
talks later. That's what's needed: relaxed parent-teen discussions regarding sex.

Many books have been written on teen sexual behavior, guides for parents hopeful of helping both themselves and their teen better cope with this highly charged topic. You and your spouse must spend some time together talking about what you both see as important. The disparities might be surprising! What are your expectations regarding your teen and sex? Concerns you have not even thought about will surface continually through these years. What you believe greatly influences your teen's sexual expression: *"Elaine, we hope you choose to wait until you're out of your teens and have a chance of making a lasting commitment. It is such a special thing."* When parents have not resolved their own feelings, teens are likely to pick up on the disparity and to act out their confusion somehow.

The authoritarian father who sneers, *"Just let me catch you having sex with some guy and I'll show him just what the barrel of my shotgun looks like,"* invites rebellion. Be clear and respectful: *"Our rule is that you will wait until you are out of your teens to have sex."* The wishy-washy parent who says, *"Well, whatever I say doesn't really matter, since you'll do whatever you want anyway. Just make sure you protect yourself,"* is unhelpful, sets no limits, and invites experimentation.

Realizing that you can't follow your teen around; the best thing is to offer clear guidelines. *"We hope you will choose to wait . . ."* or, *"We want you to think carefully and realize that it is your decision. You do have a choice. We hope you choose wisely."* If you are dogmatic in your statements to her, she will have something to rebel about. If you leave the decision to her, she will have to handle the responsibility. You did not fail to protect her. She chose to make a different decision. Of course, you will not go into *"I told you so"* if she comes home regretting a bad decision. She already knows you were right. You do need to support her and help her not to make the same mistake twice.

Your young teen is growing fast. As she develops, she may become more private and you may feel pushed away for the first time. You may want to talk with her, but lurking inside is a cautious voice: *"Is this really any of my business?"* *"Hasn't she already learned from the school's sex education program or her friends?"* *"Will what I say be believed or useful to her?"* *"Will she say, 'You're just dumb and old-fashioned,' and distance herself more from me?"* Your young teen is adjusting to new sexual thoughts and feelings. Boys are surprised with sudden erections and wet dreams. Many girls begin menstruating at eleven or twelve. Boys and girls alike are curious about masturbation, petting, and intercourse, and many actively discuss sex with their friends.

Don't let shame or embarrassment keep you from talking with your teen. You may have answered his questions about the birds and the bees when he was much younger, but his body has been changing and so have the issues. Life-and-death concerns have replaced fear of pregnancy, and many parents are truly panicked.

Thirty or forty years ago, kids who were sexually active were ostracized, reflecting a society where sex before marriage was not acceptable. It broke the rules. Today, the rules have changed. Movies, the soaps, and other media are a major influence. Sex is shown as a casual pastime, with ads portraying sex as the ultimate outcome of using their products. Television doesn't portray Mom and Dad in twin beds anymore. The sexual escapades of prominent political leaders, sports heroes, and other celebrities are depicted in every detail by the press. These messages are out there at a time when your teen is forming very personal ideas about his sexuality, and your anxiety about how he is influenced is valid.

Another important influence is peer pressure. Kids sometimes encourage one another to have sex. A senior girl warned her freshman sister to watch out for the senior boys: *"The guys have bets about which girls will have sex with them."* One eleventh-grade couple said they were teased into having sex: *"How could you guys say you're an item if you're not doing it?"* Discussions with your teen about responsibility and values can help her "stick to her guns."

Prepare yourself for the fact that sometime in the not so distant future, your teen will be tempted to become sexually active. Both boys and girls are often confused about what being sexual means. Too often it translates to "having sex," but sex and intimacy are not synonymous. A kiss does not have to be followed by intercourse, as portrayed in the movies. When a girl has been dating a boy on a regular basis over a period of time, sex may become part of their relationship. A prepared parent will feel confident in stating the family value: *"No sex in the teens."* Your expectation is clear but is no substitute for discussing your values and checking your teen's perception of what safe sex means.

A prepared parent also knows the health ramifications of risky sex today and learns to share this knowledge openly and honestly. Today, sex can harm and kill. Though AIDS is the best-known sexually transmitted disease (STD), the National Institute of Health strongly warns that others are rapidly on the increase throughout our country. Chlamydia, gonorrhea, syphilis, herpes, and viral hepatitis, without treatment, have long-term harmful effects. They are believed to cause sterility, pelvic inflammatory disease, and cancer.

Outdated assumptions that boys are interested in sex all the time, that girls have to be talked into it, that girls say no when they mean yes, and that girls always play hard to get are based on slim evidence, yet they remain a part of our culture. These assumptions are not helpful to teens, and you and your teen should discuss the fact that they are false. The good news is that the word *abstinence* is beginning to make a lot of sense to a lot of teens. They are beginning to use it in the same way as they say, *"I don't smoke."*

WHAT TO SAY AND DO

Talking about sex may virtually paralyze you, but many parents find that when they admit to feeling vulnerable, their teens listen and talk more: *"I'm uncomfortable talking about sex, but it's very important to me because I love you. I'm willing to be uncomfortable, if you're willing to talk with me."* Ask sincere questions—she's the expert. She will open up when she feels she can speak without being judged. And you will be one step closer to having her consider your ideas. Verbalizing them makes them more real.

Your own sexual experiences are private and it is not helpful to share any details. Be ready for common questions such as, *"How old were you when you had sex for the first time?"* Answer, *"What I did or didn't do probably has little to do with you."* This is an opportunity to discuss an awkward topic. Say, *"I'm glad you brought the topic up because you are not me—you live in a very different time, and many issues regarding sex have changed."*

Many parents wait until they suspect sexual activity, then feel pressured to discuss it. Don't wait. In this era of teen pregnancy, AIDS, and other sexually transmitted diseases, what and how to advise our teens about sex has taken a clear direction. Informed parents find it easier to express safety issues: "Wait! *The odds are too great for contracting AIDS or another venereal disease or to get pregnant. Your life and future are too important to risk!"*

Be sure to add, *"Alcohol and drugs will alter your clear thinking. Unwanted sex occurs most often when drinking or drugging is part of the scene,"* and, *"Pregnancy changes your life. Whether you keep a baby or not, you will have complicated your future beyond necessity. Have you both talked about what you want for your future? It may seem natural to have sex because your body is ready. But it is not best for you. I care about your future."*

Do not leave sex education entirely to the schools. These discussions belong in your home as well. One pamphlet had the catchy and very wise title, *Sex Is Never an Emergency.* Teens do not always feel this until they think about what it really means. It is an important topic for discussion. Other discussions might include concepts such as commitment, love, friendship, abstinence, and so forth: *"Sex between two people who have made a loving commitment is very special. This takes maturity. Sex is not dirty, and shame and guilt are not attached to it when two people are older and have had a longer time to learn about themselves. Sexual activity adds a complicated piece to the lives of teens when they're already struggling with their own identity."*

Discuss the fact that your teen can change her mind and her behavior: *"If you've had sex and then thought it over, you do not have to do it again. People can change their minds, especially after thinking about the consequences. You're not marked for life."*

Some teens are hostile when parents bring up the topic. He plots, *"If I'm angry enough, maybe she'll leave me alone."* Don't be silenced by an irritated or seemingly uninterested teen. Find a good talk time. Sometimes a television program or even an ad will spark the topic. One mother read aloud a letter to the editor published in her daughter's high-school newspaper, another from a parenting book: *"Barbie, listen to this and tell me what you think."*

Model what you expect from her. The single parent asks, *"How do I tell her sex isn't okay? She knows I don't abstain."* It is hard to win cooperation when all you can say is, *"I am an adult and can decide for myself at my age. At your age, I expect you to abstain."* Single parents who abstain or are very discreet can set a positive example.

Convey early on that both boys and girls have equal responsibility to set personal boundaries. Boys need to hear, *"You are not helpless to control your sexual urges."* Likewise, girls need to hear, *"You are intelligent and can make good decisions based on what you believe. You can say no. You are not a victim. Don't feel guilty for rejecting a pushy date."*

So, what do you do when you find him in bed with a girl? (You are a lucky parent if you have thought this through before such an incident occurs.) Do not overreact. If you rant and rave, you replace the teen's guilt with anger at you for overreacting. Be calm and say, *"Okay, you two, get dressed and I'll meet you in the kitchen in five minutes."* Then take several deep breaths and be as calm as possible when they appear. House rules have been broken, the teens have been caught, and they are very, very embarrassed and perhaps terrified. They expect the worst, but their embarrassment is more than enough pain for the moment. Why not turn the tables? Ask them how they feel about being caught and what they think you should do about it. Their solution might be harsher than necessary, as they will probably be very tough on themselves. One mother who found herself in this situation with her seventeen-year-old and his girlfriend said, *"You have broken the family rules. I want you to have a time out for two weeks—no dating, no phoning, no contact outside of school."* This was designed to give them each a break to consider where they wanted their relationship to go. The couple decided to break up, but they remained good friends.

Your teen may sound confident and appear to have thought through whether or not to have sex with her serious steady. One mother said, *"Ginny's been a good student, dependable, active in sports, and has had a year-long relationship with a boy. She says, 'It's right for us, I know it is, Mom. I'm protected.' "* You feel confused, and you wonder, *"I just don't know. She sounds so convincing. What do I tell her?"* You are her parent, you're more mature, and you care! *"It is your body. I know you feel you should be able to decide whether to be sexually active. I do not believe it is best for either of you at this time. I wish you would choose to wait."* This might be a good time to suggest a visit for them to Planned Parenthood or a similar organization. There, they will meet with a counselor, discuss abstinence, and learn about alternatives to intercourse. Petting and masturbation are alternatives to intercourse. Condoms can be effective if used properly, but abstinence works better. These are the kinds of messages your teen needs to hear, from you too. You can't control what she will do sexually, but you can help her think things through logically and be very clear about your hope.

Teens harass one another in many ways, not uncommonly by begging for sex. Such requests and remarks often end up making everyone feel uncomfortable. Your teen needs to recognize sexual harassment. The bully may threaten and coerce, and giving in will probably mean several things, all of them bad. *"Ally, you will feel used, because he will move on; he doesn't show that he cares as deeply as you do. I don't appreciate the way he treats you."* She may be defensive: *"Mom, you don't know him!"* Say, *"Ally, I know enough to see that he's pushing you much faster than someone who cares would. Watch out."*

When your teen turns sixteen and has more freedom to go places with friends, sometimes in cars, and especially if she has a steady, you begin to realize that sex may become a reality. Though teens may be well aware of possible repercussions of unprotected sex, many continue to put themselves in danger. Remind him, *"Sex should never be an emergency, and alcohol and other drugs promote unwanted sex."*

Should you leave condoms around for your teen? There is a concern that this will mean that you condone teen sex: *"If my mom put condoms in the bathroom for me, I would think she subtly expected me to have sex. I wouldn't like that. I want that to be my decision."* Some teens say that if they are responsible enough to have sex, they should be responsible enough to get their own condoms.

PREVENTIVE TIPS

At a good talk time, discuss his personal goals. Focusing on the future is one of the best ways to relieve peer pressure: *"Jack, what would you like to be doing five years from now?"* *"Bradley, you seem to be a born leader. Have you thought about working toward team captain? Have you considered school government?"* Strengthen his ability to be an individual.

Be a playful parent. Have a sense of humor. Our stress-filled lives sometimes shortchange us. Have fun with your teen, both with her friends and with her alone. Show her she can feel good with and without a boyfriend.

A boyfriend doesn't have to be a lover. Encourage your daughter to have both female and male friends.

Be a prepared parent. Read about and attend conferences, talks, and workshops on adolescent issues. Think through your ideas on the subject of sex before you discuss them.

Questions make younger and older teens think about who they want to be with and perhaps date. *"Randy, what do you like in a girl? What beliefs and values do you think you should have in common? Is it important that she have a good sense of humor? Do you care that she is intellectually interesting? What interests and hobbies would you like her to have?"*

Teens need practice saying no without feeling guilty. Discuss parallel situations where someone's rights are being ignored. All kids need to be able to recognize when they are being coerced. This takes sensitivity. Such observations are real lessons that have wide applications in all areas of life, and should not focus just on sex: *"Did you see in the paper that . . ."* Values including respect and consideration need to be discussed on a regular basis.

Go to school and meet the teachers. Volunteer to work with other parents on a committee. As you talk with teachers and parents, discuss alcohol and other drug use, peer pressures, and sexual behavior. Your presence in the school may help your teen feel loved and therefore less likely to engage in destructive behaviors.

For more information on this topic, read *A Parent's Guide to Teenage Sexuality* by Jay Gale (New York: Henry Holt & Company, 1989); *It's Perfectly Normal: Changing Bodies, Growing Up, Sex and Sexual Health* by Robie H. Harris (Cambridge, MA: Candlewick Press, 1994); *What Every Teenager Really Wants to Know About Sex* by Sylvia S. Hacker and Randi Hacker (New York: Carroll and Gray, 1993); and *Everybody's Doing It: How to Survive Your Teenager's Sex Life (And Help Them Survive It Too)* by Andrea Warren and Jay Wiedenkeller (New York: Penguin Books, 1993).

WHEN TO SEEK HELP

Troublesome behavior includes excessive interest in the opposite sex at a very early age, dressing and acting provocatively, dating older teens or young adults, and major curfew violations. If you see this kind of sexual acting out, talk with your teen's school counselor, who may have a better perspective.

If you suspect past sexual abuse, your teen needs counseling. Abuse can be a roadblock to healthy sexual relationships during the teen and adult years. A trained therapist who specializes in cases of sexual abuse can provide incredible help that will have lifelong benefit.

See also: Body Image; Chapter 1, What Happens During the Teen Years; Counseling; Curfews; Dating, Parents; Dating, Teens; Mealtimes; Safety; Trust; Values

SHOPLIFTING

"Annie was reported for shoplifting. I'm so humiliated!"
"It wasn't that big of a deal. I never thought I'd get caught. Anyway, it was a good try."

UNDERSTANDING THE SITUATION

When your daughter is caught shoplifting, you're rightly distressed. This situation is loaded with legal problems and emotional issues. You may question your teen's innate sense of honesty, you may struggle with guilt, and you're likely to be confused about where to turn for support, knowing that family and friends may be critical and misunderstanding.

Shoplifting usually is a response to several things.

- As your child gets older, she is increasingly interested in having nice clothes and other possessions that help define her. Though it is illegal, shoplifting among teens is common. She may wish to conform to the group of friends she hangs out with. If your daughter feels different from her peers (and clothing can be a factor in this), it may be a tragedy for her. Her self-esteem has a lot to do with how she thinks she looks to her friends. The items she has taken will, she thinks, make her more acceptable.
- Peer pressure may be a factor: she may have shoplifted on a dare.
- There may be other factors in her life that are troubling her.

Is she missing an older sister who has gone to college? Are there money worries, illness, or school-related pressures such as receiving bad grades or not making a team sport? Shoplifting may help her feel in control when control over other things in life eludes her.

- There is a part of every teen that wants to test the rules. Shoplifting is a common way to do it. Your son may dare himself, trying to get away with something for the sheer thrill of it. He may think he won't get caught, and he may not even have contemplated the repercussions. This cavalier attitude makes shoplifting more like a game to him. He may think, *"Jessica got caught, but I won't,"* even though Jessica had to pay a fine and do community service.

- Shoplifting, like overeating, can be a symptom of feeling left out, being treated unfairly, feeling unloved or hurt. Taking physical objects can be an attempt to fill an unconscious psychological emptiness: *"I deserve this sweater."* Shoplifting for this reason usually also indicates depression.

WHAT TO SAY AND DO

Maintain the calm, despite your shock. Underlying your anger is: *"I love him; I fear for him."* Find ways to release your anger or frustration so that you will not lose control when you confront your son. Very angry, out-of-control parents act to exonerate the teen's bad deed. It gives him more control than his parents. Say calmly, *"Taylor, I love you, but shoplifting is wrong. You have made a very poor choice."*

Don't accuse. Do not say, *"Did you steal the jacket? How could you do that?"* This will cause defensiveness and lying. Instead, express your true feelings, then give him time to think: *"I'm shocked and disappointed that you did this. I need more time to think about what this means, and you do too. We will talk later."* *Later* is a scary word to a teen. He will suffer as he reflects and wonders what is coming.

Then, later, remind him that shoplifting is a crime. Get down to basics! *"It is against the law to take things without paying for them. Until they are paid for they are not yours!"* He will need to take the item back or pay for it.

Getting caught shoplifting is embarrassing but can be helpful in the long run. If the police are called, it reinforces the seriousness of the crime. Sometimes a fine is charged by the store; and the police may send the teen to first-time youth-offender programs. These programs also assign community service hours, counseling, and other significant tasks. The goal is a meaningful consequence without having the shoplifting appear on a permanent record. Find out what is customary in your community.

After your child has confessed to you, returned to the store, or gone to court, then is the time to comment on his efforts and your love for him: *"Thank you for being honest. It must have been very embarrassing for you to return those items. I love you."* Sincerely ask him, *"How do you feel about how you handled it?"* Then, let it go.

Assume it is over. Your son needs to know that tomorrow is a new day and that you feel this mistake will not happen again.

You may need to hold on to this assumption. For example, your daughter claims her vest is from a friend, but since she was caught shoplifting, you are beginning to wonder. Remember, kids do swap stuff, and you do not want to confront her if she is not stealing. To suggest that she may have done so would be likely to bring a torrent of "you never trust me" accusations and might force her to lie. Without proof, do not accuse.

One serious pitfall is to label your child a thief. This is just plain mean and may cause her to see herself as just that and to repeat her behavior.

Above all, do not panic! The good news is that the problem is now in the open and you have an opportunity to help. Do not base your actions on the fear that your child will be a thief for life. Heavy-handedness may lead to more shame and thus more illegal behavior. It is because we love so deeply that we may overreact with regretful anger, criticism, or rejection. The shoplifting may recur. Keep the faith. With your encouragement and loving firmness, "this too shall pass."

PREVENTIVE TIPS

You need to love him unconditionally despite your anger at what he has done.

At a positive talk time, explore with questions and empathize with feelings: *"Irene, do you feel out of it because you don't have as many clothes as some of your friends? I can relate to that feeling. I'd like you to feel that you fit in with your friends,"* and, *"What do you think you need? Let's brainstorm some ideas."*

Teenagers like to earn money—it is a grown-up thing to do. Take an interest and help her find baby-sitting or odd jobs. When she sees you taking an interest in her developing responsibility, she will feel better and much more capable, and shoplifting will probably become a thing of the past.

Do you snack on grapes while grocery shopping or accidentally walk out of a store without paying for the potatoes at the bottom of your basket? Do you actually return and pay for the potatoes, or do you pretend not to notice? Your teen watches, and you can bet she's learning.

Find times when you can share your values without moralizing or lecturing. This can be done without even realizing it during moments when the family is watching a video or TV show that involves social issues. For example, to see how shoplifting is a self-esteem issue, watch *The Karate Kid* together. The young boy in the film overcomes great odds.

WHEN TO SEEK HELP

If shoplifting occurs repeatedly, it is time to consult a professional.

If your child is stealing food or alcohol, this may be a sign of an eating disorder or alcohol problem that needs to be addressed professionally.

Compulsive shoplifting can be likened to an addiction and needs treatment. It can be related to compulsive symptoms of depression. Accompanied by therapy, medication may be helpful.

See also: Bullied; Clothes; Depression; Friends, Choosing; Lying; Trust; Values

SHYNESS

"I worry about him. He's always been shy, and now I wonder if he'll ever ask a girl out. He doesn't make friends, boys or girls, easily."
"They want me to be like them, but I can't."

UNDERSTANDING THE SITUATION

Like many other parents of a reticent teen, you may worry that life will pass him by. You know it takes tenacity to tackle this tough world. It gets embarrassing as others notice his lack of involvement in outside interests. Many parents feel a sense of urgency as their shy kid turns into a timid teen.

Some teens spend more time observing situations than joining in and may never feel comfortable with the crowds in the halls at school, the party scene, or lighthearted teen banter. After attempting a keg party on the beach, one somewhat reticent teen said, "It's just not me." He admitted that he was a bit lonely, but he seemed to accept it. Shy teens usually have a few friends but may never join in with the usual teen scene. In many respects you can be thankful, because your teen is thoughtful and less apt to be pulled into potentially dangerous situations.

Shyness is often the result of a lack of confidence. You may need to back off, let her be. The more you pump her to perform, the more you deliver the message that she isn't okay. Meant to be helpful, your suggestions are interpreted as discouraging criticism. She may actually become more timid and reclusive, and may rebel against your efforts.

Kids grow more confident when they feel that they belong, are needed, and are capable. Rather than push him, help him to discover what he does best, then help him to follow up on his interests. Each success builds on the next. It may take leaving home after graduation, going off to college, and being more on his own. You can be a very supportive parent by encouraging him to discover what works for him. Letting go is not easy, but if you keep your faith and trust that he is capable, he will feel it, and the process will be easier for all of you.

To be a confident, popular person is usually what the shy teen wishes for himself. Instead, he is embarrassed, thinking that he's the only one who feels self-conscious and unable to converse and be accepted. What he may not know is that most teens feel this way to some extent and are busy overcoming it too. One man sagely said to his granddaughter, *"Do not be so self-centered as to think they are all looking at you."* This helped her gain perspective and take some responsibility for her feelings, and to her relief she found that he was right.

WHAT TO SAY AND DO

You may be distraught over his reluctance to join others, his being left out—you may even feel embarrassed. Do not make a big deal about it. Unlike you, he may be happy and comfortable with his few friends. He may want to change and be the person you think he should be, but he is probably a quiet person by nature and will continue to be so. Your anxiety is your problem. Stay calm.

Check out your worries with people who know him in different settings, such as his teachers and coworkers, to find out what they have observed. You may be pleased with what you learn.

Perhaps you can help her explore interesting activities. One shy teen enjoyed volunteering at a ranger station helping with bird counts. Another's uncle hired her to bus tables in his restaurant. She was good, and she began slowly to make friends with the other workers, who appreciated her efficiency.

Music can be a wonderful outlet for people who are not outgoing. Not infrequently, those who are uncomfortable in conversation are perfectly comfortable playing a musical instrument. Teens who like sports but are not interested in playing may be encouraged to become a manager of a school sports team.

Do not label your teen shy or timid or bashful. Don't compare her to yourself or to other teens. You may be very relaxed with people, and she may never be—and for her, that's just fine. However, she needs to hear positives from you as you talk to others: *"She's contemplative, she's thoughtful, and she's analytical."* Describe her in these more helpful ways. Children tend to fulfill parents' fears as well as hopes.

PREVENTIVE TIPS

A worried parent may be the shy teen's worst enemy. If you find yourself constantly wanting to make excuses or "do it" or "say it" for her, perhaps you are the one with the problem. You need to take a look at your expectations for her. Are they realistic? Are they in line with her strengths? What is her nature? What are her capabilities? Find a trusted person to talk with. Honestly admitting your hopes and your disappointments will help you to accept your teen's individuality.

It will be a relief for your teen to know that you accept her for who she is rather than for what you think she should be. You may see her blossom if you can truly accept her. Discuss with her the things she wishes she could get involved in, such as volunteering in a hospital, helping with the after-school activities at the Boys and Girls Club, or getting a paper route. Remember, for her these might be big steps, and she will want to consider them before jumping in. A simple, *"Janet, you always like teaching us about things. Do you think you'd like to be a teacher's aide for the after-school program at the elementary school? I'll bet Mrs. Demsey would be interested in help from you. She's such a great teacher."* A nudge may be added later: *"I have to be at the school tomorrow. Would you like me to ask Mrs. Demsey if she could use a helper?"*

WHEN TO SEEK HELP

Shyness in itself is not alarming. However, isolation can lead to loneliness and depression. If he truly does not have any close friends and seems withdrawn, seek professional help.

Some timidness can stem from fear. If your teen is able to do many things comfortably yet has trouble with others, such as not wanting to drive or leave the house after dark, help may be needed. Excessive fears are treatable and should be evaluated by someone who is familiar with phobic reactions. It is very important to begin treatment before fears expand to other areas of her life.

See also: Depression; Friends, Choosing; Friends, Left Out; Hanging Out; Jobs

SIBLINGS

"Megan is so excited that Piper will be in high school with her. She says she and her friends will protect her. They do tangle, and there are times when their arguing seems constant. I just want them to be friends."

SIBLING: *My little sister is such a wimp. She's so annoying. She starts a fight and then yells for help.*

SIBLING: *My brother is a jerk. I've never hated anyone so much in my whole life. He's so rude to me, and he pounds on me. My parents don't know the half of it. They think he's so perfect.*

SIBLING: *They say, "Why can't you get good grades like your sister? Her teachers love her." Or it's, "I hope you make the team just like Heather did."*

UNDERSTANDING THE SITUATION

Most parents wish for lifelong happy, healthy, loving relationships among their children. And, as most parents will agree, encouraging positive relationships at home takes a lot of work. Glimmers of friendship are priceless moments. Adolescence adds another dimension to sibling relationships. Self-absorption, irritability, mood swings, and the extreme need for privacy are all hard to live with, and siblings tend to be intolerant. Battles can be big and seem endless.

If you're distressed over sibling fighting, it is not too late to remedy the situation. The necessary skills are easy to acquire. All it takes is change: You change the family atmosphere by changing your ways, and your children will change as well. Sibling fighting is normal, but those who are consistently hurting one another are losing something priceless.

The struggle to be the best and the most loved child in the family is an almost universal sibling issue. It is relieved when parents create an environment of mutual respect, work hard not to label or compare their children, express appreciation for the uniqueness of each child, celebrate each one's contributions, and limit the competitive climate that so pervades our society. Be patient and keep the faith. Some days it may seem that the bickering will never stop. One of the best things about having more than one child is that your children have one another on whom to practice important life skills such as negotiation, compromise, competition, sharing, understanding, and loving. Sometimes they will argue. Siblings often have ambivalent feelings for one another; intense hate and fierce love can and do coexist. Your work is to maintain an atmosphere of mutual respect—an ongoing challenge. The fruits of your labor will show when you least expect it. Be sure not to miss those rare moments of support and protection an older brother offers, or to appreciate the gales of laughter coming from two silly sisters (even though sometimes it is so annoying), or to wonder over the mischief siblings can dream up.

When the time nears for a teen to leave home, you may see for the first time what a tremendous impact he has on his younger siblings. One mother noticed that when her son left for college, her daughter Lilly, two years younger, began going to more parties and staying at girlfriends' to avoid family curfew. She felt that Lilly's sudden wild behavior reflected her brother's leaving. Lilly admitted she missed him. Wanting to leave herself, she found an alternative—acting out.

WHAT TO SAY AND DO

When parents recognize individual strengths and value the importance of interdependence, caring and mutual respect develop. At the family meeting, discuss family commitment.

One family calls this the Full Value Contract. Their commitment is designed and signed by all members of the family and provides structure when concerns arise.

THE NEYLAND FAMILY COMMITMENT:
Laugh together
Support one another in all areas of our lives
Treat one another with respect
Accept one another's uniqueness
Follow our daily family schedule
Ask for help when necessary
Give help cheerfully
Play together daily
Learn from our mistakes
Speak positively to and about each other
Strive for high personal and family goals
Meet life's challenges as a strong team
Practice unconditional love

Stay out of squabbles as long as no one is being hurt emotionally or physically. Unknowingly, parents often create an atmosphere conducive to sibling fighting. Change your common reaction to fighting. At the family meeting, say, *"I've been getting much too involved in your fighting. From now on, I will not interfere when you argue. I'll trust you two to work out your differences. I'll probably leave the room to save my sanity."* Be sure to do as you say you will.

When you stop interfering with their fighting, arguing may increase. They are looking for the attention they have always had. Be consistent. Notice when they are getting along well and comment specifically about what you see: *"Brian, you really helped Kristin out cleaning the family room. Thank you. You made it possible for her to be on time for her dance class."* Appreciate improvements when you see them.

Don't ignore physical or emotional hurting. Teach your kids how to use a "time-out." Time-outs offer space and time to cool off and consider the situation. Nothing is ever resolved with anger. Derogatory comments can be devastating. When Eric yells, *"Lisa, you make me sick. You'd make any guy sick. You'll be lucky if you ever get a date,"* stop, and teach with an example: *"Ouch, Eric, that hurt! Obviously you're angry with Lisa. Tell her you're angry and why. This has nothing to do with whether or not Lisa will ever have a date. This is about how angry you feel."*

Take time to teach the long-term importance of a good sibling relationship: *"You kids need to work on being better friends. There will be a time when your dad and I will be gone. Fifty years from now, you may be the only ones left in the family. Your friends may be gone as well. You'll want to be very close, because no one will know you as well as you know each other. Only two of you will share your important childhood memories: ice-skating at Grandma's on Thanksgiving and baking black-bottom cupcakes, learning to water-ski, Rufus having her litter of puppies, and you having the chicken pox together."*

Teach strategy. Both the bully and the bullied can learn cooperative skills that will help when away from home. One mother said that when she knew her daughter was getting her period, she was sympathetic to her situation: *"She doesn't need her little brother teasing her."* She coached her daughter to think of strategies: *"He only bugs you to get your attention. Think of some ways to ignore him when he bothers you—and, more important, think of some ways you might make him feel special, and show him that you care about him."* This mother stayed out of the next fight. By walking away, she sent the message, *"It's your deal. I know you can figure out a way to solve this."* Her daughter shut the door and did not interact with her brother.

When teaching your kids to resolve their conflicts, wait until all concerned have had a good cooling-off period. Never try to resolve a conflict in the heat of the moment. When all are calm, call a family meeting. Try using the following steps for conflict resolution.

- Equipped with pens and paper for all, state the ground rules: *"Each of you will have an opportunity to talk and to be heard. Please do not interrupt one another."* Listen to each one talk, uninterrupted, and record what you hear.

- Then ask each individual, once, if they have any more to add. (Remember, no interrupting, and no arguing.)
- Next, empathize sincerely! Show appreciation for each one's feelings: *"Wow! Do I hear two very angry girls with two very different perceptions! I'm amazed at how two intelligent people can see the same situation so differently! It doesn't necessarily mean one is right and the other wrong."* Read back to them what you recorded: *"Libby, you _____ and felt _____; Laurie, you _____ and felt _____."*
- Give each individual an opportunity to add to or correct what you have read to them.
- Brainstorm together how the situation might be remedied or changed. It is not okay to put down anyone's ideas with remarks such as, *"Oh, that's dumb, I already tried it. It won't work."* Record all ideas.
- Together, go back through each idea, cross off what won't work, choose one or two to try.
- Schedule a follow-up meeting to check whether the situation has been remedied. It may be necessary to repeat this process many times.
- Finally, shake hands before ending. Celebrate their cooperation. Humor is extremely effective when encouraging friendship: *"You three are the only brothers you will ever have. When I'm gone, you'll have one another to help you remember the barbecue sauce recipe."*

PREVENTIVE TIPS

Model respectful behavior with your partner and others. Your teens will resolve disputes far better when your approach is the one you expect of them.

Try beginning family meals with "appreciations." When siblings learn to say something positive about one another on a daily basis, they will begin looking for the good in each of them.

Catch your kids having fun and being pleasant together: *"Gosh, it's nice to see you two getting along together."* Show your appreciation by commenting when they are good together:

"Jen and Mike, we had a good time tonight. It's wonderful when we can have fun together like this. I know we'll have a great vacation."

Make time to take off with your kids, sometimes with and sometimes without their friends. When friends are along, siblings sometimes show off and gang up. On the other hand, sometimes inviting a friend along changes the dynamics so there's less sibling fighting.

Good one-on-one time together is important. Each child needs some time alone with each parent to feel special.

Discourage comparisons. Refrain from using labels: *"She's my worker, I can depend on Jessie. Jake is my couch potato."* Parent put-downs are absolutely forbidden. They become self-fulfilling prophecies.

Discuss anger control as described in the section titled Anger. At a good talk time, not in the heat of the moment, say, *"Suzy, I notice times when you get very angry with your brother. Would you be willing to discuss some ways to handle your anger and still get what you need from Daniel? These are ideas that have helped me. I just wish I had known them when I was your age."*

Take time to listen to each child. Pay close attention to her perceptions. One young teen said to her neighbor, *"When there's a younger kid and an older one who's just starting high school, the younger one feels left out a lot, especially when at dinner the older one has more to tell my parents than I do. It isn't fair. It makes me feel like I don't matter."* The neighbor listened to and discussed this with understanding, and the young girl was able to go home and tell her parents how she felt at the dinner table. With their awareness and help, she is now feeling more included and important.

Whenever there is severe sibling rivalry, it is your responsibility to swallow your pride and honestly evaluate your own feelings. At some level do you feel more positive toward one child than the other? Is some preference seeping into the picture? This can happen; if you find it to be the case, you should be able to rectify your feelings through awareness. The rivalry will decrease.

For more information on this topic, read *How to Talk So Kids*

Will Listen and How to Listen So Kids Will Talk by Adele Faber and Elaine Mazlish (New York: Avon, 1982).

WHEN TO SEEK HELP

If your family is seriously disrupted by physical violence or emotional abuse, don't leave family members alone together. You need to get help. The problem may not be as overt— some family members distance themselves by withdrawing emotionally, which can be equally painful. Family therapy is in order. *"We cannot go on like this. It is time we got someone to help us find ways to get along."*

See also: Anger; Bullied; Bullying; Divorce; Jealousy; Mealtimes; Mood Swings; Stepparents

SMOKING

"Gregory will not listen to reason. I'm afraid that if he gets started smoking, he won't ever be able to stop."
"Oh, Mom, don't worry. It's only a cigarette. I'll quit before I go to college. If it was crack, then you could worry!"

UNDERSTANDING THE SITUATION

Smoking is a critical topic for today's teens. New scientific evidence supports the many reasons why teens should not smoke; however, this information is difficult both to sell and to enforce.

Cigarettes can cause a chemical addiction, just as alcohol and other drugs can. It is certain that the earlier smoking is started, the harder it is to stop. Often, by age fourteen or fifteen, before informed decisions can be made, teens who smoke are addicted.

Cigarettes are easy to obtain and use, which increases the likelihood of addiction. It's possible to smoke twenty or thirty a day and not display altered behavior such as drunkenness from alcohol. Most teens reach the stage of addiction before they have any desire to quit. Recent research has found that addiction to cigarettes is as hard or harder to break than addiction to heroin. Fortunately, studies show that if kids don't smoke before age eighteen, they probably never will.

Teen smoking is on the rise and is linked to deadly diseases in the adult years, and some believe cigarettes are a gateway to other serious drug use. Experts tell us that most teen drug addicts in rehab are smokers. Unfortunately, teens usually don't worry about their long-term health—they feel invincible. Many do not see dying as a threat because it is too far off. As one teen said, *"I may as well smoke and enjoy it; I'll die of something sometime. What's the diff?"* They have a hard time taking seriously the fact that smoking is very bad for them, especially if their parents smoke. Rather, they're preoccupied with being accepted, being cool, and being "bad." Smoking cigarettes is one of the most common ways to act out. Cigarette advertisements are slanted to give rebellious teens the message that to be sexy or macho, all you need is a cigarette.

Younger teens usually begin smoking because of peer pressure—some as early as nine or ten. Thirteen- and fourteen-year-olds often begin in order to gain group acceptance: *"If I smoke like they do, maybe they'll let me hang out with them."* Some teens smoke to rebel: *"I smoke to tick my parents off."* Others do it because they are bored, and some smoke to lose weight. A fourteen-year-old explained, *"Other kids won't push you to smoke. They aren't proud of it and usually want to quit. The peer pressure is from within yourself, to be in a group that you want to be part of."*

Experts confirm a common parent concern that smoking may be the first step toward other harmful drugs. For instance, marijuana is easy to get, and inhaling is now a learned skill. Street-available pot is said to be dangerously stronger than it was even five years ago. All parents need to be better informed about smoking and its effects. The youth of today need nonsmoking role models, sound information, and perhaps intervention. These can empower teens to make good decisions for themselves.

WHAT TO SAY AND DO

Keep calm. You may be worried and infuriated when you see your teen with a cigarette. You may feel that you need to control the situation, demanding, *"I never want to hear of you smoking ever again!"* It worsens matters to issue unrealistic threats: *"If I ever catch you smoking, you will never drive the car, use the phone, or see your friends again!"* This dogmatic approach will probably serve only to reinforce the behavior. This situation won't get resolved overnight. He is more likely to stop smoking with encouragement from you and others who love him than with punishment.

Don't ignore this behavior, either. She may be testing the water. One sixteen-year-old said, *"Sometimes kids just take a cigarette to light it to look cool. They don't inhale."* Approach her with love and trust. When calm, say, *"Tammy, I'm really confused. I never thought smoking would interest you. How long have you smoked?"* Calm problem solving together will help her to think about what she's doing and to consider the situation responsibly.

When you share how you feel, show concern as well as firmness: *"Anna, I love you. I do not want you to smoke. It is a health risk and it is addictive. There is a no-smoking rule in and out of our home for everyone."* You cannot ensure that she won't smoke when she's not with you, but you can leave her with your trust and set limits at home based on the health of all family members.

If you smoke, you may have a far more difficult time convincing her that she should not. Avoid a double standard. This may be a good time for you to quit. The house rule of "smoking outside only" or "no smoking" must be mandatory for all.

Instead of blaming (*"You disgust me"*; *"You smell like garbage"*), make sure your comments are not related to his sense of self-worth. Tell him what you feel and what you wish specifically, using the *"I feel _____ about _____ because _____, therefore* _____" approach. For example: *"I don't like the smoke in the house because it isn't good for anyone, so please smoke outside."* Attaching shame and guilt is not helpful and almost never works.

Don't depend on the schools to make the point. One fourteen-year-old girl reflects on how her father played a video for her showing the lungs of cows raised in a heavily industrial area in New Jersey and those of cows raised in clean country air. The lungs of the cows in the industrialized area were black and torn, while the lungs of the cows in the country were pink and healthy. She never forgot that image. Education at home as well as at school is needed to counteract peer and advertising pressures.

If your young teen is showing interest in smoking, appeal to his sharp thinking. This may help him to make a better decision. Have him figure out how much cigarettes cost him, based on a pack a day. *"Jason, you're a good thinker. Figure what it will cost you to smoke per year, by the time you are eighteen, twenty-four, and fifty years old. If you put that much away in a savings account, you would also have interest on it. The fifteen hundred dollars you'll spend in two years will cover your car insurance. The tobacco industry depends on you to get hooked so that they can get rich. It's a real racket!"*

One twenty-year-old remembers his father saying, *"If you quit smoking and bank the money you save from not buying a pack a day, I'll give matching funds when you turn eighteen."* This was especially meaningful to this teen, as his father was not wealthy: *"I knew what this meant to him. I did quit smoking, and Dad's money went toward my college."*

Share your personal struggles. One father talked about his smoking as a teen. With loving sincerity he told his daughter, *"I wanted to be accepted. That's the only reason I did such a stupid thing."* It is almost impossible to overemphasize the power of the teen's need to be accepted. Our job as parents is to help them get into sports or other activities in which smoking is not considered cool, so that other forces work on our side at a time when our influence is less strong than before.

PREVENTIVE TIPS

A talk with a drug counselor may help convince her that smoking can lead to use of other drugs. Use all the resources available to you.

Ask your young teen why kids start to smoke, even if she doesn't. At a good talk time, say, *"Liz, would you like to look at this article with me? It says most kids begin smoking to be accepted by a group. Sometimes boredom is the reason, and some kids do it to rebel against their parents. Why do you think kids smoke?"* This leaves the door open for her to share what she feels.

Use books or personal examples to educate him about smoking-related illnesses. You do not need to lecture or moralize to make an impression.

Community action is important. Talk to store owners about selling tobacco products to minors. Emphasize local law enforcement. Store owners may be held accountable if their clerks sell to minors.

Be aware of the advertising your teen sees daily. The brands that advertise the most are those most widely smoked by teens. Discuss how the ads attract teens. What is it they're really advertising?

WHEN TO SEEK HELP

If your teen has started smoking and you cannot help feeling angry and distant, you need to talk with someone who works well with teens. Salvage your relationship. You need to be a supportive parent in all areas of his life. He needs your love and your trust. See the school counselor, the principal, or a favorite teacher or coach. Definitely seek professional help if you suspect this is leading to use of other drugs.

See also: Alcohol and Other Drugs; Friends, Choosing; Friends, Left Out; Trust

SNEAKING OUT

"I overheard the girls planning to sneak out. What shall I do?"
"We'll wait 'til they go to bed. They'll never know."

UNDERSTANDING THE SITUATION

One parent described his shock, anger, and then panic when he discovered that his son had sneaked out of the house. In this two-part scenario, Dad checked on his son Martin and a friend, Bruce, at midnight on his way to bed. The lights were out. Not convinced that the boys were sleeping, Dad turned on the light—and saw the empty beds stuffed with pillows. Part two: He called the police and was further shocked when the boys were found giving a party at Bruce's empty house.

Leaving home without permission, daring to be adventuresome, and living "on the edge" are part of growing up for many teens. Your teen is likely to be practicing "doing it on her own," without permission. Sneaking out to meet friends in the middle of the night to go skinny-dipping or to "toilet-paper" a house can be fairly harmless. It is daring and a bit thrilling, like the star athlete risking a play against his coach's advice. The attitude, "I won't be caught," is part of this behavior. Your teen is not thinking of all the possible, dangerous ramifications. To her, it's an adventure.

Young teens who sneak out to share a stolen cigarette with their friends may do it a couple of times and then be finished with it. The excitement gets old after they find out that they can do it. However, sometimes the daring can go too far, and they lose touch with issues of safety and common sense. Taking the family car for a midnight drive, or hitchhiking to a friend's house, is not sensible and is potentially dangerous.

WHAT TO SAY AND DO

Unless a problem has been reported, most parents learn about the sneaking after the fact, from another parent or a witness. Stay calm. Never attempt to resolve this issue in the heat of the moment. Tell her you need some time to calm down or to collect your wits.

When you feel ready, win her attention by identifying her feeling: *"Sarah, I understand you were feeling adventuresome Saturday night."* Show understanding: *"I remember some experiences when I was your age."* (It's best not to describe them at this time.) Next, ask her to share her perception: *"Would you be willing to tell me about your leaving the house after we'd all gone to bed?"* Be specific. And be sure to let her hear how much you care. You may be angry, but the anger is because you love her: *"I worried about your safety when I found out you'd sneaked out. I want you always to be safe."*

Finally, in a confident tone, state the rule and the consequence: *"Sarah, I appreciate your honesty. The family rule is that we must know where you are at all times. Do not sneak out. If I'm not home, leave a note. Since this is a first offense, no consequence. If it happens again, you will stay home without contact with your friends for two weekends. But I'm sure it won't happen again."*

She may get angry when caught. Expect responses such as, *"It doesn't affect my schoolwork, so what's the big deal?"* and, *"You're such a cop! You don't trust me."* Do not be afraid of her anger. Stay calm and firm, and do not let her manipulate you. Say, *"This isn't about trust, this is about being safe. When you're calm, we'll discuss the consequences."* The wait gives the responsibility back to your teen and avoids a power struggle. You both win.

PREVENTIVE TIPS

At a good talk time, ask questions that will make her think:

- Why is it fun to sneak out?
- Why do you think parents worry?
- What is the best-case scenario when . . . ? What is the worst-case scenario when . . . ?
- When do you suppose sneaking out would be no fun?

Introduce yourself to her friends' parents. Share your family rules with them. You will be helping all concerned. If Marie sneaks out with Andrea, it is helpful for both teens' parents to use positive parenting. It is also important to plan opportunities for the girls to have good, safe times together in the future.

Join or form a parent support group and stay informed. Parents need one another, especially single parents.

WHEN TO SEEK HELP

Sneaking out may indicate other problems. Perhaps he is meeting friends for sex, drug use, or other dangerous or illegal behavior. Talk to the school counselor about what she knows about the friends he keeps and their activities. Talk to his friends' parents.

If you suspect dangerous activity, you need to confront your teen with your suspicions. This may involve calling in an authority figure. You may need to check with the police to learn the local laws, your legal responsibilities, and your options.

See also: Alcohol and Other Drugs; Chapter 3, Tools of the Trade, Parents networking; Dating, Teens; Running Away; Safety; Shoplifting

SPOILING, OVERINDULGING

"Tracy is so irresponsible. Her one chore is to feed the cat, but Fexie would die if I left it to her. This is the third jacket and second pair of running shoes she's lost this year. I can't let her go without, but she shows no appreciation for what she owns. She acts so spoiled!"

"Now I'll get another lecture about losing things. Every time I hear, 'You are so irresponsible,' I tune out. Later, I'll say, 'Sorry,' and she'll forget about it and buy me a new one."

UNDERSTANDING THE SITUATION

Many parents and grandparents complain that the entire younger generation is spoiled. Do any of these comments sound familiar? *"She must have twenty-five sweaters and she's whining that she has nothing to wear"; "I let him get the cat and now he won't take care of it or pay for the shots as he promised"; "He just opened fifteen Christmas presents and he's complaining that he didn't get the kind of presents he asked for"; "She came home crying, saying that she's quitting French because the teacher hates her. That will be the third class she's dropped this year."*

In part, it is our response to their struggles, disappointments, and desires that make for overindulged teens. What's a parent to do? We've loved our children, in good faith, perhaps so much that we've overindulged, pitied, rescued, and lost perspective about what the role of the parent should be.

Are you now able to buy your teen more than you ever dreamed of having at her age? Do you delight at her excitement at gifts that you never had, or that you had to earn yourself? The irony is that she may never appreciate these gifts as you would have because she has never been without. Instead of showing appreciation, she appears uninterested, then demands more.

Could it be that because you work long hours, you feel guilty that you are away from him too much? Many working parents feel guilty setting limits.

Do you give in over her chores or following through on her personal responsibilities because you're too tired to argue? *"It's just easier to do it myself."* Tired, overextended parents often do not have the energy to follow through when needed. It is understandable but does not help your teen to develop a sense of responsibility.

Do you fear losing in a battle of wills? *"If I argue, I'll get caught in a losing battle, I'll give in, and she'll win."*

Could it be that you can't bear to watch him struggle, when you know that one phone call from you could clear up the mess? That would certainly end his turmoil—but would it teach him to do the same for himself? To be accountable?

Could it be that when you set rules and stick to them, you feel like a mean and uncaring parent?

Do you worry that she won't be popular if you do what you feel is right? Do you give in when she says, *"No one will want to have me around if I'm the only one who has a curfew!"*

Are you concerned that she won't love you if you challenge her wishes? Setting limits can be very hard. All she has to say is, *"You're the meanest person in the whole world."* Do you doubt your convictions and cave in when she begs?

Life demands that children grow and learn to make decisions and take care of themselves. Support her in becoming more capable. Some teens control the house and invade their parents' privacy. Some even persuade parents to write phony excuses to teachers. The good news is that it is not too late to change your approach. Overindulgence is curable. It's the discouraged teen who feels that *"Life isn't fair,"* or *"You owe me,"* or *"It's not my fault."* When you stop indulging and begin to act responsibly rather than out of guilt, your teen will begin to act more responsibly also. This isn't easy. It takes the patience of Job and a great tenacity, especially if you were overindulged. But you can do it, and you'll probably end up with a happy, competent offspring who will love you and be your lifelong friend.

WHAT TO SAY AND DO

Be up front when changing your behavior. Have a family meeting to discuss a new agenda. *"Jasper, we've made a big mistake. In trying to let you know we love you, we've rescued you and overindulged you. We've denied you the opportunity to struggle and learn and stick to it when things get uncomfortable. You'll never feel better about yourself than when you have to work through some problems on your own. Sometimes I'm too quick to fix them for you. So if you notice I'm asking more of you, it doesn't mean I don't love you. I do love you. I want you to feel competent and able, and if I keep doing everything for you, you'll never be happy."* He may look at you like you're crazy. From then on, demonstrate what you mean, consistently.

Changing your approach may be very tough for him. He may act out in order to convince you to revert to your overindulgent behavior. This is the time to be very consistent; it isn't easy for either the parent or the teen.

Teach how to problem solve, and don't bail him out too fast with your solutions. This can be very hard to do and painful to watch. Here is an example: William was fourteen when he lost his bus pass. He said to his parents, *"You have a problem. I lost—well, maybe someone stole or picked it up—my bus pass and the driver says I have to buy another one."* Mom said, *"Wait a minute. Whose problem is this?"* Mom felt for her son. He didn't make mistakes often, being the responsible first child. She wanted to jump right in and pay the forty dollars for the new ticket. Wisely (perhaps because of a look from Dad), she said, *"I paid once; I don't have it to pay again. I'll sleep on this tonight, and meanwhile you think of a way to resolve this for yourself. We love you and know that you can handle this."* By the next morning, William had come up with a plan. He wrote a note to the bus driver and had Mom sign it. It told the driver he was looking for the pass and hoped he could ride until he found it. He talked to the principal, had a note put in the school bulletin, and alerted all his teachers and friends. The pass never turned up, but the driver let him ride the month out, knowing he was trying. William felt far more confident having solved this problem on his own than he would have had his mother bailed him out. And he was very happy that he didn't have to come up with the forty dollars, which might well have been Mom's solution!

Ask your teen to meet you halfway. When she wants something more expensive than you think is reasonable, for instance a better-quality trumpet to play in the school band, ask her to pay the difference. Likewise, ask her to share the load when it comes to major privileges such as driving a car or a hobby such as horseback riding. She should pay for her car insurance and gas, or pay something toward her riding lessons. When she begs for designer shoes, say, *"I'll pay what Penny's high-tops cost and you come up with the difference."* These are the shoes that won't get lost.

When she loses her jacket or gym shoes, ask her to replace them or pay you back for replacing them. Or visit the school's lost and found or a thrift shop for a temporary replacement. Do not replace lost items with a brand-new match just to appease. Chronically "lost" articles may be no accident. She may be giving them away to appease or to be popular, mimicking your pattern with her. She may have been "conditioned" to be an irresponsible pleaser!

For more information on this topic, read *Raising Self-Reliant Children in a Self-Indulgent World* by Stephen H. Glenn and Jane Nelsen (Rocklin, CA: Prima Publishing, 1988); and *Punished by Rewards: The Trouble with Gold Stars, Incentive Plans, As, Praise and Other Bribes* by Alfie Kohn (Boston: Houghton Mifflin, 1993).

PREVENTIVE TIPS

Don't feel you have to provide everything on your teen's wish list for her birthday, Hanukkah, or Christmas. Kids today are possession conscious, but the worst that's likely to happen is that she'll complain or feel a little let down. She'll survive. She may have to ask for it next time around, or perhaps she'll decide to earn it on her own.

Make time to spend alone with your teen, with one or more of his friends, and with the family as a whole. The more fun you have together, the stronger your relationship will be, and the less inclined you will feel to overindulge her with "things" to make up for not being there. This may mean setting new priorities and perhaps changing your work schedule. Talk with a good friend or other parents about ways to make more time. It may mean unplugging a television set and turning down the heat so that everyone gathers around the fireplace in the evening. One wise grandmother said, *"The breakdown of the family started with central heating. The family dispersed to different parts of the house."* For a start, play games or read together. This may be slow going at first, but in time, you will find that you both look forward to it.

See also: Arguing; Chores; Complaining; Jobs; Lying; Money; Safety; Values

SPORTS

"Sports for teens are so different from when I was in school. She has many more choices and time commitments. At times I feel unsure about how to advise and support her."

"I really like my team. I feel good wearing my letter jacket, and the older kids like me because I made the team. Sometimes I feel really stressed, though. It's hard keeping up with all the demands."

UNDERSTANDING THE SITUATION

You may feel that every spare moment you have is spent on a basketball court, soccer field, dance floor, gymnasium, or swimming pool. And if you have more than one child, much of your free time may be spent in the car, juggling a multitude of sports events. How many sports should you allow your teen to get involved with? How much is too much? Coaches seem to put so much emphasis on winning, but how competitive should parents be? We are asked to buy uniforms, bags, and team jackets, and then to travel to all points of the state. How much involvement is okay? The coach says she's really good and wants her to train for a state team. How far will she have to go and what will happen with her schoolwork? When will you have family time?

If your teen is athletic, as he matures, so will his interest and ability in sports. More teens today are playing sports with a strongly competitive attitude. Some teens push themselves beyond what they enjoy in order to win their parents' attention and approval, and this is unhealthy. Other teens, fearing failure, will underestimate their athletic abilities and welcome a loving, helpful nudge from Mom or Dad to try out for a more competitive team. You want to be an encouraging parent, sensitive to the needs of your child, not an overpressuring parent.

Athletics are recommended for all ages. Good coaching, understanding and encouraging parents, and a determined teen make for a good experience. Participation in sports provides your teen with many lifelong skills and advantages—physical health, commitment, sportsmanship, concentration, teamwork, exercise, endurance, and responsibility, to name a few.

Generally, your teen will find the sports he likes best. Keep in mind that some teens prefer to sing in the school chorus or play in the band, or join debate or chess clubs or 4-H. Much like sports, these activities teach individuals to share and work toward a common goal. There are jobs on the teams for the nonathlete such as team manager, scorekeeper, and the like. The camaraderie of a well-led group is very personal. Contribution, participation, and pride build healthy self-confidence.

Teen sports are important for other reasons as well. The insecure teen feels important and has a strong sense of belonging when she can say, *"Yes, I play volleyball."* Sports are also an outlet for appropriate expression of anger or bravado. Many teens have an abundance of energy and need to express it. Sports offer excellent opportunities to make new friends, usually providing a solid peer group as well as good adult role models. Sports offer structure, rules, and boundaries at a time when a teen may be rebelling against the rules of his parents' generation.

It may be very hard to attend all the games, but you are very much appreciated on the sidelines. This is especially hard for working parents of two or more kids, but your dedication will be rewarded. You will always be your teen's very best cheering section.

WHAT TO SAY AND DO

Listen to what your teen wants from sports. Does she want a fun social experience, or is she very serious about playing com-

petitively? A recreational club or junior varsity may be lower
key than a full varsity team. Both are wonderful experiences,
and teach the same basic skills, but with a different emphasis.

Help him plan for success. Physical limitations may determine
the sport at which your child is most likely to succeed. Not
everyone can be a football jock. Weak ankles may rule out cross-
country running and make swimming a better choice. Cheer-
leading and drill are considered sports in many schools. Some
kids thrive on individual pressure and like sports such as gymnastics or wrestling, while others prefer team sports. Subtly and
openly, you can guide your teen toward the activity most suited
for her. Handicapped children need not feel left out. There are
horseback-riding programs for the handicapped as well as skiing
for the blind and other sports included in the Special Olympics.
Your job is to help determine which sport fits best.

The coach may want a teen who is athletically very talented
to work toward the professional level. Taking him away from
home, friends, and studies needs to be discussed and evaluated
with your teen and with school counselors and the coaching
staff. Each teen has his individual needs. What will his peer
group be? How will he continue high school? Will he graduate
on time? Are you willing to put family life on hold for him?
What will the expenses be, now and down the line? What is
the commitment now and in the future?

Many select teams request contributions toward travel, team
jackets, uniforms, and so on. Car washes and bake sales allow
families to defray the costs. Discuss how much money you can
afford to support his sport before he tries out for the team.

Volunteer to do what you can for the team—snacks, phone
chains, fund-raising, transportation, or officiating. Learn the
rules of the game so that you can intelligently discuss what's
happening. Close friends, grandparents, and other relatives make
wonderful cheering sections for kids of any age. Even teens
comment that they really like the support. However, when he
is in front of other team members, he may not show his delight
that you're there watching him.

Sportsmanship is a life skill. Teens do lose control at times.

He may have handled defeat better in elementary school. Don't overreact or criticize. Let the coach handle the situation. Later, discuss your teen's reaction, and problem solve together: *"Charley, you were pretty upset with that off-side call yesterday. That's understandable. How do you feel now? Is there another way you wish you had handled it? Angry feelings are natural in those situations. I know losing control may have felt bad later. How would you deal with it if it happens again?"* Finally: *"Yes, you blew that moment, but that doesn't mean you'll do it again, despite how you feel. Practicing good sportsmanship is as important as ball control. They both take time to handle well."*

Your sportsmanship on the sidelines is equally important. Cheer for the whole team, not just your teen. When there is a bad call, it is up to the coach to respond, not you. Don't make it hard on the coach or embarrass your child. Your behavior reflects on the whole team and certainly on your teen.

Rather than give criticism (that's the coach's job), make encouraging comments. Be specific: *"Paul, in the first quarter when you passed the ball, you set that goal up beautifully."* Find as many ways as you can to support all members of the team. Comment on effort rather than on outcome.

Before giving your opinion, ask his evaluation: *"How'd you feel about the game?"* *"What have you all practiced recently that helped the team?"* *"What would you like to see happen next time?"* This approach offers a chance for an honest, rewarding discussion.

If you can't get to the game, find time to ask about her performance. You can still be there for her. Especially if she is down in the dumps after an error, she needs your comforting ear. You can't play for her, but you can acknowledge her pain and disappointment. *"I know that must have been very embarrassing and you felt you let the team down. That is hard. I also know that you are very quick on your feet. I know you did your best. I'm proud of your effort. You will enjoy baseball for many years, and there will be other good and bad days."*

Keep a healthy perspective. There is a danger to the thought, *"My son must get that scholarship or else . . ."* It's wonderful for everyone's ego when the teen is elected the best quarterback in the state. However, a teen who works only for his sport, to the exclusion of other aspects of his life, faces eventual injury or defeat and the feeling that nothing else matters. Support a well-balanced lifestyle. Suggest that he play more than one sport, according to season, and encourage family activities, academic goals, and other interests such as music, drama, and community service.

Sports teach commitment. When your teen seems to lose interest in going to practice, remind him of his commitment. Firmly say, *"Roy, I know the movie sounds like more fun, but you need to go to practice. You can be with your other friends another time."* Your guidance is important during these emotional years.

If she constantly complains about the coach, take time to observe practice or games and to talk to other parents. Learn what qualities a good coach should have for this age group. A firm, demanding coach may get complaints from the team because he is strict and takes them to task. As long as he is not overly critical of his players, he may be a very good coach. Better to help your teen (and yourself) understand his style than to get between the coach and his players. Life requires adjustment to all sorts of personalities.

PREVENTIVE TIPS

Encourage healthful habits at home and model what you want to see from her. Eat well and exercise.

Carpool with kids whose parents are not available and cheer for them, too.

Consider your teen's busy schedule and commitments as you plan family activities. Coordinate mealtimes according to sports schedules as much as possible.

Encourage the whole family's interest in a variety of sports. Attend local sporting events. Participate actively as a family in as many activities as you can. Active vacations that include hiking, swimming, fishing, boating, skiing, skating, and so on are terrific reinforcement.

Qualified teens can officiate at games for younger children and get jobs in summer camps or with parks and recreation departments, or they can volunteer to work with disadvantaged kids in sports-related projects. A job in a favorite field can lead to a career in doing the things you would choose to do for fun. Your teen may not think of this long-range concept on his own.

WHEN TO SEEK HELP

The competition in organized sports today is terrific; however, too much pressure on performance can lead to future problems.

Some teens can become so competitive that they feel winning is the only important outcome of the game. Self-esteem plummets, a black cloud descends over the family, and everyone stays out of the teen's way after he has lost or played poorly. If so much of his well-being depends on winning, something has gone seriously wrong. Consider your own attitude and talk with the coach. Your teen must regain perspective and balance. Counseling can be found outside of school with professional therapists who are experienced in working with adolescents.

See also: Chapter 1, What Happens During the Teen Years; Friends, Choosing; Jobs; Stress; Values

STEPPARENTS

"My goal is to be a friend to her, but I'm having an impossible time getting even that far."
"You'll never be my dad, so don't even try."

UNDERSTANDING THE SITUATION

Becoming a stepparent is an enormous "step." One man, joining a woman and her three children, said, *"It's the toughest thing I've ever done in my life! It's almost been too hard to do."* This man had to form relationships with four people, and two of the three children were adolescents! He added, *"They had the advantage—they only had to get to know one person!"*

Stepparenting adolescents is more than just a challenge; it is enormously difficult. Bonding with teenagers is not an instant process. The teen is separating emotionally and intellectually from his parents and will soon physically leave home as well. He is trying to find out who he is, by moving away from his parents, while at the same time he is expected to form an attachment with this new parent. It is extremely complicated.

An added complication occurs when two families with children merge. This is called a blended family and can cause havoc in the dynamics of both parent and sibling relationships. The Brady Bunch makes this look too easy. One woman reflected years later on her stepparenting: *"I still feel guilty for coming down on my own children too hard. I guess I felt I knew how much they could take and I tended to be harder on them than on my stepchildren. That increased sibling rivalry and was hurtful for all."* A father reflected, *"I never did set limits well with my own children, even after I remarried. I guess I felt so guilty about what happened with my first marriage that*

I wanted to make it up to them when I remarried. It was hard to say 'No' and not overindulge, and that led to a lot of risky teenage behavior." Both parents agreed that ideally you need to be proactive and seek help to merge two families and establish disciplinary approaches and boundaries before major issues evolve.

The bonding process is serious. One father said, *"Laura was on the way to being the wicked stepmother. The group we went to saved us all. We had no idea how complicated this would be. Laura became Jamie's personal chauffeur for about two years, and this became the ticket to being accepted by her. There was something wonderful about being in the car together that allowed them to share and subsequently bond. It was just the right thing!"* If bonding does not occur, family life can become unbearably strained.

When parents work together with a positive attitude and seek support through their church, community, family and friends, family counseling, stepparent groups, and so forth, healthy bonding becomes possible and even probable.

WHAT TO SAY AND DO

Because your presence changes family dynamics, you may be considered an intruder. Take time to understand the children's positions before you entered the scene. Family counseling can help. For example, Robert was thirteen, the oldest of three children. Having been his mother's dependable helper for several years, his self-esteem was tied up in this role, and there was no question that a stepfather made him feel unneeded. *"At first we were terribly angry with Robert, and were at a loss to explain his sullen, angry outbursts, which were directed at me and his stepfather. We were lucky to have taken a friend's advice and gotten into family counseling, which allowed Robert to tell us how bad he was feeling. This made all the difference."*

Legally the stepparent has no rights or responsibilities in regard to the stepchildren unless she has adopted them. Ironically, teens often feel the stepparent has no rights or responsibilities in regard to them either. The wise stepparent will nurture the children and support the natural parent's rules. *"Brian, your father has asked that you be home by midnight. I support him one hundred percent. That's late enough.* " You will avoid the wicked stepmother label if you are a supportive team player.

One on one, you have a chance to discover each other as individuals. Ask your stepson if he wants your thoughts on critical issues. When your opinions are invited, it is more likely that you can be of help. One stepfather invited his fourteen-year-old to help at his office on a Saturday. She was thrilled and acted maturely and respectfully—quite different from her behavior at home. Each time he planned an activity with her, such as a bike ride or a day skiing, she began to know him better, she felt valued, and they were on their way to becoming friends.

Use the family meeting to establish rules and to settle differences. Many blended families have found this approach very helpful.

Be patient through the initial period. Timing is crucial to developing trust. Being a stepfather is a balancing act between wanting to help the mother but not wanting to take the place of their father.

Be mature. Make it clear both that you like him and that you will step aside for his real parent: *"Michael, I am your stepmother. I will never try to be your real mother or take her place. I enjoy being with you and I love having you around, but I will never interfere with your mother or your need to be with her."* This role is tricky, and envy can rear its ugly head. You may feel rejected or resentful at times, and that is understandable. Find someone to share your feelings with, but do not take them out on the rest of the family.

Keep your sense of humor. Teens do try to manipulate parents, and stepparents sometimes get singled out for the worst of it.

PREVENTIVE TIPS

The needs of children are very important when one parent dies or leaves because of divorce, and then again when the other parent remarries. Family counseling is recommended, even before it seems needed. It takes mature adults with good parenting skills to manage children and teens through the traumas of both the losses and the celebrations.

Make time for yourself and your new spouse. You have your relationship to attend to as well. It is easy to lose sight of that in the face of children's needs.

Seek out self-help groups through hospitals, schools, and so on; meeting with other stepparent families can also be very helpful.

For more information on this topic, read *The Stepfamily: Living, Loving and Learning* by Elizabeth Einstein (Ithaca, NY: E.A. Einstein, 1994); and *Parenting Without Pressure: A Whole Family Approach* by Teresa Langston (Colorado Springs: Naupress, 1994).

WHEN TO SEEK HELP

A teen who has any fantasy of his parents' reuniting may resent the new stepparent. Unresolved issues, such as deep-seated anger about the divorce and remarriage, can be indirectly expressed through rebellious behavior or depression. Until such issues are worked through, you all may have a difficult time. Be sensitive and patient. He's discouraged and expressing his hurt indirectly through unhealthy actions. Seek an experienced family counselor who understands teens.

See also: Counseling; Divorce; Jealousy; Losses and Grief; Siblings; Stress

STRESS

"I worry about Len. He's so irritable and hard to get along with, and lately so forgetful. I know he's not sleeping well."

"The kids will laugh at me during my speech and I know I won't get a good grade, and now I have soccer tryouts and I haven't had time to practice. I haven't even mowed the lawn. Dad's going to be so mad."

UNDERSTANDING THE SITUATION

It is indeed worrisome when your teen begins showing symptoms of too much stress. Kids may be worried and anxious, unable to slow down, easily irritated and angered, or unable to focus; they may develop sleep problems, ulcers, or eating problems, or begin using alcohol or other drugs, and show signs of frequent illness, to name a few. Yet stress can also lead to positive growth.

Experts agree that everyone needs a certain amount of stress in order to be healthy, to develop character and maturity, and to be productive. Healthful stress makes us excited, enthusiastic, and eager. Stress itself isn't bad, it's the way we handle it. Being overwrought makes for excessive worry, anxiety, and fear of failure. Teens often feel a pull to do what their friends are doing, even if they're not entirely comfortable with it: *"Should I join in and risk my parents' disapproval?"* Such conflicts are stressful, though they may be an effective test of your teen's sense of right and wrong. His discomfort helps him decide his standards and develop good character.

Entering junior high school is usually one of the most

stressful transitions of the teen years. The jump from the secure elementary classroom to the big junior high or middle school is fraught with unknowns. Hormones trigger emotional as well as physical changes. Young teens are concerned about being accepted by peers and, for the first time, by the opposite sex. The world has suddenly become much more complicated.

Family transitions such as moving, illness, divorce, remarriage, and job loss are all potentially stressful. When family roots are altered during the teen years, she must readjust her perception of the world, and this can be very disconcerting and confusing. She may find it hard to study. Schoolwork increases, chores are redistributed in the family, and she worries about keeping up her grades and continuing with her outside interests. Stress is unavoidable. She may begin to feel out of control. Sometimes it seems that teens are managing well when in fact they are suffering from headaches, not sleeping well, or experiencing other symptoms of too much stress.

Your job is to recognize unhealthy reactions to stress and to guide your teen. Give less advice and more reassurance. Direct with good listening, and help with understanding. This positive parenting approach will help her to handle the "daily stuff" with better organization, emotional control, and practical choices. As hard as it may be, be patient and stay calm. Your anxiety will only add to her confusion.

WHAT TO SAY AND DO

When your teen is rude, angry, or irrational, recognize that this may be due to stress. Do not overreact. Punishment won't help. There is a feeling underneath that needs to be understood and expressed, rather than repressed. Instead of losing your temper, act confused, which probably won't be too hard: *"Keith, wait a minute. I'm confused. All I asked was, 'Please set the table.'"* State your limits: *"Throwing the saltshaker across the room—what's going on?"* Listen, then reflect: *"Oh, I see. Yes, that does sound difficult."* Once he learns to get in touch with his feelings, he will have better emotional control.

Instead of filling his head with unwanted advice, ask questions to help him think: *"You aren't sleeping well lately. How can you help yourself?"* or, *"You feel stressed over all that's due in that one class. What would help you prepare for next week?"*

Do not rescue her because you want to save her from stress. Your teen will learn to do her best when you allow her to make mistakes and perhaps to experience a failure. We never feel better about ourselves than when we overcome a challenge. Yet there is a fine line between feelings of independence and those of abandonment. Your teen needs you to empower her by listening, sympathizing and empathizing, and encouraging.

Help her learn the difference between her problem and someone else's. A primary issue is problem ownership. Watch for blaming phrases: *"He made me go with him,"* or, *"She needed me."* Say, *"Heather, no one can make you do anything you don't want to. Learn the difference between what someone wants you to do and what you feel is best for you."* This takes practice, and you will need to have this conversation again at different stages.

Help her to practice saying no. Overcommitting is a major source of stress. We all need to be realistic about what we can take on. Typically, parents do a poor job at this. We work, drive our kids everywhere, make dinner, clean the house, do the laundry, listen to everyone's problems, meet their schedules, and, if we're smart, find a minute for ourselves. The stress is unhealthy, the pace a killer. Taking control of your life will help your family for the rest of their lives. Striving to be a perfect mother is bad for you and is bad modeling. "Good enough" is all that's required: *"Kim, I notice that you're trying to be everything to all your friends. I do the same in different ways. We need to learn to stop at good enough, to say no, and not to feel guilty about it. Don't forget the most important person—you."* Or, *"Jody, much of your stress is due to taking on too much. Listen to your body. I feel a tightness in my stomach when I need to say no."*

Model stress control. If you tend to procrastinate, she may, too. Planning helps to avoid the last-minute panic before guests arrive. Ask your teen's opinion: *"What am I doing wrong? I always get myself into a panic before guests arrive."* Listen to her suggestion. She may say, *"Why don't you set the table at two o'clock so this won't happen."* Let her help you "fix" it. She'll feel good and learn from it, too.

Model a positive attitude about stresses that cannot be avoided, such as a natural disaster, a new boss, or a failing grandparent: *"Maria, we all need to learn that there are some situations we have no control over. We'd better learn to handle them, because they're part of life."*

PREVENTIVE TIPS

In order to model a healthful lifestyle, you need to understand stress reduction. An aware parent recognizes when she needs personal counseling. This can be accomplished with a good parent support group, clergy or other spiritual support, positive talks with close family and friends, adult education, and/or professional therapy.

Learn the signs of stress and pass them on at a good talk time: *"Billy, watch for signs of stress. Listen to your body—you may feel your stomach tighten, you may lose your temper and pick fights, you may be forgetful or feel disoriented, and so on."*

Teach stress-reducing skills. Your teen can learn to do visualization, yoga, and meditation, relax in a hot bath, listen to her favorite music, or talk to a calming friend.

Stress management is a learned skill not unlike anger control. Both involve reducing the problems that create the stress. Brainstorm with him: *"Colin, you have been running a very fast pace. What could you do to help reduce the stress?"*

Use less directing and less reminding and coaxing. If necessary, use neutral reminders: *"What will you need today in English?"*

A sense of humor is vital. Leave notes: *"Have a great day! Love, Mom and Miss Kitty,"* and, *"Please hang me up! Love, your towel."*

Help your teen with positive self-talk. Rephrase the negative: *"I don't believe in the word* can't. *I'll try hard, I will give it my best effort!"*

Flexibility is helpful. Discuss "going with the flow" and not arguing over every little point. Talk about letting others be the way they are and not trying to change them.

Talk about friendships. Your teen is seeking peer approval rather than yours. She may feel the anxiety of being left out.

WHEN TO SEEK HELP

Upset stomach, tense muscles, grinding teeth, bowel symptoms, irritability, depression, changes in sleeping or eating habits, or poor grades and incomplete schoolwork may be signs of too much stress. Help can be found through your physician, school counselor, and various support groups.

See also: Anger; Depression; Friends, Left Out; Home Alone; Rudeness; Worry

SUICIDE

"I'm in a state of shock. I knew Ellen was depressed, but I never suspected it would come to a suicide attempt."
"No one understands. No one cares. No one notices. There's no use. The world will be a better place without me."
"They will really miss me [appreciate me] when I'm gone."

UNDERSTANDING THE SITUATION

To imagine suicide happening to your teen is paralyzing, which may be one of the reasons why so many parents are caught unaware.

If you know your teen is feeling unhappy, you may worry and seek advice, but generally you will feel able to help him deal with the pressures and to comfort and encourage him. If his behavior is irritating, you may grow intolerant and tend to ignore the situation, hoping he will resolve his unhappiness on his own, as he has in the past. Unfortunately, teens do not always believe that things can get better. Your passiveness may appear to him to be uncaring, and therein lies the danger.

To think about suicide is not abnormal. Most people, teenagers included, have had thoughts such as, *"What would it be like to be dead?"* or, *"What would my family be like if I died?"* These are normal. You should worry only if such thoughts are persistent or become an envisioned solution to problems. You should take action if you find notes, stories, or poems about suicide or if she begins to talk about killing herself. Such behaviors must be taken seriously.

Developmentally, teens are extremely vulnerable. Normal adolescent separation involves moving out of the protective environment of family and trying out newly acquired skills of independence. The process is scary. Mistakes happen, often leaving a teen feeling very inadequate and ashamed. When teens think of suicide, generally it is not death per se that they want. They are trying to get away from an intolerable feeling (shame, hopelessness, worthlessness) or what they perceive as an impossible situation. Both teens who are struggling academically and those who are straight-A students and student council leaders are at risk.

Lynn got drunk and ended up sleeping on her boyfriend's family-room floor after vomiting. In the morning, she felt humiliated at having to face his family and was so despondent that she took an overdose. What she considered an intolerable event was combined with other overwhelming adolescent anxieties. At that moment, she could not forgive herself. Shame is a frequent precursor of teen suicide.

When a person is suicidal, he usually gives hints. Symptoms of depression such as changes in sleeping and eating habits, withdrawal, a flatness in the voice, and decreased energy are common. Grieving over the loss of a close friend or relative, especially if the person killed himself, may lead to thoughts of the same. Listen for comments like, *"There's nothing to live for."*

Some teens will give away their favorite jacket, tapes, or other treasured items in unexpected gestures of friendship. Generally, communication with parents is poor.

If your teen is suicidal, you will have difficulty dealing with your guilt, self-blame, and shame. To ask for professional help may be uncomfortable, but it is a must. It is imperative not to overreact but to take your observations and his pain very seriously. To "give it one more day" may be one too many. Your procrastination could be interpreted as, *"I'm worthless. No one cares."* Most teens are highly emotional and do not handle delay well. Signing her up for activities to keep her busy is not likely to be helpful. A depressed person who is suicidal is a medical emergency. No matter the origin, suicidal feelings are very difficult to overcome. Commanding her to "keep your chin up" is not enough.

WHAT TO SAY AND DO

The suicidal person considers death a way to solve problems. If your teen is depressed, be aware of additional changes in her behaviors, a family history of suicide, or a teen suicide in your community or in her school. A depressed teen may identify with a suicidal act, and this could trigger an attempt: *"Frank did it; I can, too. See how the newspapers gave him front-page coverage? I can get that, too."* This is known as "copycat" suicide. Watch for signs of depression—sad or morose moods, unusually sensitive or defensive reactions or distant behavior, and comments such as *"I wish I were dead,"* or *"I won't be here then . . . I won't be around. . . ."* Unfortunately, most teens who kill themselves do it by accident. *"I just thought I'd try it and see how it felt. I didn't want to really kill myself."*

It is hard to know whether a few scary comments are serious indications of suicidal thinking or just a way of asking for attention. Always err on the side of caution. Take all suicide comments seriously. You may hear hints such as *"I won't be here to worry about it,"* or *"You'll be sorry when I'm gone."* Even if these are not accompanied by other signs of problems, be sincere and directly ask: *"Tell me, are you thinking about hurting yourself or killing yourself?" "How often do you think about it?" "Do these thoughts happen once or twice, or do they persist so that you can't get rid of them?" "How would you do it?"* If your teen, or any of her friends, answers yes to *any* of these questions, you need to act.

Reflecting your teen's sadness and hopelessness allows your teen to know you are able to connect with exactly how bad life feels at this moment, and it may be a welcome relief to him to know that you care enough to ask. It does put some responsibility on you—you need to assure him that you will do everything in your power to get help and to prevent him from hurting himself. Say, *"It sounds to me as if it's not death you want, but a way to escape those feelings. I know that we'll be able to find other, healthy ways to get away from feeling so inadequate and guilty. I care so much for you. I want to help you."*

You have not failed him. You do care, after all, and you do not think he is worthless. It is likely that you have given him some hope, even if he has not been able to say so. Tell him that you are going to see a specialist who can help, that you will take days off from work, and that you will be with him every minute or have someone else be there until he is feeling better. In other words, you will not let him hurt himself.

At this point, counseling is nonnegotiable: *"Look, I can't possibly feel what you are feeling, but I do want to help you feel better. We're going to talk to someone very helpful. You may not want to go, but I will find someone who understands and can help us both."* Your teen needs a risk assessment for suicide. You can take her to a hospital emergency clinic, a mental health or social service agency, or a psychiatrist or other mental health professional who is experienced in teen depression and teen suicide. Go together, immediately.

Living with a suicidal teen is very hard. Parents feel many pressures. You feel strung out at work, you're the chauffeur and the cheering section, you try to put healthful meals on the table, do the laundry, and tend to younger children. Time is scarce, but you are urgently needed now to comfort her. Your physical presence is not enough; you must be there emotionally as well. When she wants to talk, listen. If the moment is allowed to pass, it may be hard to get back to it later. As hard as this is, the effort and time spent will be the best investment you ever make.

PREVENTIVE TIPS

Your depressed teen will be exquisitely sensitive to your attitude toward him. He is looking for any reason to think less of himself. Watch your body language and your tone of voice.

Classes on parenting teens offer training in conflict resolution, as do many high schools. Learn to settle your disputes fairly and lovingly. Closure is imperative. If you walk away from your teen, you model running away from problems, and suicide is often a means of running away.

Teens need stability in their lives, a constant and solid source of identity. If you are intent on helping, search for an activity that she really likes. It must be her interest, not yours. (If you love golf, she may try to like it to please you, or hate it because you love it.) Is there a hobby to support a favorite interest? A sport? Having something that is hers, something meaningful and real, may sustain her through a lot. A new CD player may encourage an interest in music. A loving family, a pet, an outside person who believes in her, or a cause she believes in, are all important stabilizers.

Be alert. Put yourself in his shoes. Is he doing well? Does he have a life away from home? Good friends? Is he involved meaningfully with clubs, sports, or other interests? What are the things he worries about? Is he a high-level worrier, or can he let things go? Are you able to listen to his dreams and concerns?

Be a part of your teen's life. You are still needed for direction, for feedback and support, and for comfort and love.

If raising teenagers is an ongoing challenge, coping with a suicidal teenager is a crisis. Search for weapons and ammunition, and for medications and combinations of medications that could be dangerous. Get them out of the house and seek help.

For more information on this topic, read *Too Young to Die: Youth and Suicide* by Francise Klagsbrun (Boston: Houghton Mifflin, 1985); *Straight Talk About Death for Teenagers* by Earl Grollman

(Boston: Beacon Press, 1993); and *On Death and Dying* by Elizabeth Kubler-Ross (New Haven: Yale University Press, 1968).

WHEN TO SEEK HELP

As stated above, it is imperative to respond to a teenager who is talking about or showing signs of wanting to kill himself. Offering your love and help is generally a much-needed relief. Therapy and/or medications may be in order. Hospitalization, too, may be necessary. This may seem drastic, but it may be required to keep her safe. Even if your teen hates you at the time you take her to the therapist, the emergency room, or to an in-patient treatment unit, beneath it is the knowledge that "my parent is trying to help." Most teens do not want to kill themselves but realize that they are out of control. Parents may be the last to know this, even if they ask.

See also: Counseling; Depression; Eating Disorders; Hanging Out; Homosexuality; Mood Swings; Stress

SWEARING

"I'm shocked at the language I hear her friends using. Every sentence is, 'What the _____?'"
"It's no big deal. What the _____?"

UNDERSTANDING THE SITUATION

Four-letter words commonly fly in school hallways and locker rooms and at sports practices, and, despite the teacher's presence, often in the classrooms. You may begin to think you're the odd one—*"Oh, Mom, you're so old-fashioned. Get with it!"*—

as you listen to popular lyrics, Oscar-nominated movies, and interviews with sports figures. Because these words feel powerful, most kids will experiment with them. If you do not lose control and let it become an all-consuming problem, it will probably dissipate.

Young adolescent boys are especially prone to swearing; they even have group competitions. They find it wonderful fun to see who can make the loudest comments and/or obnoxious sounds! The best defense is to keep out of it. Do not overreact.

Your job is to set the standards in your home and in public when you are with them. Keep your sense of humor, and realize that you will have to draw the line about far more significant issues in the years to come.

WHAT TO SAY AND DO

Boundaries teach respect. Be clear and concise: *"We don't use those words in this house."* Turn around and walk away. Don't hang around to lecture or argue.

When his friends are at the house and you hear swearing, stop them as a group: *"Please, guys, the language has to go, but we'd like you to stay. Thank you."*

In public, he may swear to show off or to feel a part of the group. He may use crude language to shock others, or to embarrass you. If possible, let it go. A knowing glance may work. If he is really out of line, invite him into another room to discuss it in private. Don't embarrass him. Simply say, *"Ian, the rules here are the same as at home."*

Don't be a prude. Occasional swearing can offer relief at times of great frustration. At a good talk time, discuss words that are expressive yet not too offensive.

Use humor. You may be able to stop it with a joke. With a sniff, say, *"I didn't know we were in a locker room."*

PREVENTIVE TIPS

Model what you expect from your teen. Don't swear.

At a good talk time or family meeting, discuss excessive swearing: *"Rod, we cannot control what you say when you're with your friends. We have a no-swearing rule when you're at home with the family. Swearing once in a while, or in pure frustration, I can overlook."* Stating your standards expresses your values and teaches respect.

Find youth groups that have strong values. Young leaders who believe in high group standards set good examples. Mature college kids can be good influences on high-school-age kids; mature high-school kids are good for younger teens. When an older teen tells your son that swearing isn't cool, it has an effect.

Help your teen find other ways to feel powerful. Allow negotiation. Listen to and reflect feelings: *"Oh, so you disagree with me. You feel _____. I can buy that. You're certainly thinking."*

When possible, show interest in your teen's activities. Invite friends to favorite family haunts and have fun together. Spend time together skiing, hiking, camping, and so on. When you expand his world and help him to feel more confident, he may be less drawn to swearing.

WHEN TO SEEK HELP

If your teen seems to be rebelling across the board, and swearing is just one of the many issues on which he refuses to cooperate, you need to talk with an experienced friend or relative who knows him, or to a professional.

See also: Rebelliousness; Values

TELEPHONE

"The phone rings nonstop until after I go to bed. I can't even make a call myself. At times I'm awakened at eleven o'clock with, "Ring! Ring! Is Gina there?""

"My parents are so rude. My dad actually hung up on my call with Julianna. I was right in the middle of an important conversation."

UNDERSTANDING THE SITUATION

Home from a hard day, you sit down, put your feet up, close your eyes—and the phone begins ringing. The conflict is clear. You need quiet, and your daughter needs contact with her friends.

As she chats about music, jobs, schoolwork, parents, teachers, peers, and other people, she is learning what others think and feel. This is important to her understanding of her feelings and opinions. The phone also offers an easy way for self-conscious teens to get to know one another, especially the opposite sex—while safely at home.

Telephones can help teens inform their parents of their whereabouts. Cell phones are costly, but serve a good purpose. One mother liked her daughter having a phone in her car. She felt she was safer driving alone at night.

A word of warning regarding teens, beepers, and responsibility. Beepers are becoming a mainstream mode for parents to locate their teens. Isn't this backward? Shouldn't the teen's responsibility be to notify her parents of her whereabouts?

Together with your teen, make clear ground rules about the

telephone and other modes of communication. Be aware of your teen's activities with them. These devices definitely should not be allowed to interfere with his schoolwork. Nor are these "extras" a God-given right, even if your teen is paying for them. He can lose it as well as use it.

WHAT TO SAY AND DO

Rather than nag and argue, agree on telephone rules that fill her needs and yours. For example, one father, a doctor, agreed to a fifteen-minute limit unless he was on call, in which case his daughter was to keep conversations to five minutes. His rules were:

1. Quiet time between 7:00 and 8:00 P.M., no TV, no phone. Parents will take messages and try not to embarrass you with your friends.
2. Phone use okay before and after quiet time, if calls are kept to fifteen minutes, unless prearranged.
3. No playing on the phone; no crank calls.

Losing phone privileges is a common consequence for breaking rules. Because the phone is so important to teens, restrictions should be reasonable and related to the misbehavior. For example, because Kathy brought home low grades, her privileges were limited to using the phone only to discuss schoolwork or to make appointments. This meant five-minute conversations only, until her grades showed improvement. Her parents agreed that if she needed to talk longer about schoolwork, she could.

Some parents who can afford it install a separate kids' line. The same telephone rules apply, including maintaining good grades as a condition of use.

Discuss your rules with your teen before charges appear on your bill. One daughter's best friend moved to another state, and before anyone realized what was happening, there were three hundred dollars' worth of calls.

Consider carefully before you allow your teen to use your calling card. Is he responsible? This is a privilege for him and a liability for you. Discuss the ground rules thoroughly: *"Matthew, calling cards and PIN numbers are for family use only and are not to be shared even with your best friends. These numbers and cards are parents' private property. When you are old enough, you can get your own. Pay phones work, too."* Consider having your teen memorize the numbers rather than carry a card.

PREVENTIVE TIPS

Your teen is watching you. Don't tell him to limit his calls if you don't do the same.

Teens complain, *"My mom is on the phone constantly."* Try to be available for your teen. He may want to share an idea with you, and if you're always on the phone, he may feel that *"She doesn't care,"* or *"She's too busy to listen."*

WHEN TO SEEK HELP

If your teen is receiving many short calls, carries a beeper or cell phone, and seems to be busy meeting others beyond what you might think is normal, you may have to think about drug dealing. If you ask him if he is dealing, he will deny it. It is better to watch and learn. What are his friends like? Does he always seem to have money? Talk to his teachers and school counselor and try to get to the bottom of the situation.

See also: Alcohol and Other Drugs; Friends, Choosing

TELEVISION

"Kate can't possibly be allowed to watch that trash. It's suggestive and vulgar. With all the drugs, sex, and violence in the world today, that's the last thing we need in our home."

"My mom is so freaked by MTV. What's the big deal? She doesn't understand that a lot of it is good. I know what I can handle."

UNDERSTANDING THE SITUATION

MTV and *television* are often synonymous to today's teen. Many teens will agree that most rap music and videos are about sex and violence. However, one teen said, *"It's true that there's crummy stuff on MTV, but most of it is good. Like, I learn about what creative jobs kids are getting right out of high school. And it's neat to see the singers sing their songs. They have really good groups on, singing really good music. They always dub out the bad words. Most kids don't even listen to the words, mostly the beat."* Oddly, though, this teen could sing all of the words to the songs she claimed not to listen to. The words often reflect what the teen is struggling with.

Television exposes children of all ages to subjects we would not have chosen. You may have screened programs when your teen was younger, but the bottom line is that you cannot see everything he watches, nor do you want to.

As your teen enters the adult world, she needs to be able to establish values and know right from wrong. Some programming addresses real-life issues such as resolving conflicts, peer pressure, violence, and ethics. Television "police" are struggling to ensure a balance of choices, but much of the programming is of dubious value. Be aware. Have her show you what she watches. Help her separate fact from fiction and interpret what she is seeing. Many families jointly select weekly programs, and teens agree to follow the system. Keep the faith. When strong, good values are well communicated, over time teens become more selective.

Playing home video games and watching television are sedentary activities and can be somewhat addictive. Overeating can result. When a teen is happy at school and involved with outside activities, occasionally watching MTV and other television is not detrimental. Moderation and a sensible balance in life are vital for healthy living. The electronic media vie for your teen's attention. Do you want it to dominate your teen's life, or do you want her to make good choices about its use and take control?

WHAT TO SAY AND DO

Permanently placing televisions in teens' rooms is a big mistake. Totally unsupervised viewing, especially when there is access to paid channels, leads to watching much undesirable junk. It also means that your teen is missing learning how to share with other members in the family, negotiating which programs to watch, debating the fine points of one program over another, and making trades when there are conflicts. This sort of process teaches how to share and how to live interdependently with others, which is a valuable, life-long skill.

At a good talk time, ask, *"Shelby, what programs do you like to watch? Why? What do you think about rap videos?"* Mind you, she's more likely to talk when she feels safe from criticism. She probably has well-formed opinions.

Watch with him. You may not feel welcome at first, but if you keep quiet, he may appreciate your interest. Replace the unhelpful, judgmental *"I can't believe you like that junk! What are kids coming to?"* with a nonjudgmental assertion: *"When you*

_____, I feel _____ because _____, so instead, _____." For example, say, _"When I'm home listening to the rap you watch on MTV, I cringe. I don't like the words, I don't want that language in our home. Please, just keep it off rap. I can live with all the rest."_ The consequences of not cooperating are simple: you unplug the TV. You will not be able to control what he watches when you're not home, but you are modeling your values, and your message is clear.

Use the family meeting to compromise and plan alternatives. Trade an hour of sedentary activity for an hour of bike riding or a free family swim at the YMCA two to three times a week.

PREVENTIVE TIPS

Teens appreciate a place to bring friends where they can hang out together without parents, ideally a room with a television, a stereo, and some games. If you can make this available, she'll spend more time at home with her friends.

At the dinner table or at the family meeting, discuss what teens are viewing today. What are the best television shows? Listen without criticism. Then take the time to preview these shows.

Select one or two programs a week that everyone enjoys. This means compromise. A favorite sitcom can become the one event during a busy week that everyone enjoys together and looks forward to.

How much alone, idle time does your teen have? One teen said, _"I don't have time for that much television by the time I finish soccer, practice the piano, and do my homework. When I have time, I like to talk to my friends."_ Some teens are out of school by 1:30 or 2:30 P.M. and come home to an empty house. Too much time alone often results in too much television.

WHEN TO SEEK HELP

For some teens, television is a way to avoid socializing and physical exercise. Are his grades dropping? Does he spend an inordinate amount of time in front of the tube? Is he isolated? Ask, *"Are you worried about how much time you spend watching TV?"* Many teens will admit their concerns. You need to help her to alter her direction, and that may involve counseling.

See also: Computer; Depression; Home Alone; Laziness; Overweight

TRADITIONS

"I dread Thanksgiving. Erin hates sitting around with all the old people at Aunt Alice's." Or: *"This will be a terrible Thanksgiving. Ruby wants to go to her boyfriend's family dinner. We've never been without her."*
"I feel bad for my mom. I know she wants me with the family, but I want to be with Tom." Or: *"Aunt Alice's is boring."*

UNDERSTANDING THE SITUATION

Adolescence is a time of growth and change, and that means *letting go*. Intellectually, you know that at some point she won't be there for Thanksgiving dinner, yet you are shocked and taken aback the first time it happens. This is part of the "empty nest syndrome." Traditions offer security to the entire family during the years of transition, providing a much-needed anchor at a time when children are juggling schoolwork, friends, sports, and jobs. Family traditions are about belonging. In this day of divorce and separated, extended families, parents have to work a little harder to keep traditions alive.

More than family celebrations, customs, and beliefs, traditions define a family's way of being and doing. In our family: *"We do an old-fashioned spring cleaning"; "We have Grandma to dinner every Sunday night"; "Weekends include church"; "Cooking is done by the girls; the guys do cleanup"; "We go to Hawaii every year."* These are customs that everyone in the family is proud of. If Grandmother always had a centerpiece of fruit on the Thanksgiving table, you may, too. If zinnias always decorated your August birthday table, you may want them now. These little things matter; they become "the way life should be," and without them "it doesn't feel right." We are saddened when they are absent. Yet, unless you are willing to be flexible, your traditions can become an albatross.

WHAT TO SAY AND DO

To avoid unrealistic expectations, check your teen's perceptions, the what-to-expects. Tell her directly: *"Christmas will be different this year. Todd is staying at college and we're going to the cabin to be with cousins. This change may be hard. What is important for you to have happen?"* This gives your teen a sense of control and shows that her concerns matter to you. Talking to Todd on the phone on Christmas Eve may be important for her, and you'll have avoided disappointing her.

Be flexible. Traditions should not become so rigid that you miss the spirit of the holiday. Maggie remembers her mother sending her three teenage brothers to cut the Christmas tree and set it up for the family decorating party. When Maggie arrived home with Mom, there was the family tree all right, but hanging upside down from the ceiling. And that's the way it was decorated!

A nice tradition is to have small, personal (sometimes discreet) celebrations about almost any first-time event, such as having to shave for the first time, her first period, his first job, reaching six feet on the height chart, baking Grandma's ginger pound cakes from scratch, and so on. These moments can be as memorable as when she took her first step. Wouldn't it be wonderful to express that level of enthusiasm for life more often? This builds healthy self-esteem and says, *"You are grow-ing, maturing, and becoming a wonderful person. I'm excited for you."*

Holiday traditions will change as your teen grows, and this may affect the whole family. After a holiday, debrief; decide together what should be changed next year. Take advantage of your teen's insight. Sometimes families have to make a break from tradition to escape an uncomfortable situation—for instance, the drinking at Uncle Walter's has spoiled the fun. Your immediate family may decide to celebrate with an intimate dinner at a favorite haunt instead. You may agree to your teen's missing the family dinner this year but decide that he will be home next year. You may decide that gift giving is out of hand and to draw names and give to only one person next year.

Be sensitive to aspects of your celebrations that your teen has outgrown. Be creative. Evan and his eighteen-year-old sister now fill the family Christmas stockings for a tired Mom and Dad. A reluctant mother gave up the beloved family egg hunt; instead, she set a basket of hard-boiled eggs on the breakfast table with felt markers. The contest was for the funniest egg, best dog face, most creative, and so on. Traditions resurface with the coming of grandchildren.

PREVENTIVE TIPS

Teenagers have two groups to satisfy: family and peers. *"It's Thanksgiving but it's also my girlfriend's birthday. Where do I go?"* This means compromises and hard choices for the entire family. This is a normal aspect of separation. It may be further compli-cated by divorce and the demands of two households. Be a good sport. No one needs to live guilt. Be aware and be sensitive.

Keep family histories alive. It is important that your children understand and appreciate their heritage: *"You were named after _____, and there is a history to that name."* Family lore becomes fabric for the next generation: *"You have great courage in your blood. Great-great-grandmother walked the plains while Wild Bill Hickok rode his horse beside her,"* or, *"You have very smart genes.*

Your grandmother skipped two grades and started college at age fif-teen." These stories need to be told and retold.

Older folks take pride in participating, too. *"There's nothing like your mother's homemade jams and jellies."* A father wants to pass on a recipe for pickling. A grandmother teaches her grand-daughter to crochet and to make Ukrainian Easter eggs.

Videotape your activities and events. One family made a video for long-distance grandparents. Over a year's time they created "Our Family's Ways." They documented eating, clean-ing up, brushing teeth, learning to drive, doing homework, wrestling, playing football, and so on. Family occasions were mixed in with wonderful, funny scenes—one with the teenage boys running around one side of the house in winter clothes, in the snow, then coming from the other side of the house in the summer sun, in bathing suits. Without intending to, these teens documented their family traditions.

Encourage your teen to use family stories and traditions in school assignments. History is more meaningful when it is per-sonal. Perhaps you can find an old family picture of a relative during the Civil War or some other historical event.

Remember, when adolescence ends (does it ever?), the young adult will look forward to being with her family for holidays.

See also: Birthdays; Grandparents; Mealtimes; Values

TRUST

"I used to trust him."

"I know my parents don't trust me. I screwed up sneaking my boyfriend in. Now it doesn't matter what I do, they'll never trust me anyway."

UNDERSTANDING THE SITUATION

A leading issue for parents of teens is trust, especially after a crisis. *Dilemma:* How to have faith in your teen after she has been caught shoplifting. *Dilemma:* How to believe her when she tells you the beer in her closet belongs to her best friend. *Dilemma:* How to believe he really didn't invite all those kids over when you were gone. *Dilemma:* How to trust her word that she isn't sexually active.

Trust is vital to healthy self-esteem. Can you imagine going to work and having no one trust you? Making an error and then having your phone tapped, you would soon begin to doubt yourself, and the same happens to teens when parents lose faith. Your trust says, *"You are truly loved. We know you are capable of good thinking and making good choices. We trust you!"* Your teen will err, but rather than being admonished, he must know that you will forgive and support him as he learns. He will believe in himself if others give him the confidence to try very hard, without fear of repercussion if he fails.

It works best if all significant adults indicate their trust. One teen puts well what seems a common situation: *"My mom will always forgive, but my dad never forgets."* One girl said, *"I think even if I got pregnant my mom would be hurt and everything, but she would forgive me and understand and help me. I think my dad would take me out of his will."* Parents differ in their responses, and this scenario could easily be reversed. A teen's impression of how a parent will respond may not be accurate.

The issue gets clearer when safety enters in. For example, giving Craig the car is not just about trust, it's about safety, training, and experience. Dad trusts Craig to be capable. He makes sure his son has had driver's training, he makes sure Craig understands the family car rules, and he gives Craig more freedom as he gains experience. When Craig makes an error, Dad reduces privileges until he sees an indication that Craig is ready to try again. Craig never feels that Dad has lost faith or trust in him as a person.

WHAT TO SAY AND DO

Frame issues around responsibility, safety, and consideration, rather than *"I don't trust you."* Say, *"You forgot _____. You told me one thing but did another. That is not responsible behavior."*

Comment on her good judgment: *"Nora, I know you wanted to sneak out with the others at the retreat. You used good judgment and leadership in deciding not to join them. It doesn't always seem like the most fun choice at the time. How do you feel about it now?"*

When your teen asks, *"How long before you will trust me?"* she may be really asking, *"How long before I can _____?"* or, *"When will you let me _____?"* Shift the focus to: Is safety or family values an issue? Has there been time for teaching? Has she shown responsibility with recent, related privileges?

Your teen will make poor choices. Give yourself time to cool off and think: *"Melanie, I can't discuss this right now, I need time to cool off. When I've settled down we'll discuss the consequences."* This will take the pressure off and keep you from angrily saying *"I thought I could trust you,"* or doing something that you might regret later. More important, it will also give her time to consider her responsibility.

Most issues concern safety. *"Robby, most of our arguments are not about trust. I may worry too much, but I trust you. I also want you to be safe."* Explain the difference between being a trusting parent and a naive parent: *"For example, your curfew isn't about trust. I am not naive. 'Stuff' happens after midnight. You have enough time after the game to have a Coke with friends and take Cindy home."*

Family rules make expectations clear. She needs to know what you trust her not to do. Rather than lecture, ask her what she knows: *"Carrie, you're riding with Morgan tonight to the party. What is our agreement about driving to parties with others? What would you do if Morgan drinks? I feel good knowing you would call us."* Encourage, and be sincere: *"We do love you and trust your judgment."*

The argument, *"You don't trust me,"* is manipulative. Do not respond with sarcasm: *"You're right. Give me about ten more years."* It is unhelpful to bring up past hurts and mistakes: *"Trust you? After you shoplifted last March and lied about where you were going last month?"* Instead, respond matter-of-factly. Use role reversal: *"The dilemma for me is that I want to know I can depend on you. If you were a parent and your daughter had lied to you, how long do you think it would be before you felt you could depend on her?"* Listen to her reply with an open heart and mind, and constructive problem solving will result. She must know that she will be forgiven, yet she must be held responsible for what she's done. You will always love her and trust that she can try again. Never shut the door and lock it.

Use the word *confidence.* For example, if your daughter is asked to baby-sit, say, *"Lee, this is a big deal! They must have confidence in you. They trust you to care for the most precious thing in their lives."*

Your teen now needs to be trustworthy with friends' secrets, promises, and commitments, or she will have trouble keeping friends. This is a life lesson. At a good talk time, discuss friendships. Check out what's going on with her and others. Listen to her share and observe what she does. Point out what you notice that is good: *"Betty, you were thoughtful to invite Nan."*

Have ongoing, open discussions about trust. Do not lecture. Many teens learn best by concrete analogy. *"Pam, trust is built on a foundation of many layers. If the foundation is strong enough, it will endure a few cracks along the way. Mistakes will happen; we learn from mistakes."* Or use the expanding-corral theory: *"Pam, think of our trust as an expanding corral. You're allowed to do more and more as you demonstrate more dependability. For example, we allow you to drive near home during the day. Next, the corral expands to the city, and with more experience and a good record, we will permit you to drive after dark. As long as you are responsible, the boundaries will expand."*

Ignorant trust is naive. Learn about your teen's world.

Read the school paper as well as your local paper.
Attend parent meetings at school.
Have your teen's friends over and meet their parents.
Attend school events.
Watch your teen's favorite television shows and movies.

Share ways to build trust with your teen at a good talk time: *"Jerry, you can increase your privileges by increasing your responsibilities. You have many areas to work with."*

Contributing to the family:

Doing chores as agreed
Watching younger siblings
Helping, even when not asked
Joining family activities
Expressing your feelings verbally rather than sulking, yelling, hitting, or throwing objects
Listening to others and respecting their feelings and property
Caring for pets
Being polite to Grandma and other adults

Personal growth:

Caring about personal hygiene
Developing organizational skills

Being on time
Keeping appointments and commitments
Being honest

School:

Completing homework—daily assignments as well as long term
Preparing for exams
Participating in class
Participating in other school activities

Sports, music, outside activities:

Committing to practice
Finishing what you start

WHEN TO SEEK HELP

If you feel that your teen is in a constant state of rebellion and you fear something is terribly wrong, you cannot trust him. You need to seek help. Sometimes a close family friend may offer it. A school counselor may give you insight as to what is happening at school and elsewhere outside the home environment. Keep in contact with your teen's friends' parents. Family counseling may help to pull you all closer together. Your trust is vital to your teen's healthy self-esteem. Work on building it.

See also: Anger; Driving; Safety; Values

VALUES

"I don't understand it. His ideas and values sometimes seem so foreign. I want him to make good choices and show strong character."

"I don't think she trusts my judgment. I don't have to do everything her way to be a good person."

UNDERSTANDING THE SITUATION

The teen years are a time for separation, and this can be extremely trying. Your teen may struggle more than others to find new ways and new ideas. He is seeking his values—a search that includes his attitude toward sex, which messages he wants on his T-shirts, how he treats his friends, how he treats you, how honest he is, his priorities, and so forth. He may select a church, and even a faith, different from yours. Some teens, raised in an environment of financial ease, surprise parents by turning to pawnshops, thrift stores, and food co-ops because they worry about pesticides, waste, and recycling. Adolescence is the time kids examine and reaffirm your values. Remember, "the apple doesn't fall far from the tree." As hard as it is to watch your teen search for his identity, show your faith and trust, and gently let go. Growth usually occurs at what seems a time of crisis. Developing good character is a lifelong process of trial and error. Show your teen that you believe he is capable of growth, and help him to think through difficult decisions.

You need to take advantage of the opportunity teens give you to instill values at this time in their life when they are trying to make sense out of the world around them. They will listen to reason and heed consequences. Help them feel good about their decisions; be proud of their good judgment. Give them real responsibilities and real discussions. The payoff is very great. They will remember your lessons and become good citizens.

Adolescents have an uncanny way of finding the right buttons to push. Your teen may tease you by flouting your most deeply held ideals, which can result in a full-blown power struggle. Something as small as insisting that he take off his baseball cap in a fast-food restaurant can lead to a ruined evening, with him retreating to the car and refusing to eat. The more you dictate, and the stricter your threats, the more rebellion you invite. Threat creates fear—not a good atmosphere to promote respect. One boy failed to report a gun that he'd found in his locker for fear that he would be expelled or arrested. The more you let go, listen, try to understand his perceptions, and involve him in solutions, the better the outcome. Do this, and your teen may handle situations you could never have imagined at his age, and increase his self-esteem in the process.

Over the last decade, the media have offered plenty of less-than-wholesome values. In response, many schools are promoting moral issues as an academic subject, because kids are looking for answers to the most basic "what is right and what is wrong" questions. Younger teens have developed the intellectual maturity to understand subtleties, cause-and-effect relationships, and mixed messages. Realistic role models can help. Imagine a drug dealer approaching a fourteen-year-old with the question, *"Want to take something that'll make you feel better than you ever felt before? Want to make a pile of money?"* Teens need practice to understand limits, learn refusal skills, survive being "different," and feel good about their moral convictions. Teens basically strive for parental approval. They usually want to make choices that will bring positive affirmation.

WHAT TO SAY AND DO

Values are best communicated through actions and encouragement. For example, working hard to achieve goals may be a strong value to you. Notice her good decisions. Reaffirm, and be specific: *"Lauren, you make good choices. I think this dance class was one of your best decisions. All your hard work and commitment showed up at the recital. I especially liked the tango. This is proof of a lot of self-discipline."*

Do you model a proper work ethic? Do you often complain about going to work, or do you model enjoying·your job and balancing it with other fun in your life?

Teens are often faced with decisions that seem monumental and create a great deal of tension: *"If I don't go to the movies with Rita and the gang, I'll miss the fun, and they might not ask me again"; "If I don't go with Laura to choir performance, I will not be supporting her"; "If I invite Margo and Lisa to my party, no one else will want to come, but they will hate me if they find out I had a party without them."* Such problems are challenging but can be broken down into lists of pros and cons.

Suggest questions: *"Is there a right or a wrong in the two decisions?" "Which decision will make me feel the best? I understand that I may not always feel good, but what steps can I take so that I won't feel guilty?" "Which decision will take more courage?" "Is this a situation where I do something for others or to make me feel good?"*

Follow through after she has struggled with a value-based concern: *"Christine, it's been a month since you decided to go to Laura's recital instead of the movies. In hindsight, would you do it the same way?"*

Because teens tend to go for the short-term reward, help her see the long-range view. For example, *"Becky, the job at the restaurant looks great. You'd like the money,"* or *"School seems hard and long. However, it is an investment in your future job satisfaction."* She can reason and consider based on what is ultimately of value to her.

The family learns from shared decision making. Invite your teen's perspective: *"I need exercise. An aerobics class would be really fun, but it's expensive. If I ride my bike, I'd save money toward our family vacation. Plus, I could have some fun time with your little brother on my bike. Your grandfather would be proud of me. He always had time for us kids. What do you think I should do?"* Involving your teen reinforces family values, which will help when she has to make tough decisions with long-range repercussions.

Use every possible moment to teach and model important values. Kids are good observers but not great interpreters. Ask how your teen feels about a situation; try to understand him. For example, Nathan's father is often very late picking him up and is never on time for his football games. Dad is being inconsiderate. However, the message that comes across to Nathan is, *"You aren't very important to me. That's why I leave you waiting."* Internalized, this kind of situation can result in low self-esteem. This father is modeling that being on time is not an important value: *"It doesn't matter that I'm late for my son's football game, or for my job interview or having dinner with friends."* This self-centered attitude has cost him jobs, friends, and his son's respect.

A short quote may stick, when a moral lecture would be ignored. One young teen said, *"My mom always said, 'First impressions are lasting,' and 'Do unto others as you would have them do unto you.' "*

PREVENTIVE TIPS

Your teen needs to dream and set goals. She needs your encouragement to nurture her ideals. Long-range goals will often keep a vacillating teen on track.

Get involved with a support group at church, at a community center, or with a few friends to discuss the tough questions about raising your teens.

For more information on this topic, read *How Good People Make Tough Choices* by Rushworth M. Kidder (New York: William Morrow & Company, 1995); and *When Good Kids Do Bad Things* by Katherine G. Levine (New York: Norton, 1991).

WHEN TO SEEK HELP

There may be times when you or your whole family want to meet with a rabbi, minister, or other mentor to help with concerns based on values.

See also: Dating, Teens; Lying; Mealtimes; Sex, Talking About; Trust

WORRY

"Mandy worries so much, it's affecting her self-confidence. She used to love to be onstage, but now she won't try out for the school play because she feels uncomfortable in front of others. She worries about her hair, her clothes, and whether anyone likes her."

"No one said they liked my new shoes. I wonder what's wrong with them. I'll never wear them again. My mom is bugging me to try out for the school play. No way— I'm not going to make a fool of myself."

UNDERSTANDING THE SITUATION

A bit of worry can help us to function and do well. Worry is like stress. Learning to handle the right amount helps us to work hard to be good at things, and encourages our teens to study and to do their best.

At times, teens feel competent to head into the adult world, yet at other times they feel pulled back into childhood. Independence is thrilling but scary. Your teen may act capable and self-assured one minute and clingy and dependent the next. Many teens experiment with drugs, car racing, unchaperoned parties, and so forth, so it's realistic for them to be worried and concerned.

A self-conscious teen rarely shares that she is worried. Instead, she acts stubborn: *"I won't do it. I just don't want to, that's why!"* or angry: *"Leave me alone!"* or she cries: *"It's not fair, you're so mean."* You feel her childish frustration, and she wallows in anxiety and self-pity, feeling totally misunderstood. Many teens worry all the time about peer acceptance: *"Will I be popular?"* *"I shouldn't have said that, it sounded so dumb."* *"Why wasn't I asked to her party?"* *"Now he's going for her—how can I keep him?"*

Performance anxieties are often cause for extreme worry: *"Am I going to pass or fail?"* *"Tests freak me."* *"I'll never make it through my speech!"* *"I'll die if I don't score. The coach will kill me."* Teens may share parents' concerns about very adult issues. For example, if a parent is in between jobs and money is tight, a teen might worry excessively about financial security. When parents divorce, a teen may worry about where she will end up, and whether she caused the breakup. When an acquaintance dies, a teen may worry, *"Will this happen to me, or to someone I love?"*

A worried teen needs a great deal of parental encouragement and understanding. You wanted him to be strong enough to take on the world with the confidence of a winning politician or the aplomb of a great opera singer. Learning to deal with worry is part of the process. *"How do I encourage her and help her overcome worry?"* and, *"How do I know when she's using fear to gain attention and stay 'little'?"* are good questions to ask yourself.

WHAT TO SAY AND DO

Most fears can be overcome with positive exposure and experience. Older teens see the promise of moving on after high school and are less tormented by peer acceptance. When a teen sets goals, makes good decisions, and succeeds, he feels more capable and builds self-esteem, and as a result, he fears less. This takes time. Be patient. Show confidence in your teen. Listen closely to him, and don't get lost in his actions, which often hide the real problem.

He may be extremely difficult to live with. You may have to deal with his anger, and it may take weeks for the underlying worry to come forth. Be available. When he is ready to share, he'll need you to be there for him.

Sympathize, no matter how silly you feel her concerns are. Young teens especially tend to worry. They worry about the obvious things: their weight, if they'll be asked out, if they should try out for cheerleader, and what their grades will be. As they worry their moodiness can increase. They need space, and they need parents who will listen and be generally sensitive.

Set an example by doing as you say you will. Follow through with promises of being home by a certain time, and set up "safety nets" with neighbors or relatives for a teen who worries excessively. Be aware that her worrying is likely to increase if she is pushed to take on responsibility before she is ready to.

Ask her if she'd be interested in taking a martial-arts class. She may like it better if she can invite a friend to join her. These classes develop agility and concentration and can help to build self-confidence.

PREVENTIVE TIPS

Set a healthy example. It is important to be optimistic about life, to help your teen look ahead, and to be hopeful.

Support her through her mistakes. These are learning opportunities. Life can and does go on.

Help him set realistic goals. Nothing helps to build confidence more than the tangible results of success.

Volunteering at senior centers, food banks, or hospitals can also boost confidence.

WHEN TO SEEK HELP

When she has a hard time with normal, daily functioning, it is time to seek help. Excessive worry, anxiety, and phobic reactions can be confused. Sometimes phobias go unnoticed until the teen feels immobilized. Strong anxieties about leaving home, about going to school, about large crowds, and about illness and death can be very debilitating. These fears can develop into repetitive thoughts called *obsessions*, which can lead to depression. Treatment and/or medication can make a big difference. Seek professional help.

See also: Depression; Mood Swings; Stress

READING REFERENCES

Armstron, Thomas, *Seven Kinds of Smart*. New York: Penguin Group, 1993.

Bass, Ellen, and Kate Kaufman, *Free Your Mind*. New York: Harper Perennial, 1996.

Bettner, Betty Lou, and Amy Lew, *Raising Kids Who Can*. New York: HarperCollins, 1992.

Bluestein, Jane, Ph.D., *Parents, Teens, and Boundaries: How to Draw the Line*. Florida: Health Communications, 1993.

Brodzinsky, David M., Marshall D. Henig, and Robin Marantz Henig, *Being Adopted: The Life-Long Search for Self*. New York: Anchor Books, 1992.

Buscaglia, Leo, Ph.D., *Fall of Freddie the Leaf*. New York: Henry Holt & Company, 1982.

Caron, Ann F., *Don't Stop Loving Me: A Reassuring Guide for Mothers of Adolescent Daughters*. New York: First Harper Perennial, 1992.

Clark, Jean Illsley, and Connie Dawson, *Growing Up Again: Parenting Ourselves, Parenting Our Children*. San Francisco: HarperCollins, 1989.

Cline, Foster C., and Jim Fay, *Parenting Teens with Love and Logic*. Colorado: Piñon Press, 1992.

Coloroso, Barbara, *Winning at Parenting . . . Without Beating Your Kids* (video). Littleton, Colorado, 1989.

———, *Kids Are Worth It*. New York, Avon Books, 1995.

Dimoff, Timothy, and Steve Carper, *How to Tell if Your Kids Are Using Drugs*. New York: Facts On File, Inc., 1992.

Einstein, Elizabeth, *The Stepfamily: Living, Loving, and Learning*. Ithaca: E. A. Einstein, 1994.

Elkind, David, *All Grown Up and No Place to Go: Teenagers in Crisis*. Reading, Addison-Wesley, 1984.

————, *The Hurried Child: Growing Up Too Fast*. Boston: Addison-Wesley Publishing Company, 1981.

Faber, Adele, and Elaine Mazlish, *How to Talk So Kids Will Listen and How to Listen So Kids Will Talk*. New York: Avon Books, 1982.

————, *Siblings Without Rivalry: How to Help Your Children to Live Together So You Can Live Too*. New York: Avon Books, 1987.

Gale, Jay, *A Parent's Guide to Teenage Sexuality*. New York: Henry Holt & Company, 1989.

Glenn, Stephen H., and Jane Nelsen, *Raising Self-Reliant Children in a Self-Indulgent World*. Rocklin: Prima Publishing, 1988.

Goleman, Daniel, *Emotional Intelligence*. New York: Bantam Books, 1995.

Gralla, Preston, *Online Kids: A Young Surfer's Guide to Cyberspace*. New York: John Wiley & Sons, Inc., 1996.

Grollman, Earl, *Explaining Death to Children*, 3rd Edition. Boston: Beacon Press, 1980.

————, *Straight Talk About Death for Teenagers*. Boston: Beacon Press, 1993.

————, *Talking about Death: A Dialog Between Parent and Child*. Boston: Beacon Press, 1967.

Hacker, Sylvia S., and Randi Hacker, *What Every Teenager Really Wants to Know About Sex*. New York: Carroll and Gray, 1993.

Harbeck, Karen, ed., *Coming Out of the Classroom Closet: Gay and Lesbian Students, Teachers, and Curricula*. Binghamton: Harrington Park Press, 1992.

Harris, Robie H., *It's Perfectly Normal: Changing Bodies, Growing Up, Sex and Sexual Health*. Cambridge: Candlewick Press, 1994.

Heuer, Marti, *Teen Addiction: A Book of Hope for the Parents, Teachers, and Counselors of Chemically Dependent Adolescents*. New York: Ballantine Books, 1994.

Joslin, Karen Renshaw, *Positive Parenting from A to Z*. New York: Ballantine Books, 1994.

Kidder, Rushworth M., *How Good People Make Tough Choices*. New York, William Morrow and Company, 1995.

Klein, Donald F., and Paul Wender, *Understanding Depression*. New York: Oxford University Press, 1993.

Kohn, Alfie, *Punished by Rewards: The Trouble with Gold Stars, Incentive Plans, As, Praise, and Other Bribes*. Boston: Houghton Mifflin, 1993.

Kubler-Ross, Elizabeth, *On Death and Dying*. New Haven: Yale University Press, 1968.

Langston, Teresa, *Parenting Without Pressure: A Whole Family Approach*. Colorado Springs: Naupress, 1994.

Levine, Katherine G., *When Good Kids Do Bad Things*. New York: Norton, 1991.

Levine, Melvin, M.D., *Educational Care*. Toronto: Educator's Publishing Service, Inc., 1994.

————, *Keeping A Head in School*. Cambridge: Educator's Publishing Service, Inc., 1990.

Louv, Richard, *101 Things You Can Do for Our Children's Future*. New York: Doubleday, 1994.

Madaras, Lynda, *The What's Happening to My Body? Book for Boys*. New York: Newmarket Press, 1984.

————, *The What's Happening to My Body? Book for Girls*. New York: Newmarket Press, 1983.

Mayle, Peter, *What's Happening to Me?* New York: Carol Publishing, 1975.

McCoy, Kathleen, *Coping with Teenage Depression*. New York: New American Library, 1982.

Mednick, Fred, *Rebel Without a Car: Surviving and Appreciating Your Child's Teen Years*. Minneapolis: Fairview Press, 1996.

Miles, Miska, *Annie and the Old One*. Boston: Little Brown and Company, 1971.

Muller, Ann, *Parents Matter: Parents' Relationships with Lesbian Daughters and Gay Sons*. Tallahassee: Naiad Press, 1987.

Nava, Michael, and Robert Davidoff, *Created Equal: Why Gay Rights Matter to America*. New York: St. Martins Press, 1994.

Nelson, Jane, *Positive Discipline*. New York: Ballantine Books, 1987.

Orenstein, Peggy, *School Girls, Young Women, Self-Esteem and the Confidence Gap*. New York: Doubleday, 1994.

Packer, Alex J., *Bringing Up Parents: The Teenager's Handbook*. Minneapolis: Free Spirit Publishing, 1992.

Papolos, Demitri F., and Janice Papolos, *Overcoming Depression*. New York: Harper & Row, 1987.

Parenting Insights: Quarterly Magazine for Parents of 7 to 14-year-olds. Susan Palmer, ed. Woodinville, WA: (800) 790-7889.

Pipher, Mary, *Reviving Ophelia: Saving the Selves of Adolescent Girls*. New York: Ballantine Books, 1994.

Rodriguez, Luis J., *Always Running: La Vida Loca: Gang Days in L.A.* Willimantic: Curbstone Press, 1992.

Satter, Ellyn, *How to Get Your Kid to Eat, But Not Too Much*. Palo Alto: Bull Publishing, 1987.

Schaffer, Judith, and Christina Lindstrom, *How to Raise an Adopted Child: A Guide to Help Your Child Flourish from Infancy Through Adolescence*. NAL-Dutton, 1991.

Schnebly, Lee, *Out of Apples? Understanding Personal Relationships*. Tuscon: Fisher Books, 1988.

Singer, Bennett L., ed., *Growing Up Gay/Growing Up Lesbian: A Literary Anthology*. New York: New Press, 1994.

Steinberg, Laurence, and Ann Levine, *You and Your Adolescent: A Parent's Guide for Ages 10 to 20*. New York: First Harper Perennial, 1990.

Tobias, Cynthia, *The Way They Learn*. Colorado Springs: Focus on the Family Publishing, 1994.

Vail, Priscilla I., *Smart Kids With School Problems*. New York: E. P. Dutton, 1987.

Viorst, Judith, *The Tenth Good Thing About Barney*. New York: Macmillan, 1971.

Wallerstein, Judith, and Joan Berlin Kelly, *Surviving the Breakup:*

How Children and Parents Cope with Divorce. New York: Basic Books, 1980.

Wallerstein, Judith, and Sandra Blackslee, *Second Chances*. New York: Ticknor and Fields, 1989.

Warren, Andrea, and Jay Wiedenkeller, *Everybody's Doing It: How to Survive Your Teenager's Sex Life (And Help Them Survive It Too)*. New York: Penguin Books, 1993.

Wolf, Anthony E., Ph.D., *Get Out of My Life: But First Could You Drive Me and Cheryl to the Mall? A Parent's Guide to the New Teenager*. New York: Noonday, 1992.

INDEX

ABOUT THE AUTHORS

Karen Renshaw Joslin, M.A., holds a master's degree in Education and is a certified public school teacher. She is the author of *Positive Parenting from A-Z,* which was published in 1994 to widespread acclaim, and has been translated into several languages. She teaches her "positive parenting" curriculum in hospitals, schools, and corporations in the greater Seattle area. She has two grown children and lives with her husband and teenage daughter in Bellevue, Washington.

Mary Bunting Decher, M.S.W., A.C.S.W., is a clinical social worker and affilliate instructor of the School of Social Work at the University of Washington. In her twenty-year professional career, she has worked extensively with teenagers and their families in foster care, hospital, school, and non-profit social service agency settings. She is the mother of two grown daughters, and lives with her husband in Bellevue, Washington.